FAITH: AN HISTORICAL STUDY

THE MACMILLAN COMPANY
NEW YORK · BOSTON · CHICAGO · DALLAS
ATLANTA · SAN FRANCISCO

MACMILLAN & CO., Limited
LONDON · BOMBAY · CALCUTTA
MELBOURNE

THE MACMILLAN COMPANY
OF CANADA, Limited
TORONTO

FAITH

AN HISTORICAL STUDY

By
STEWART MEANS

With an Introduction by
ERWIN R. GOODENOUGH

NEW YORK

THE MACMILLAN COMPANY
1933

SET UP BROWN BROTHERS LINOTYPERS
PRINTED IN THE UNITED STATES OF AMERICA
BY THE FERRIS PRINTING COMPANY

TO MY CHILDREN,

MARGARET, TOM, HELEN,

AND GLENN.

From whose lives and characters
I have learned more of the meaning of History
than from many volumes.

ὅπου ἂν ἦι Χριστὸς
Ἰησοῦς, ᾽εκεῖ ἡ καθολικὴ ἐκκλησία.
Ἰγνάτιος

PREFACE

In a book very much read by thoughtful people during the middle of the last century the writer says in one place, "There are cases in which more knowledge of more value may be conveyed by the history of a word than by the history of a campaign." The method of the study that follows was largely inspired by this sentence of Coleridge. It is not a church history in the ordinary sense of the word, or a history of doctrine. It is an attempt to discover what forces were at work to shape the different forms in which the interpretation of the word Faith found expression. The search was long and slow as the seeker came increasingly to apprehend how complicated those forces were. The amount of ground I covered in the thirty years in which I was engaged in this investigation I can hardly estimate. So far as I could discover no one had ever sought to follow this particular path before me. The difficulties of the task begat doubt as to its value. Perhaps the real reason for my persisting was that I wanted to satisfy my own mind. I wanted to know. The work is now done. Not well done, as I painfully realize: but if I have helped any one to see that there is a problem here, and a very vital one, I shall feel that the chief purpose of the book has been achieved.

I am truly grateful for the facilities I have enjoyed, facilities exceptional for a parish clergyman. My first gratitude is to the Library of Yale University and its staff. For fifty years I have had the free use of that great collection, and the interest and generous assistance of its most intelligent staff. Then I have had the privilege of knowing and associating with men who knew far more than I ever have known or will know. Also I have felt always that the daily life of the people with whom I was in close contact was helping me to escape the dangers of mere pedantry. Among the many, dead and living, to whom I am conscious of my obligations two stand out in clear relief, both living and both different. They are the Reverend Francis B. Whitcome of Poughkeepsie, New York, and Professor Erwin R. Goodenough of Yale. Both men went over the manuscript closely and ruthlessly and suggested many changes. The matter of the book is my own, but if it possesses any attraction for a reader it is due to the wise and generous criticism of these two dear friends.

STEWART MEANS.

New Haven, Conn.
Jan. 19, 1933.

INTRODUCTION

A READER of Dr. Means' *Faith* hardly needs to be told that the book is a rare combination of learning and insight. To those of us who know the author its significance is even greater as being another expression of his personality. He asked me once to write an introduction for the book in case he died before it was published; I see no reason why the fact that he is happily still with us should keep me from doing so.

The life of Dr. Means is a wholesome reminder that great ministries rest upon deep foundations. As a boy his educational opportunities were such as would seem to us very poor; it was at Union Theological Seminary and the Episcopal Theological School at Cambridge that he first came into contact with profoundly learned men and great minds. He learned to know the importance of the past for the present, and to face the problems of life aware of the ramifications of those problems which thoughtful men of all ages had perceived. Still not a "trained man" in the sense that he could be certified as a master scholar in any field, but with an insatiable hunger for knowledge he entered the priesthood of the Protestant Episcopal Church.

In a very few years he came to St. John's Church in New Haven to begin a ministry unique in the history of the city. University professors of all and no denominations one by one took pews in his church. The discussion groups of Yale's scholars asked him to join them and still refuse to listen when modesty prompts him to resign to make room for younger men. In later life, after his books had made known to the world the soundness of his scholarship, Yale's Doctorate of Divinity was inevitable. At the same time the great number of artisans and office clerks in the congregation showed that his appeal to the untrained humbler classes was as great as to the learned. As a preacher his power was not so much in brilliant oratory as in the cumulative effect of sincerity expressed in that simplicity which only profound thought and genuine emotion combine to produce. Not only his parishioners but all New Haven felt the quiet influence of his ministry. In a day when sex was unmentionable, and prostitutes and unfortunate girls, far from being a subject of discussion at theological seminars, were simply cast out into the darkness of social taboo, Dr. Means faced misinterpretation and derogation for years to found and conduct the first house of refuge for such girls the city had ever seen. He told me he could not have done otherwise in view of the life of his Master.

Throughout this active ministry he kept reading, especially Church History, but everything else as well. He finally lost touch with modern science (though he did not give it up without a struggle) but every other sort of reading still engrosses him. Extremely sensitive to a fine style, he has always taken more pleasure in books that would inform than in those which would merely amuse or inspire. He learned languages only with great difficulty, yet he knew that there were priceless treasures which only French and German could give him, so he has kept digging away at them for years. The footnotes which he originally planned for the following pages were largely references to German and French works. The names he included and the works he used constitute a roll call of the great Church Historians of a century and a half, from those esteemed in his youth to the most modern authorities. He has always been eager to get the latest scholarship; but he has read Gibbon, F. C. Baur, Ritschl, Renan, Milman, and dozens of others too well not to know that though subsequent researches have disclosed many details unknown to those masters, their conclusions about the past may be paralleled and supplemented but can never become obsolete. So he sees antiquity from the point of view of Baur and of Reitzenstein and Cumont simultaneously. But most of all he sees the past through his own eyes: if he can look over Harnack's shoulder at the picture he is painting, Dr. Means knows how to paint his own.

None of this concentrated study has ever alienated him from life. It has helped him to understand it better, to live more fully himself, and to respond more sensitively to the lives of others. The ignorant person who came to him for comfort only knew that he had comfort to give, and no matter from what step on the intellectual ladder a visitant might consult him the experience was the same.

The book that follows is then only one of the many accomplishments of the long period during which Dr. Means was writing it. Now in the rich twilight of his eighty years, as he sits still working in his study, one wonders where his successors are to be found. Perhaps these learned and passionate pages may inspire young men to emulate his learning and share his passion.

ERWIN R. GOODENOUGH.

CONTENTS

FAITH: AN HISTORICAL STUDY

CHAPTER I

THE ORIGIN AND DEVELOPMENT OF THE JEWISH CONCEPTION

THE significance of Jesus Christ has been so overpowering that we often fail to realize the fact that history records a continuous movement. The importance of Jesus Christ was not recognized until his influence had long been at work in the world, and the forces which He set in motion had entered deeply into the life of the Empire. In our eyes the birth of Christ divides the old from the new by such a wide chasm that we forget that the stream of human life flowed on unbroken and undisturbed. As L. H. Mills has said: "No psychic development in the history of the human race has ever taken place without its long antecedent causes, which form a part of an ever-continuous chain of being of which the special development is but a link."

So, to change the figure, we can understand the history of the Christian Church and the new spiritual life of man only by seeing the great streams from the past which went into what we now visualize as the new river.

In the spiritual evolution of the Jew there are many stages, some fairly clear and well defined in his literature, and others dim and confused. For he did not stand alone in the world and have a free and independent development. He was in contact with many nations, and great waves from their powerful and intense life again and again flooded his history until his identity was threatened with destruction. Just how deeply the life of the Jew was affected by these influences we cannot clearly determine,

1

but we must believe that they were an essential and integral portion of his history and are part of the great inheritance from the past which makes our world to-day what it is.

As in the case of all primitive peoples the Israelitic tribal consciousness seems at first to obscure almost entirely that of individual personality. Among the Hebrews the whole religious life was woven into the conception of a Covenant between God and the Nation. Jehovah at first is a tribal God. The individual is simply a member of this tribe or nation and bound in with its history and life. The strong consciousness of a personal and separate character, with the clear note of individual reponsibility, which are the distinctive features of the highest Christian civilization, are not developed. Great individuals were not lacking, yet the religious side of Hebrew life resolved itself into a tribal acceptance of a Covenant established between God and the Nation. Acceptance on the part of the individual is simply an act of submission or obedience to the laws which are given to the people as a whole.

But whether the consciousness of personality existed or not, the forces which make for it were working there increasingly as the religious instinct developed. Man is primarily a religious being in the sense that his spiritual nature develops through all the vicissitudes which beset his path. The essential meaning of religion is the recognition or apprehension of man's relations with that which is invisible, eternal, and more or less universal. Regarded on its purely subjective side, such an apprehension may be described by its generic term, Faith. Faith exists long before the name appears, though in its lower forms it may be so modified and conditioned by external or internal elements as not always to be easily recognized. The Hebrew words or phrases which are translated in the Septuagint as "Pistis," do not bear the same meaning as even the classical use of that word. More than that the psychological state expressed by the New Testament "Pistis" or Faith did not exist among the early Hebrews except in a very rudimentary form. The word itself, as understood by St. Paul, is not found in the Old Testament. Taken in the later sense as the active spiritual force within the soul it is nowhere regarded as the indispensable subjective condition of salvation.

The absence of the term might lead to an assumption too wide and too sweeping to be sustained by the facts if it is not clearly kept in view that the essential capacity may exist though it be imperfectly formulated. The Prophets expressed the firmest hope and the most unbounded confidence in the promises of God, and this confidence is regarded as the prerequisite of all Hebrew piety. Yet their trust is passive rather than active and expresses itself in willing obedience to the law of God and hope in the promises which are annexed to obedience.

The Captivity, which brought to a close the long history of the monarchy, was even more significant for the inner than for the external life. Before considering in detail any of the effects of the Captivity one must realize the position which Babylon held toward the world of Western Asia. As Greece was the "Holy Land" and Athens the "Holy City" of cultivated paganism in the West, as Jerusalem was the Holy City of the Jew, so was Babylon the "Holy City" of Mesopotamia. From the remotest period of their history the Hebrews had been directly or indirectly under the influence of the ancient civilization of Babylonia. So widespread and so powerful were the underlying Babylonian ideas of the world that we may say they became, especially through the biblical creation stories, the conceptions which governed human thought from the conversion of the Empire up to the time when the new scientific point of view began to influence the European mind. At no time were these influences concentrated upon the Hebrews with

more power than during the era of the Captivity, and
their whole subsequent history bears the marks of this
contact.

Two results wrought by the Captivity in the external
fortunes of the people stand out in striking prominence.
In the first place, the Hebrew nation as a body was
totally destroyed. Only a fragment remained unabsorbed
by its conquerors and even this remnant no longer bore
the name of Israelite, but the people were henceforth called
Jews. In the second place, during the Exile the people
forgot or lost their ancient tongue and adopted that
which was known as the Aramaic, which had been, ever
since the age of Assyria, the speech of business and
diplomacy.

The Captivity which bid fair to end the national history and wipe the name of the Hebrew from the list of
nations was ended by the hand of Persia. The power
which wrought the deliverance of the Jew also broke the
might of the ancient kingdom which had taken him cap-
tive, and Persia became in turn the dominating influence,
for a time at least, in the new life of the people. The
attitude of Cyrus toward the Jews and of the Jews
toward Cyrus indicates a larger degree of understanding
and sympathy than might at first have been inferred.
The relations between them seem to have been friendly
and intimate, and in the Persian dominions, Judaism had
a free development, but must have been profoundly
affected by its intercourse with its powerful master.

The Persian religion contained a close union of religious and ethical ideas of the most powerful nature
and this combination appealed most strongly to the Jewish spirit. The movement of Persia toward the West
is one of the most important facts of this period of history and also one of the prime factors in the later development of religious thought and life in all the territories
to which its power spread. The mutual influence which

the various nations of Western Asia exerted upon each other were vastly increased. Indeed, the Jewish Captivity laid the foundations of a great syncretistic movement which continued during the two centuries of the Achæmenidæ, through the Alexandrian period, involved the entire Orient, and can hardly be said to have ended even when the Roman power welded the whole Mediterranean basin into one huge empire.

Through the destruction of the national states which continued through this long period, all the religions of the East lost their earlier national character. State and religion were no more united as they had been. Hence religion sought a new basis. More than that, the early authority was broken. The national life, as such, having ceased to be, the individual lost the protection of ancient institutions and traditions and oftentimes became the center and subject of powerful and foreign religious ideas and influences. The breakdown of the early limitations of life has always the utmost significance in the development of the soul. A keener sense of the soul's solitude begins to penetrate into consciousness. From this isolated and personal position, with its wider outlook, the divine relations are felt in a more individual way and members of other nations and races are dimly seen to be included in the divine purpose. When this consciousness begins to stir, the movement toward a universal religion has set in.

Amid all the confusion of this huge welter of peoples and religions, two points of supreme importance begin to emerge. The first is what we would call Individualism or the sense of personality, with its dawning self-consciousness and the growing worth of the soul. The second is Universalism, with its dim apprehension of the unity of man as well as of God. On the other hand, the immense ferment threw up much which had slowly been sinking away from the purer and nobler thought of the past. Man was, so to speak, thrown backward, and ancient and primitive superstitions which lie at the base of all old religions came again into prominence.

For Judaism the most important fact in the time immediately subsequent to the return of the Exiles is the establishment of Judaism as a Church through the rebuilding of the Temple. In the formation of the restored people as a Church it has been asserted that Persia played a very prominent part, and, if religious ideas are significant in the life of an institution, it cannot be doubted that Persia made large and important contributions.

The religious value of the new Temple was not so great as has often been assumed. The long agony of the Exile had given a pathos and a passion to the religious feelings of the more pious Jews which the Restoration and prosperity could not entirely destroy. But this spiritualizing process, this growth in religious self-consciousness, was somewhat checked by the rebuilding of the Temple, which placed an external object as a center of the religious life of the Jew and narrowed and hardened the horizon before the groping eyes which were dim with new desires.

Hitherto, Asia and its peoples had pursued their own path and worked out their own destiny practically alone. Oriental influences had, it is true, spread to the farther West, and Hellenic theology was everywhere pervaded by ideas and religious sentiments coming from the Orient. After the Persian War many foreign religions were brought to Athens, most of them from the East. Hitherto, however, the West had failed in any decided way to influence the course of Eastern history. But in the fourth century before Christ Alexander invaded the East. The crash of falling kingdoms followed his swift and wonderful march and in a few short years the East was forever changed. The ancient and powerful enemies of Israel were broken by the arms of this youth from

Macedonia and before his death Judaism was facing a new and wonderful future. The old races of the East lost more and more their separate character: the blending of the various types was accelerated; the blinding confusion which so many and rapid changes had brought about, was intensified; and, as the strong fabric of the ages crumbled and passed away, the earth seemed to rock under the hesitating feet of thrice-bewildered men. It was an age of national dissolution, of the blending of many races, the fading of old differences, distinctions, and languages. New ideas and new thoughts flowed through old channels of the human mind and strange religions met and exchanged arms in the wild ferment of this changeful period.

For the first time the bright sun of Hellas shone into the dark secrets of the East and oriental races felt that the old mysteries of life had new interpretations which they were eager to know. In the dissolving of old ties and the release from hereditary limitations the new not only found a foothold but the old was set free to gain new territory. Great as the political significance of the Alexandrian period was—and it practically rearranged the whole map of the world—the religious significance is even greater. With the destruction of the old states and institutions the national religions fell to pieces and a mass of secret sects sprang up everywhere filled with a common feeling for the awful and the unknown. The vivid oriental imagination, with its strange and grotesque phantasms, wandered half blinded in the clear light which Greek thought flung upon the world. The hideous demon-worship of the past emerged from the darkness of the primitive stages of the race and made its appeal side by side with the calm and lucid demonstrations of the Greek mind. Everywhere a vast collapse seemed to overwhelm the old faiths. As Bousset has pointed out, there appears to be some unknown and mysterious psychologi-

cal law, in accordance with which, when the old faiths
break down, still earlier superstitions revive and primitive instincts spring up again in new vigor. Palestine
was the retort into which the life of the old world was
flung and in which all the different elements were mingled
and blended together. It held them all in solution, indeed, but it could not give them vitality. In vain Judaism
tried to shut itself within itself and exclude all these new
and foreign influences. It was at the very heart of the
storm and felt all its power. The new forces flung themselves upon it and swept it into the vast current which
was setting toward the future. Greek speech, Greek
knowledge, and Greek thought, as well as Babylonish and
Egyptian theology and magic, together with all the characteristic influences of the Ancient World freely entered
and affected for better and for worse the life of the
people. The Jew at the end of this period was quite different from the Jew at the beginning.

Western Asia now became organically related to
Europe and the two parts mutually influenced and
affected each other. Greek, the Macedonian dialect, was
the prevailing language in the Western civilization, and
Aramaic became the common speech of the East. During
the Macedonian period the Jew spread everywhere: east
and west, north and south, from Media to Spain, from
the Crimea to Ethiopia he wandered with his austere
thoughts and repellent ways. The two most important
facts in the external history of the Macedonian period
of Judaism are the Diaspora and the establishment of
the synagogue as a widespread institution. They stand
in the closest relation to each other and are deeply significant for the future of Judaism.

The new life of the Greek Diaspora presented many
and striking contrasts with the existing Palestinian Judaism. In the first place, the Jews again adopted a new
language and even the Aramaic speech of Palestine was

almost entirely lost among them. This new language opened up another world of ideas and the richest philosophic literature of Antiquity. The calm sanity of the Greek thought sprang from an entirely different source from that of their accustomed circle of ideas. The danger was lest they should be absorbed in the dominant mass of heathenism which surrounded them as had occurred again and again to portions of the people in the past. The struggle to maintain the old religious convictions under the new circumstances was, in spite of the popular view of the origin of the Septuagint, undoubtedly one of the strongest motives for its translation. Yet nothing could protect the Jew of the Diaspora from the effects of the Greek influence. Remoteness from the old life, wide differences in the intellectual and social atmosphere, in the habits of life and in language, could not be without the most marked effects upon the Jews scattered throughout the West. This was more particularly the case in Alexandria, which was the meeting point for the two great streams that had been flowing toward each other during the long centuries of the past.

The Septuagint translation was itself much influenced by its environment. The very fact that Scriptures could be read in the idiom of the Greek market place robbed them of much of their exclusively national character. Even more important was the fact that the contact of the Jew with Greek philosophy and Greek science revealed a striking contrast with the archaic and concrete forms of early Hebrew literary expression. This contrast made some modifications necessary in order to bring the translation abreast with the more modern and scientific ideas which filled the new environment. The old anthropomorphic phrases of the past were repellent to more philosophical modes of thought. The transcendental conceptions of the philosophical faith of Greece, the tendency to abstractions, the purely intellectual way in which the problems of life were conceived and expressed, made the ancient Hebrew literature appear simple and childish. As a consequence, in the course of the translation the earlier language was often modified and softened, and, in some instances, passages were changed or omitted. Yet even with the most careful readjustment it was impossible to reconcile the old texts with the prevailing views.

A new mode of interpretation was therefore applied which had already done service in the reconciliation of the early Greek literature and mythology with philosophy. It was long before this received a scientific form and became the recognized method of Scriptural interpretation; but the Allegorical Method as it appears in Philo is but the systematizing of a hermeneutic which had long been in use. Passing from him into the Christian Church it became the "damnosa hereditas" of biblical interpretation for nearly two thousand years.

The Jew in contact with Hellenic culture and science found presented to him not only a different theory or mode of conceiving God, but also a contrasted conception of man. A different psychological factor was brought into play which inevitably widened and deepened his own consciousness. In the days before the Exile the Jew had heard the voice of God from the mouth of the prophet, and followed, with a placid freedom from self-analysis, the commands which came to him. In the ages following the Exile the same attitude continued, though the source of authority was the Book of the Law, and the interpretations of its recognized teachers became the legal expression of the Divine Will. The aim of life was righteousness, which meant obedience. So the appeal of Judaism in Palestine was made directly to the will and a strenuous and continuous effort to obey was regarded as the foundation of the religious life.

The aim of Hellenic thought was also righteousness.

But the meaning of righteousness was not primarily obedience to an objective external law, but rather the development of man by the upbuilding of his powers; all the various functions of mind and body were to come to their realization and fullness in the ideal man. The ideal of Jewish piety was the saint or the prophet, with the eye directly fixed upon God and the soul silent and passive until the command came to it. Duty and service to a revealed will, expressed in obedience to specific commands and regulations, were the fundamental characteristics of this religious ideal. These constituted righteousness and this was the end of life. Energy, action, passion, and awe were the strongest elements in the individual life. Strenuous as it might be, there were certain elements of simplicity in it and an absence of self-consciousness which made it seem to the Greek, with his more complex problems and deeper reflective nature, elementary and primitive. The differences which existed had their roots in certain psychological contrasts which lay at the bottom of the opposing ideals, though they might not be recognized. Virtue, as the Greek conceived it, has its roots not in an external law, nor primarily in the human will, but in an internal process. By an evolution in the mind itself and in the disposition of the man himself, in which thinking is the most important part, and which is in close and organic relation with the will, is the end reached, which is virtue. The human reason is the instrument and origin of virtue, for it is only through reason that man can understand either God, himself, or life. All statements, definitions, or thoughts about God or man must be founded upon and make their ultimate appeal to reason. There is no authority which can supersede this final court of appeal. The worth and meaning of man must then consist in reason, and religion must necessarily have the same aim—the highest reason.

For the Jew the reason was only subordinate. Act

seemed to him more than thought, and so he regarded the will as the essential and primary factor in the human soul. Thus from Greece came the high regard for the powers of thought; from Jerusalem the deep appreciation of the human will. Is there any unity which will include them both? Is there any syncretism which will recognize and reconcile these opposing truths? The problem pressed with strange surprise upon the Jew of the Diaspora when he set out to the West from Asiatic shores.

The harmony between the moral instincts of the Jew, rooted as they were in the very fiber of his nature, and the scientific ethics of the Greek, produced a deep and lasting effect. The contrast between his intense emotional apprehension and the sharp precision of the Greek logic roused his own intellectual interest and led him to attempt a more formal statement of his faith than he had hitherto sought. So long as religion did not pass beyond the national limits it did not know and it did not need any statements, dogmas or creed. Broadly apprehended by the soul of the people, it was largely tradition, national custom, or use. It had grown up through many centuries and was rooted in the soil of the national life. It was not keenly self-conscious, and required and called forth no reflection or theoretical statements. When, however, the Jew was separated from the national life, or this national life for him had ceased to exist, his religious life assumed a somewhat different character. An effort, deliberate or unconscious, was put forth to state his religious ideas or convictions in definite form.

The attitude of the Jew to his environment was not merely receptive. In the Jewish life since the Exile two different conceptions were present governing the relations between Jew and heathen. According to one, Israel is the servant of God who shall bring the true light to the world. He is a missionary, a preacher, sent for the redemption of mankind in general. It was not a new view. It lurked in the heart of many an Hebrew of the past and burst forth in passionate words from many of the greatest prophets. The other view is that God has chosen Israel for His people and left the world to the guidance and government of angels and spirits.

Generally speaking, the Jew of the Diaspora, whether consciously or unconsciously, seems to have adopted the former view, and a widespread and eager propaganda was carried on among the heathen nations with which he was brought in contact. Since the Exile the proselytes had also grown to be a great and powerful element in Jewish life notwithstanding the exclusiveness of the Pharisaical party. Philo believed in this Jewish propaganda and advocated it very strongly.

In order to find points of contact and make the appeal stronger, the teachers of the Diaspora presented Judaism chiefly on its moral side and suppressed almost entirely the legal aspects which had already lost some of their significance to the foreign-born Jew. Ethics gained a prominence which they had not hitherto possessed, save in practice, and spoke with a more deliberate and universal authority when they had behind them and within them the religious root and inspiration. The ethical mood which had taken possession of heathenism and which was manifest particularly in the philosophy of the Cynics and Stoics augmented the force of this appeal and led many to Judaism. The peculiar character of this influence was totally unlike that which the philosophical school exerted. The cardinal Jewish doctrine, the Unity of God, was asserted with the utmost emphasis and its acceptance drew the proselyte within the wide fold of Judaism.

The mixed character of Jewish feeling, however, should not be overlooked. On the one side, it is true, the conciliating propaganda was carried on with the greatest zeal, but on the other still remained, to a greater or less degree, the old inherited national particularism. All were invited to the new light and the stranger who walked in the fear of the Lord was held in high esteem and respect. Yet the ritual law of circumcision, which was a necessary prerequisite to full incorporation in the Jewish family, kept many heathen from full membership. As this could not apply to women, we find the gains were proportionally larger among them than among men. Greek philosophy had already begun to teach, especially through Stoicism, the unity of the human race, and the widespread Jewish propaganda brought this new idea into a clearer light and gave a deeper and more solid foundation in religion than the dogma of philosophy possessed. Thus, as the Jewish Diaspora grasped more clearly its own mission, there came into view a new philosophical and religious principle, that of Universalism. But the growth of this new idea deepened the sense of personality and individualism and amid the immense confusion of men's thoughts paved the way for new ideas and vast changes which no man could foresee. The spiritualizing of the nature of God which was a necessary basis for a genuine Universalism had, as its inevitable correlate, an intensifying of the personal consciousness and a decided and positive growth in individualism.

One of the most effective agencies in this powerful propaganda was the synagogue, whose character and influence will be set forth more fully in dealing with the inner religious life of Judaism. The synagogue did not arise in the Diaspora but was of Palestinian origin and was taken into the Diaspora when Jews left their native land. The relations between the two portions of the people were, however, very close and the emigrant Jew always looked back with unabated affection to the far-off hill of Zion and the mysterious Temple with its sacrifices and songs in which he perhaps had never personally shared. No change took place in the thought or fortune of the one without affecting in some degree or manner those of the other.

The years between the conquests of Alexander and the birth of Christ are, as we have seen, filled with changes which wrought a revolution in the whole nature of Judaism and give us some of the most interesting pages in its history. The outer fortunes of the race reacted upon the national mind and gave it new impulses and new directions. We need to know what was passing in Judea as well as in Alexandria in order thoroughly to grasp the significance of these centuries for the spiritual revolution or evolution in the history of the western world. The historical material which we have for this period seems to show that Hellenic thought and culture were received with great enthusiasm by a large part of the people. The syncretistic movement begun in Babylon was about to take a great leap forward. A political and skeptical priesthood, an eager intellect and the fascinations of a new and wider horizon led to the adoption of Hellenic customs and habits by an ever-increasing number of the people in Palestine itself. All sides of life were affected by the pressure of the Greek life and thought introduced by the new masters. The conciliating attitude of the new rulers, the reconciling tendencies which were at work in the national life, led to the strangest and most dangerous compromises. It is stated that they went so far on this path that a delegation was sent from Jerusalem to Tyre with an offering for the shrine of the Tyrian Herakles and the messengers only escaped the charge of idolatry by a dodge (II Mac. 4, 18-20).

With the reign of Antioches IV, called Epiphanes, matters were brought to a crisis. After a period of senseless tyranny and oppression by the madman, the Jews broke out in revolt. The movement began in the year 168 B.C. and forms one of the most splendid pages in

Jewish history. It was a purely national protest and
had consequences of the greatest importance not only for
the external but also for the internal life of the people.
The numbers of the Diaspora were greatly increased by
the fierce struggle which was taking place on Jewish soil
and the ultimate victory of the Maccabeans extended the
territory of Judaism and brought an increasing number
under the rule of the Law. This in turn was interpreted
with greater rigor and wider application. Under the
influence of this struggle a new spirit issued out of the
ferment into which the people were thrown. As an expression of this new spirit there arose at this time, or
very shortly after, that new institution which is peculiar
to the Jews above all ancient peoples—that is, the Synagogue. The study of the Law had grown to be one of
the great preoccupations of those among the people
whose minds were fixed upon the glories and the promises
of the past. The terrible struggle for self-preservation
intensified the national spirit and deepened and individu-
alized the piety. The more personal the religious life, the
more each soul was taught to regard itself as in specific
religious relations, the more the individual religious consciousness was developed, the more the Temple with its
external character and forms would stand outside the
growth of the popular religious life. The sacerdotal aristocracy gradually lost its preëminence, and in the place
of it there arose a pious lay democracy. The wide extension of the synagogue is one of the cardinal facts of later
Jewish history. It made religion the property of every
man by planting it in the heart of his daily life. Thus
religion was no longer a matter of the priesthood but
became a lay affair, almost entirely divorced from the
historic authority which was embodied in the priesthood.
As the synagogue could and did exist wherever the Jew
might be, it became the center of his religious interest.
Yet the movement of Jewish history was at no one time

the development of one single and powerful religious impulse. On the contrary, there was the greatest complexity. While with some the Maccabean struggle deepened the national sentiment and increased the spiritual devotion, in others the very victory gave rise to other ideals and opened the way for political ambitions which could be obtained only by the sacrifice of the more spiritual instincts of the race.

It was during this period that the parties we are familiar with in the time of Christ had their origin; or, if not their origin, they then obtained a development which they had not hitherto reached and attained a position which they never lost until the fall of the City in the year 70 A.D. Our concern with them is only in the way they reveal the religious interests of the people and advance or retard its spiritual development. The discussions about the meaning and origin of the different religious sects of Judaism are so familiar that it is unnecessary to enter upon them here. There seems to be little dispute about the Sadducees. They are generally regarded as the representatives of the old religious views which were national rather than personal and contained few of those new and vital elements which gave such an intense vividness and vigor to the later religious spirit of Judaism. They were the High Priestly Party. This older type had but little influence upon the later development and furnished none of those earnest spirits who gave such character and passion to the religious life. Some have asserted that Sadduceism was only the continuation of the Greek party among the Jews, but the majority of writers and the weight of evidence point to the view here presented.

In the time of Ezra and Nehemiah there existed an element in the national life which was bitterly opposed to the wider and more generous outlook of the prophets and the disposition to adopt foreign ideas or establish foreign relations. The slow movement of the national life and the unspiritual tendencies which were manifesting themselves indicated that a spiritual exhaustion and a vital decay might be close at hand. The outburst of the Maccabean struggle revived all the forces of the national life, and the intense sympathy of the party of the "Pious," with the new movement and aspirations, gave it increasing prominence. When the outbreak assumed more and more a political tendency the relations between it and the party of the "Pious" became increasingly strained. The intense preoccupation of the "Pious" with purely religious ideas deprived them of all interest in simply political or national views. This, in the end, no doubt contributed largely to the weakening of the Maccabean power. Yet it would be an overestimate to lay too great emphasis upon their position in the beginning of the Maccabean period. Although John Hyrcanus had closely allied himself with them he did not hesitate at a later day to separate himself from them. Had they been the dominant party among the people he would not in all probability have done this. When the Maccabean power was ended and the hand of the stranger was upon the neck of the Jew, the Pharisee turned increasingly to the inner life. The problem of his own soul and the study of the Law absorbed him more and more. As he separated himself from the purely political party he also drew away from the priestly caste which was in close alliance with the national element. In the end, national and political affairs had little interest for him because they were considered as profane. And finally the Pharisee found no difficulty in accepting the rule of the Herods, since he thought all these matters lay outside the real life of the soul. As a matter of fact, however, many Pharisees were found in almost all the political disturbances throughout the later centuries.

In what relation the origin of the synagogue stands to

Pharisaism it is impossible to determine. The growth of Pharisaism undoubtedly contributed to strengthen the interest in the synagogue, and the synagogue in turn was an instrument ready to the hand of the Pharisee. The institution of the synagogue was probably due, at least in part, to the increasing interest in the study of the Law. This study engrossed the minds of some of the most earnest and religious spirits of the age. The more the necessity of the knowledge of the Law, the more its acquisition became the task of a special body of students, who in turn became the teachers of the people. The rise of those significant figures in Jewish history, the Rabbis, dates back probably to the establishment of the synagogue, but it was through the latter that their influence became more directly felt and more widely extended. Yet the synagogue was not merely a vehicle for Pharisaism. It became the chief organ of Jewish piety through all the later ages of its history. It was far more widely spread and vastly more influential in the general life of Judaism than Pharisaism and it is through the synagogue that the religious instincts of the people express themselves today. It was here the Law was read and expounded and it was here that the young were instructed in the great principles of religion. Owing to its intimate and somewhat informal character it was an ever-present influence in the life of every Jew. The instruction of the young was one of its more important functions and the Hebrew Bible was the primer by which the youth of the land was made familiar with the will and ways of God. So much did the study of the Scripture occupy the time and attention of the young that the synagogue was often called the "House of the Book." To cultivate the highest and most personal side of the religious life, that of prayer, became one of the great aims of its instruction. One of the chief duties of each teacher was to tell his pupils how to pray. This fact lay behind the appeal which the disciples on a certain occasion made to Jesus (Luke 11, 1).

Through the agency of the synagogue the whole of life was thus surrounded by a religious atmosphere. It is true that an enormous number of petty practices were introduced by the ultra-scrupulous, and details unspeakably trivial were forced upon the mind and life. But the great body of the people, however much they might admire or revere the strict Pharisee, lived a free life, influenced only by those simpler teachings which had their home in the synagogue.

The importance of the priesthood was not only lessened, but that order itself was more or less subordinated, in the respect and reverence of the people, to the new teachers whose authority was constantly increasing.

At this point a new phase of religious development appears. It is one which has been characteristic of all religions as they advance from the stage of emotion and conviction to that of study and reflection. The great leaders are the scholars, the theologians, who, by virtue of superior knowledge, are entitled to speak with authority on matters of faith. Speculation is not necessarily destructive of piety, nor, on the other hand, can it be identified with it. The legal character of the prevailing religious conceptions undoubtedly hastened the growth of casuistry from the moment the mind became absorbed in religious problems. This was characteristically so in Palestine.

The part which the synagogue played in the Diaspora was a double one. It was the common center of the Jewish life and also the instrument by which the heathen were led to the teachings of the ancient religion. The pagans were cordially invited to the services and oftentimes formed a large part, if not the most important part, of the congregation. Of course, the tendency, if not the necessity, under the circumstances, involved the simplifying and softening of the teaching in order that it might make the strongest and most direct appeal to the awakening interest of the heathen hearers. Love of God, love of virtue, love of man, were the central points of the synagogue teaching and these were regarded as the ethical substance of Judaism. The only requisites for membership as demanded by at least a section of the Alexandrian Diaspora, were baptism and repentance; but the baptism had no sacramental character. The Palestinian Pharisee had taken quite a disapproving attitude toward the hellenization of Judaism. He had the very strongest dislike for the Septuagint and considered it an unqualified injury to Judaism. The Pharisee regarded the day upon which it first saw the light as a fast day and compared it with the one when Israel made the Golden Calf. He also looked with suspicion and dislike upon the movement for the conversion of the heathen. He did not believe in the genuineness of such conversion, for it seemed to involve compromises and sacrifices which he was unwilling to make. The religious need which drew the pagan toward Judaism did not appeal to him; and, when later he saw this same half-Jew turn toward the preachers of the Gospel, he said, "Trust not a proselyte in the fortieth generation." The contrast between the Palestinian Pharisee and the Jew of the Diaspora was most clearly manifest when Pharisaism had reached its most formal development and hellenistic Judaism was attaining a form which could not but be repellent to the formalist of Jerusalem. If the rabbi of Judea was a bitter literalist, the typical teacher of the Diaspora seemed to the Palestinian to have lost himself in dreams and in the vague abstractions of a transcendental theory. If the Jew at home held hard and fast to a cold and rigid classification of religious duties, the hellenistic Jew plunged into the most abstruse speculations and allegorical interpretations. If an exaggerated idealism reigned, for example, in Alexandria, an even more exaggerated formalism prevailed in Jerusalem. The absence of the authoritative teachers of the Law among the Diaspora further accentuated the difference. Yet, however great the influence of Pharisaism was in Palestine, it can easily be over-rated. It is the one sect with which Jesus was most frequently in conflict, and its hostility was probably the primary cause of his death. Yet numerically we are assured that it numbered scarcely more than 6,000.

Side by side with Pharisaism were working other forces less striking to the eye perhaps, but perhaps exerting a deeper influence and representing a more vital spiritual energy. The most significant of these less noticeable forces was Essenism. It has been conjectured that Essenism originated in the pre-Maccabean period before the rise of Pharisaism. The time of its origin and the elements which contributed to its formation cannot be fully determined. Many things point to foreign influences. In the beginning of its history it probably represented but a small element in the community. Judaism, as a religion, was the least ascetic of any of which we have any knowledge. It must have been out of some reaction, together with some outside force that Essenism gained its place and power. One of the laws of religious evolution seems to be, that every religion as it advances tends to organize itself in institutions and define its thought in theologies. The more outward and formal, the more rigid and positive become the statutes, the more the inherent vitality of the religious spirit protests against this inflexibility and formalism. The more objective religion becomes, the more the religious spirit turns inward and apart. No sooner is a church formed than monasticism begins to develop. As soon as religion tends to become reduced to a ritual individual spirits plunge into mysticism and contemplation.

Other reasons may be added which would lead us to

infer a greater influence for Essenism than its historic records would suggest. At first glance Pharisaism seems like an exaggeration of the moral tone of the Old Testament. When ethics and religion are identified, or when morality is regarded as in itself answering all the requirements of the religious spirit, a hopeless confusion ensues. Out of this confusion naturally springs the assertion that religion is a matter of legal prescription. It is the religious sentiment, the instinct for piety to which the monastic movement of Essenism appealed. As has been said, nothing is less ascetic than the ancient Hebrew piety, and the rise of a monastic institution at this time shows a deep revolt from the established forms of religious life, and the atmosphere which surrounded them. This break with the common rule and the prevailing modes of thought is a revelation not only of the growth of the personal consciousness, but of the syncretistic tendencies of the age. It is the expression not only of the essentially subjective character of religion as opposed to its merely outward manifestation, but also indicates the probable presence of a foreign influence. The number of Essenes as given by Josephus is not great, about 4,000. This statement refers probably to those who belonged to the order and lived according to its rules. Besides these there were many who lived in the world, scattered throughout the towns and villages and in daily intercourse with the inhabitants. Some writers think St. John the Baptist was an Essene. In many cases they were teachers of the young and contributed to the extension of their doctrines and the knowledge of the purposes of the party. Essenism seems to have been sufficiently widespread and prominent to attract the attention of the heathen, for it is mentioned by the Roman Pliny.

No popular dislike appears to have been aroused by the ceremonies of the Essenes. From a negative point of view Essenism would apparently have been obnoxious to public sentiment by its distinct and emphatic rejection of sacrifice and of the services of the Temple. Yet it stood very high in popular regard and excited both admiration and reverence in the minds of the people.

Outside the well-known parties of the Sadducees, Pharisees, and Essenes, whose numbers were confessedly small, lay the great mass of the people who were only in part affected by them. This popular element, the Am-haarez, was despised by the Pharisees. They were unable to observe the rigid legal observances of Pharisaism. It is asserted that they even rejected circumcision. The traditional method of interpreting the Scriptures gave way among them to a freer and more personal use, and works of mercy were highly esteemed. It was in this class that the large body of literature known as "Apocalyptic" had its origin. In considering the documents we realize that they throw a light upon the inner life of the period which we get no where else. We grasp the new motives and sentiments, the color and character, the religious ideas, and the type of piety which were developing among the mass of the people during these long and stormy years.

The Apocalyptic books were primarily and essentially popular. They owe their origin in almost every instance to special historical crises. Regarded from a purely literary point of view they possess but few merits, yet the absence of these is the best evidence of their popular origin and purpose. They represent the life and passion which, for two centuries, throbbed in the breasts of men obscure and despised, who found in them an expression of that which was moving them so deeply. A wild prophetic spirit breathes from these unknown writers, and a bitterness toward the old religious authorities. One of the latest goes so far as to denounce the priests as liars and bloodsuckers. It may not be possible to determine all the causes behind this literature, but there are some few very decisive ones which must be recognized. The old prophetic view of the national life and the historic destiny could not maintain itself in the face of the vicissitudes which, century after century, fell upon the people. The national interpretation of life was a failure in the presence of the hard facts. As the integrity of the nation became more and more a dream, the uncertainty of the future sharpened the spiritual depression and raised painful questions about the future of the individual. The collapse or breakdown of the traditional faith never drives the mass of a people to find any rest or comfort in philosophical speculation. It only opens the way for new ideas and hopes which will make a more direct and personal appeal than the old theory. The new literature which was born of these conditions had as its object the solution of the problem which was presented by the sufferings of the servants of God. How could these be reconciled with God's righteousness and what relation had it to the new sense of self-consciousness which was emerging? However earnestly the old point of view might be asserted, the shock of disappointment accompanying the failure to reconcile God's righteousness with the conditions of fact and thought, made the process of readjustment a manifest effort. A more vivid self-consciousness was born of these struggles. The soul of the Jew was

"Wandering between two worlds, one dead,
The other powerless to be born."

There are distinct traces of new ideas in the Apocalypses which have an inner relation to the spiritual development of the people, though, in some cases, this relation is obscure and may seem doubtful. Ideas, which appeal to the imagination and hover in that border land where superstitions have their root and strength, first catch the eye. Among these new elements the most striking perhaps is the angelology which appears first in this period and gradually develops until it becomes an established force in Jewish thought. The resemblances of this angelology to the Persian, and the fact that it appears only after the contact of Judaism with the powerful Persian and Babylonian religions, leave little doubt that it was from the East it was derived, and was not a natural product of Jewish thought. At first the angels represented only impersonal agencies which pervade the unseen world. As time passed on and the Achæmenian Empire rolled its huge waves of conquest toward the west the system became more and more developed. In time names were given to these powers which are almost identical with the Babylonian, and a regular hierarchy was formed which passed easily over into the Christian Church. Its origin is unquestionably Babylonian, but by what steps or under what influence, whether from the Orient or as a natural process of thought, the angelology became dogmatic, we do not know. It played, however, an ever-increasing part in the post-exilian period of Judaism. To determine its value in the evolution of the religious life of the Jews is by no means an easy problem. One thing seems manifest: that is, the belief in spirits, good and evil, has stood in very close relation to the religious and psychological development of man. It appears to be a stage, and almost a necessary stage, through which all religion passes on its way to a free and spiritual interpretation of life. On its psychological side belief in angels deepened the sense of personality by surrounding the individual with unseen influences which exert their power in the region of the inner life. The Dualism which it represented and which it brought before the soul contributed also to deepen the intensity of the moral discords of which the soul was becoming conscious. This growth in self-knowledge and spiritual perception was assisted by other ideas and truths, which, working side by side, moved upon the life.

The Apocalypses also reveal the emergence of a new

thought of the individual destiny, the conception of the
Resurrection, adopted in Palestine, but not, apparently,
in the Diaspora. The hellenistic Jew seems to have taken
in its place the Greek idea of the immortality of the soul.
Even in Palestine itself the distinction which exists between the Babylonish and Greek conception of the destiny of the individual comes to light. The Pharisee
asserted the resurrection of the body and the Essene
denied it. The Essene affirmed, on the other hand, the
immortality of the soul which he probably derived from
hellenistic Judaism. That this article of faith or new
element of thought and life, the resurrection, was not of
Jewish origin might be inferred from the fact that the
Sadducees repudiated it as not forming any part of the
ancient faith which they claimed to preserve intact. The
prophetic literature gives no clue to the immense development which the idea later received, nor in the piety
of the Psalmist is any root manifest from which it could
arise. The prophet had preached a hope for the people,
not the individual, and the "Land of the Living" is the
horizon of the Psalmist's praises. There seems to be no
intuition and no process of reflection out of which it
could spring at the time it did appear; so we must look
for its source in the external experiences of the nation.
An examination of the Apocalyptic literature will show
constant references to the Resurrection, Hell, an Eternal
Life in Heaven, future rewards and punishments, of
which there are no traces in the Old Testament literature
and which, therefore, must have been derived from other
and foreign sources. Renan did not hesitate to affirm the
Persian origin of these doctrines and to determine the
exact historical moment when they became the property
and faith of the Jew. "Persia believed in the Resurrection before the Jew did. The martyr was the creator of
a belief in another life. . . . The date of this belief
among the Jews is therefore fixed. Antiochus and the

book of Daniel represent the cause and the expression."
It is very fine to be able to speak as positively as Renan
does of such a difficult historical problem, but other critics
are not so definite. Bousset believes that the point of
contact with the Persian religion is to be placed in the
Mesopotamian basin or more strictly in the territory of
Babylon about the beginning of the age of the Diadochi,
and that the idea of the Resurrection became widespread
among the Jews about the year 200 B.C. Some critics,
however, while clearly recognizing the Persian influence,
have also insisted upon the presence of Egyptian elements
in the growth of the idea among the Jews. The form
which it took was largely affected by the inherent materialism of the national mind which caused it to take somewhat hard and crude views of spiritual truths. It was,
therefore, naturally inclined to interpret the new thought
in the most objective and material manner. Yet this
narrow materialism could not prevent the rise of questions which were most intimately associated with the fate
of the individual. The thought of the Present and the
Future which stand opposed to each other in the idea of
the Resurrection react upon the individual consciousness
and give an added sharpness and depth to moral sentiment. The very thought of the Future Judgment which
is associated with the Resurrection had a profound effect
upon his inner moral development. The sense of personal
responsibility which was emphasized by the coming judgment grew keener and keener, and was accompanied by
an inward feeling of uncertainty which produced the
most acute self-consciousness. The inflexibility of the
judgment of God, toward whom many looked only with
fear and dread, produced a spiritual pessimism which
filled the soul with a misery far beyond the physical experiences in which the new consciousness had its roots.
We see it reflected in the awful anxiety of the dying
rabbi who said: "Before me are two ways, the one leads

to the Garden of Eden, the other to Gehenna, and I know not upon which I shall go."

If the Palestinian Jew received his faith in the Resurrection from the East, the hellenistic Jew derived his conception of the spirit of man and that of immortality from the Greek. The spiritualizing tendency which is a peculiar mark of the higher Greek thought reveals its influence over the mind of the Diaspora in the emphasis which is here laid upon Immortality rather than upon the bodily resurrection. Although the material does not seem to warrant a strict line of demarcation between the two branches of Judaism, since the common root of faith would naturally lead to a fusion of the prevailing tendencies in both, yet Nicolas has gone so far as to say: "No Palestinian document ever speaks of the immortality of the soul and no Alexandrian ever asserts the resurrection of the body." If the bodily resurrection was held by the Diaspora, as doubtless in many cases it was, it nevertheless yielded in interest and prominence to that of the continuous existence of the spirit which is the essence of immortality.[1]

The most distinctive contribution of the period represented by the Apocalypses is the elaboration of the Messianic expectation. The growth of this idea and its reflex action upon the spiritual nature makes it, in many respects, the center of the religious life of pre-Christian

[1] An examination of the following passages will show how difficult it is to draw a sharp line between the thought of the Palestinian and the hellenistic Jew, though the different tendencies may be recognized and felt rather than distinguished. Enoch, c. 51. Apoc. Baruch, c. 30, 42, 50, 51. Test. Juda. 3.24, 25. Test. Zebulon c. 9. Test. Benjamin c. 10. Apoc. Moses c. 10. Psalms of Sol. IV. Macc. c. 14, 16, 19. Enoch, 22, 103. II. Macc. c. 7, 9. 7, 11. 7, 14, 23. c. 12, 44, 45. Baruch, c. 2, 17. Son of Sirach c. 7, 17. 48, 5. Wisdom of Sol. c. 2, 23. 4, 1, 16. 5, 15, 16. 6, 18, 8, 18, 17. 15, 3.

A well-defined doctrine of immortality is not in Sirach, I. Macc. Tobit, Judith. In the later extra Palestinian writers it is different. In Wisdom the temporal and eternal life are contrasted and opposed to each other. 3, 13 ff., 4, 2. III. Macc. the same. Ps. Sol. 13, 11. IV. Ezra 13, 23. *Die Apokryphen und Pseudepigraphen d. A. T.*, pp. 109, 112. L. Couard.

Judaism. Even the fact that it arose throws a powerful and illuminating light upon the inner life of the period.

Judaism is not alone in the feeling and expression of the desire for Redemption. The general idea which we associate with the Messiah seems to be an early and deep instinct of the race, so soon as it has reached a definite stage in its historical progress. How and to what extent the remoter and earlier history of this idea was affected by Babylonian influence would be difficult to say. If foreign influences exerted any formative power in the earlier ages, they were undoubtedly largely modified by the purely Jewish expression which sprang out of the nation's historical experience and which is manifest as one of the characteristic notes of the prophetic movement.

After the Exile, and particularly in that period which has its inner life revealed in the Apocalyptic literature and the Apocalyptic dreams of later Judaism, there are some noticeable variations from the vagueness of earlier prophetic hopes. The disappearance of the Jewish kingdom left no room for the simple and natural expansion of the prophetic idea. When, however, hope survived and exerted any power, it was in a different form and called for a catastrophe by means of which the new kingdom should be inaugurated and established. This new kingdom was not to grow out of earthly conditions at all. It descends from Heaven and includes not only the future of Israel but that of the entire world. Undoubtedly these eschatological ideas of later Judaism, largely conditioned as they were by the later experiences of the nation, were at first purely local and temporary. When, however, the horizon widened before the eyes of men and reflection showed that world-wide problems were involved, the outline of these ideas took on a dark and somber tone. Some of the changes can be traced directly to the national experience and are in closest relation to the outward history. The cataclysm which was so profound and awful an expectation of later Judaism was one of the coördinating ideas which deeply modified the Messianic expectation and left less and less room for the purely personal element in the general hope.

During the Maccabean age that family was looked upon by many as having a Messianic character. For, although the Maccabees were not of David's line, they belonged to the tribe of Levi, and to this tribe the Messianic hopes were then transferred. In the Roman period, the high authority of the Scriptures, as taught by the Scribes and Pharisees, revived and strengthened the idea of the Davidic Messiah among the educated. The mass of the people seem to have clung vaguely, though passionately, to the dream of a powerful earthly and national king. The more the pressure of foreign domination was felt, the more hopeless the older anticipations appeared and the more bewildered and confused became the hopes of men. As political and social conditions failed to offer any promises of improvement men looked increasingly to God for redemption and deliverance. A revolution was to come which would destroy the existing order and bring about the end of the present world. Such a violent and awful event could have but one author: God himself, as the great Judge, stood at the center of the catastrophe. He alone is king. Logically there would seem to be no place for a Messiah apart from God. Yet the idea appears and reappears in strange forms and hints: it is at times so confused that it is impossible to find clear and homogeneous groups of ideas upon the subject. Toward the end of this period the messianic idea was widely held and with increased intensity, if not definiteness. It was found even among the Samaritans.

Many as are the unsolved and probably insoluble details in connection with the Messianic expectations of the times, the matter of vital importance is that there were these deep desires, growing keener and more insistent with each generation, though unable to express themselves with definiteness. The longings of human nature had become vocal, and the only harmony and unity which can be found in them is in the universality of the sentiment. The form of expression was largely conditioned by the individual character. The wide interval between the grosser minds who looked merely for a revival of the Davidic line and age, and the longings of the lonely and broken-hearted who sought a revelation of love which would create in them a life of purity, peace and fellowship with God cannot be filled up by any theory. It can be explained upon no ground save the differences in individual development and the larger and wider play of a constantly growing sense of personality. Variety, individuality, are the very marks of spiritual progress. The growing distinctness in the passion for, and the clearer definition of the person of, the Messiah imply an increased vividness in the self-consciousness of the individual. For it is out of the personal soul that the need for a Messiah springs and the more man becomes conscious of himself, the more he demands a Savior. His religious consciousness must therefore make a certain definite progress toward personality before such a being as Jesus Christ could make a valid appeal to the fundamental instincts of his nature.

It is not a Palestinian rabbi nor a heathen convert who shows the highest and noblest expression of the religious spirit of this age. The one in whom the deepest sympathy with the Greek longings and aspirations were united with the most earnest conviction of the greatness of Judaism was Philo the Alexandrian. It is true, Greece was not to him as it was to the cultivated pagan, an "Holy Land," yet he speaks of the greatest of the Greek teachers as "Holy Plato." It must be admitted also that while Philo represents the highest point attained by the religious spirit of this age he also stands apart from and above

the general level of contemporaneous thought. He also
stands more remote from the Palestinian schools than
any other known man of his times who shared the great
aspirations and hopes of Judaism. He may even have
been looked upon with suspicion by the leaders of the
Pharisees. For the Jew of Palestine oftentimes had closer
relations with the Jew of Babylon than he had with the
Jew of Alexandria, at least those of the Pharisaical school
had. Among the celebrated men who taught at Jerusalem
many were born on the banks of the Euphrates, but
there is not a single mention of an Alexandrian teacher
at Jerusalem. The great Rabbi Hillel came from Babylon. Stapfer has asserted that from the Palestinian
standpoint the school of Alexandria was regarded as
schismatic. The Talmud never once mentions it, and if
Philo had come to Jerusalem, Gamaliel would have looked
upon him with dislike. He stands at the very end of this
period and his life overlapped the beginnings of Christian history. In him is represented the last phase of
religious development preceding the Gospel, a phase
which exerted a wide influence upon Christian thought.
Philo sprang from one of the wealthiest and most distinguished families of Alexandria. He was united to the
Jewish kings by marriage and closely associated with the
Empire by reason of his wealth and aristocratic connec-
tions. He dreamed of a reconciliation of the Jewish religion and Hellenic culture, an attempt which was
doomed to failure from the very nature of the ideas he
wished to combine. The profound sense of the Divine
Personality which seems to be ever present in the thought
of every Jew, while it did not disappear from the mind
of Philo or fade into a dim and vague transcendental
pantheism, certainly made the effort to unite the Greek
and the Jewish conception a failure. His language seems
to waver as the different elements of his thought come to
expression and prevailing force, but on the whole he

seems to have been more in sympathy with the Greek point of view than with the Jewish.

In spite of his defects there is much to be learned from him of the way in which some of the most serious minds of his age felt about some of the problems of the life of man. With all the qualifications which must be made, this at least must be confessed: that Philo is one whose chief interest is in religion and all his efforts are to bring into coherent and systematic form the great truths which he feels are of the very essence of man's real life. His interest in religion is primarily personal. He turns away from the mere words, the forms and ceremonies, the hard formulas of his national religion, and seeks to discover the personal ground of the spiritual life—that is, what relation exists between him and God, and what function there is in his individual consciousness or nature by means of which this relation can be realized. Words which had hitherto a national and somewhat legal conception attached to them were raised to a higher value and meaning. The psychological value of religion and its organic relations to the spirit of man came into far higher prominence, and pointed the way to the future. For example, the word "Pistis" or "Faith" was not a new thing or word either in the canonical or post-exilian literature, but there it seems to have the meaning only of fidelity or loyalty. With Philo it was to have a new meaning and mark a new stage in the evolution of religious thought and life.

We have already seen how the outward changes in Jewish history were working inward modifications or revealing new truths to the soul which looked through its own experiences to that which lay behind and beyond them. The national unity having been destroyed and the ancient religious hopes shattered, each man found himself facing alone the problems of his life. He was discovering what it was to be an individual with separate problems and a personal consciousness. The new consciousness of personality demanded a religion which should be personal also. Some personal and individual relations must exist between him and God. And so a desire for personal fellowship and communion rose above the old historic obedience and submission. The soul cried out for a dwelling in the secret places of God, where man might come face to face with his Maker. The spiritual life of the individual as such, is the new element in the new consciousness, and Philo finds its expression in the old historic word "Faith," which, as a psychological factor, becomes the center of the new life. Of course other writers of the period also speak of Faith with a somewhat different accent from the past, yet it does not stand supreme and alone as the highest expression of the spiritual life. In some it is joined to works, while in others it does not have that emphasis which shows any deep appreciation of its real function in the history of the soul.

In Philo, too, it is limited, and limited in such a way as practically to preclude the possibility of entering into its fullest meaning: this even though he calls faith the "completest virtue." His Platonic philosophy and his transcendental theology removed God so far from human relations that the first necessity was to pass beyond the veil of the material and the phenomenal world into the unseen, immaterial and real world, the world of ideas, as Plato would have expressed it. Faith, in Philo, is described as the ability to break from all earthly and material things and trust only to the invisible. It sees that which does not exist as the phenomenal, and Abraham is consequently praised as the first believer. Philo's conception of faith fell short of the Christian notion largely because it was identified with the attainment of a form of religious experience which was highly intellectualized. Knowledge, not piety, is the aim of the philosopher, and knowledge considered as intellectual perception is the method of Philo, though his ulterior aim is piety. His failure to grasp the full meaning of faith was due, in part, to his philosophical ideas and method, in part and a large part also, to his historic position, and somewhat also to prevailing religious ideas to which the syncretism of the age unquestionably contributed.

For side by side with rational activity was a deep well of emotion filled with strange and passionate feelings. The psychological meaning of this emotional force and the relation in which it stood to other elements were not understood, and yet these emotions ruled the life with mysterious power. The old world was haunted by the unknown significance of these deep emotions, which heaved like a dark and bottomless sea below it. The consciousness of the dim world of feeling was ever present behind and below the most lucid thought. When, under the sway of mysterious forces, the ordinary faculties of sense and thought ceased to perform their function, a new consciousness, keen and vivid, but, at the same time, formless and without definite content, overwhelmed the soul. This condition, apparently so independent of all the ordinary operations of human nature exercised a powerful influence upon the minds of men of all ages and still awaits a satisfactory explanation. To the men of the past it seemed to be the manifestation of a Divine Power working upon the individual. While in such ecstasy, as he called the state, he seemed to approach the very secret of life and thought, though his lips were dumb and his mind refused to think. The ancient primitive religions hovered round this spiritual mystery and built their power upon its force. The same experience was at the heart of all the Mysteries which then filled the Empire. Swayed by this world-old mood of man, Philo too placed above faith, ecstasy, higher, as he thought, than reason or consciousness. To find God, one must pass not only beyond sense, but above reason itself. This is the way the Neo-Platonist walked and Philo was one of his precursors. Ecstasy is not only above sense and reason, but it differs fundamentally from them and represents something beyond the highest conscious activity of the soul. While trying to escape from nature, it is in reality a return to naturalism with its least restrained possibilities. So as Philo brooded, his language is filled with echoes of the wild, mystical, and ecstatic piety of the Orphic religions. "The Ascent of the Soul," of which he speaks with such awe, sounds like a phrase from the Hellenic Mysteries or the cult of Mithra. There is in all his descriptions such an intense realism as to suggest the presence to his soul of some oriental influences whether Mithraic or not. It is this special religious characteristic which makes him perhaps the very first in that great order of mystics which has formed one of the noblest elements in Christian history.

CHAPTER II

THE NEW TESTAMENT

BEARING in mind the fact that Christianity arose out of Judaism, that it had in its bosom the same spiritual instincts and bore the same spiritual stamp, that the main body of its ideas are clearly impressed with their Jewish character and origin, one is struck by the fact that the great mass of Christian literature, though having this Jewish origin, is directed to pagan Christians. How great was the number of Jewish converts we shall probably never know. If there were any considerable number of Jewish-Christian communities in Palestine during the first generation they were all swept away by that sea of fire and blood amid which the Holy City sank, never to rise again as the Jewish metropolis. The Jews of the Diaspora who became members of the infant church were quickly lost in the larger number of pagans who soon formed the overwhelming majority of the members. In fact, side by side, the Jew and the Gentile left the synagogue and went on into the Christian Church. And, in addition to these, were a great number whom we have no reason to think had even the slightest connection with the synagogue or were influenced in any appreciable or conscious way by the Jeiwsh teaching. There were evidently conditions in paganism itself which made its followers susceptible to the preaching of the Gospel. The education of the world, the progress of thought and religion outside of Judaism contributed directly to the preparation of the heathen, as the course of Jewish history had led the feet of the Jew in the same direction.

When one sees the whole Græco-Roman world turning its mind and thought toward the Gospel while the Jew draws more and more away from it, one feels that the spiritual history of that past world had a deep and divine meaning. The noblest of the early Fathers saw this, and in the movement of Greek philosophy saw God's educating love. Clement of Alexandria quotes with approval the description of Plato as the "Attic Moses." One cannot over-rate either the significance or the worth of Greece in the spiritual history of western civilization. The forces it set in motion not only prepared the world for the appreciation and reception of the Gospel, but also, for at least four centuries, exercised a prevailing influence upon it. In thought and literature it still controls the forms in which the highest types of spiritual culture express themselves.

Looking at the history of the first century from a purely philosophical point of view, it presents itself as the largest if not the final expression of the syncretism which had prevailed already so widely and so long. The East and the West are here and now finally merged, and the stream of history has in the future a unity which had not hitherto prevailed. The fullness and freedom with which the New Testament writers address their readers shows a confidence not only in their character but their understanding. They are ready to feel and appreciate truths and thoughts coming from a Jew with a full recognition of their value and meaning. This in itself is significant and sends the mind back to ask how and why did the Greek enter so readily into the meaning of the Gospel and why did it make so powerful an appeal to him.

The course of Greek speculation, which began with the universe and the problem of being, turned in time to the great question of Man; and his ethical relations became ultimately the center of the most earnest thought. It was

Socrates who turned the mind to the kingdom or sphere
of the "Objective Spirit," and so became, as Nietzsche
calls him in another connection, "Der Wirbel und Wende-
punkt der Weltgeschichte:" the vortex and the turning
point of the world's history. The very constitution of
Greek society gave these investigations in the begining a
purely social, and to that degree, an objective aspect;
but the assertion of responsibility in itself involved an
inevitable concentration of the mind upon the nature and
constitution not of society but the individual. In its extreme form ethical speculation became so individual that
the social relations were pushed entirely into the background and man brooded over the meaning of his own
soul with an intensity which has rarely been surpassed.
This intensity compelled a realization that man was only
one term in the problem. Looking at man from a purely
material or naturalistic point of view the other term was
the universe, and his relations with it were necessarily
involved, at least indirectly and inferentially. Regarding himself, however, as an ethical personality the immediate suggestion was pressed with profound insistence
upon his soul of One with whom he stood in relations of
a purely moral and spiritual character. A new and
spiritual interpretation of life became more and more
involved in all the most earnest and anxious thinking.
How great were the results of this long struggle to attain
clearness and strength is witnessed by the influence of
Platonic and Stoic modes of thought through the entire
history of western civilization ever since. It affected the
development of Christian ethics to an extent which is
scarcely yet realized and possibly never can be.

The intellectual craving for satisfaction and light, and
the moral energy for realization worked together to
deepen the sense of personality as well as elevate the idea
and character of God. For later Greek thought had
entirely abandoned paganism in the sense of polytheism

and insisted on a monotheistic conception as earnestly as the Jew, though with possibly a different connotation.

At the other extreme of Greek society, far from the lofty discussions of the philosophical schools, other forces were at work which had their origin in the primitive naturalistic religions. In the mysteries which were so widespread both in the East and the West, and which had such a great revival about the period during which Christianity began its work in the world, centers one of the greatest religious problems of antiquity. Aside from the difficulty of tracing the history and character of most of these rites, we are in even greater perplexity when we ask what was the instinct out of which they rose, and why they took the peculiar forms they did?

The religion of classic Greece was marked by that permanent quality of the Greek spirit, a wonderful harmony and an æsthetic proportion and measure. The divine and serene calm which the Greek mind felt to be the unchanging beauty of their gods was quite remote from, and out of harmony with, the strange and uncouth religious ideas of the East and the spirit which filled them. Yet in the commercial life of the Greek he came in contact with many strange and alien cults. At some time in the course of things he came to Thrace and there found a worship which, for some reason, appealed most powerfully to him. From thence either Greek or Thracian merchants brought the worship of Dionysus to Greece where it seems to have become firmly established in no long time. It was joined to that of Apollo and added to the worship of the latter a new and revolutionary element. It produced a profound impression and set in motion a new movement in Greek religious life. Life had moved on into new regions of experience and the soul was finding new questions for which the past furnished no answer. A new element appeared in the religious life of the Greek which soon became an almost universal phenomenon in the spiritual life of the

world of that day. It lay at the very root of religion as a
psychological state and has always reappeared whenever
religion became the absorbing interest of the soul: this element is mysticism, and the form which it took in the new
religious development of Greece as well as in the Asiatic
worships and mysteries was—Ecstasy. In mysticism religion ceases to be only the consecration and interpretation
of life with all its varieties of experiences, and becomes
the whole of it. Its aim is to merge the consciousness of
self in the consciousness or being of God or the gods, as
the case may be. In its earlier and more primitive form
this conception or desire was expressed in the conviction
that the god could enter into possession of the worshiper
and inspire him. He, too, could in turn enter into union
with the god. The fact of this union was seen in the state
of possession or ecstasy or madness. When the "Mantic"
was in this condition he was said to be in a state of "enthusiasm" or union with god. As these conceptions and phenomena appear in the earliest and most primitive religions
they are of necessity naturalistic rather than ethical,
and the problem of character has no place in them.
Without having any philosophical aim or philosophical
knowledge the revived mysteries sought through the me-
dium of the cultus to bring about in a practical way the
union of the spiritual and natural. The philosophers,
ever since Plato, have striven to attain this end through
conceptual knowledge. The mystic strove after an inner
union with the god, which as inner and spiritual should
be raised, and was raised, above the naturalism of the usual
world of the gods. In this way lay the advance of the
whole movement above the polytheism of the popular
religions. The strange and secret character of the cultus,
which appealed to the instincts and powers of the soul,
strengthened in the participants of the mysteries the conviction that they would attain by these means the right of
way to a god who was above and free from the limitations

of nature. The spread of these mysteries was undoubtedly largely due also to the mingling of religions which
was taking place everywhere throughout the Roman
Empire. The cherished ceremonies, the vision of religious
ecstasy, the mystical-ascetic practices which were demanded of the initiated, seemed to guarantee union with
the spiritual god, for already the thought of a universal
religion had begun gradually to emerge before the minds
of men. But the baptism of the initiated, the sacramental
meal by means of which they were to bring themselves
into inner relation with the life of God were in reality
rooted in a thoroughly naturalistic view of life. They
could not in consequence raise the cult of the mysteries
above the actual spiritual level of the popular religions.
And yet the moment the individual becomes the object of
divine influences and action (and the conscious purpose
of the worshiper has this profoundly personal character), the movement toward some rudimentary ethical
relations is inevitably involved.

Philosophy and the mystery religions alike then
tended to throw their chief emphasis upon the full
development of the individual in relation with his
cosmic or divine environment. So it was quite natural that a time should come when not only did the
mysteries try increasingly to use philosophic language,
as in the Hermetica, but when philosophy itself was
lost, or appeared to be lost, in a mysticism of the type
of the mysteries. Superficially this state indicates the
collapse of Greek speculation. As a matter of fact, however, philosophy itself had grown so intensely personal in
its problems that the one urgent idea was life and practice rather than theory and knowledge. The development
of the individual soul was the final aim of philosophy and
in this purpose the mysteries, too, gained a new meaning
and a new value. It was not so much an exhaustion of
intellectual activity and interest as it was the application

of these to ethical and spiritual aims. The Stoics, Epicureans, and Sceptics emphasized the practical life and confined their efforts largely to the culture of the individual soul. The immense significance thus attached to the individual was but an expression of the new consciousness of personality, and the evolution and development of the new ideas, interests, and powers of the personal character.

This change in outlook was accompanied or caused by historic changes in the life of the races affected. The Roman Empire had destroyed many of the local social and political bonds which held men together, as the Eastern Empires had before destroyed all the national bonds and left the individual solitary and alone amid the great shipwreck of the mighty past. So in the orbit of the Roman power the movement toward individualism began to increase. But the brute force of the new Empire and the political conceptions which were developed under it tended to overwhelm the new sense of personality in hopelessness and despair. The whole order of things seemed hostile to human character. Such world-despair or pessimism is but the reflex action of the new spiritual ambitions face to face with living forces which antagonized and threatened its very life. The full realization of the new spiritual possibilities of man could only be attained by means of some new force which would so develop and strengthen human life that it could outlast and remold the social institutions or lift the soul above their numbing and deadening power. Christianity was to be the new force which would stimulate and reënforce all the noblest spiritual energies of the world, and develop out of these struggling elements a new type and a new man whose history was to be the story of the future.

As philosophy had a purely intellectual purpose in its beginnings and the old religions were so naturalistic and unmoral, we cannot find among the inheritors of the Greek past any use of the language on its deeper and more spiritual side which approaches the depth and spiritual intensity of the New Testament. So when we look for uses in this field to prepare us for the larger meanings which were close at hand we are more or less disappointed. The words are there but they are clearly less in their meaning than they later came to be.

In philosophical and later Greek "Pistis" may be said to have three meanings: a psychological, a rhetorical, and a moral. In Biblical Greek there is also added a theological. The meanings corresponding to these three categories are: First, conviction as a psychological state; second, proof; third, good faith or trust. In Philo we find the theological meaning and the connecting link between the classical and the Christian uses.[1] The popular uses of language often anticipate the great changes which find literary expression only after they have entered so deeply into the life that they have revolutionized it and inspired a new statement of its large problems. It is in the New Testament that we see the great and vital words of man's spiritual experiences pass through all the degrees of meaning from the ordinary and commonplace uses to the loftiest and most sacred revelations.

THE NEW TESTAMENT

The New Testament as a whole teaches faith in Christ as the ground of life. Later Christian writings teach the practical value of Christianity without always emphasizing so markedly this personal relation.

In the New Testament Jesus, Himself, is the primary object of faith. It is a purely personal relation. He is regarded by the believers as the source of a new spiritual life and a new personal emotion and conviction. He is not a new Law-giver whose Sayings are a new code to be recited and memorized and which believers must follow

[1] *Essays in Biblical Greek*, pp. 83-88, E. Hatch.

and obey. He is not a theologian whose doctrines about
the "Kingdom of God" must be believed in order to insure
salvation. These are the subsequent additions and interpretations of later days. Nor is He a moralist according
to whose example the life of the individual is to be
directed. These may be inferences, and necessary inferences perhaps, but they are not the primary purpose of
the Gospel story. The Gospel was told for the express
purpose that men might know in whom they had believed.

The disciples themselves were not ethical teachers, appealing in the interest of a new practical life framed in
accordance with a certain body of theoretical rules or
principles only, though these were there. Nor were they
lawgivers, although soon, too soon, the Gospel came to be
regarded as the "New Law," the "Nova Lex," and the
Apostles the first and final authorities in the ordering of
Christian history and the Christian Church. They were
not mystics, though mysticism received an impulse from
the Gospel which has made it one of the greatest and
noblest forces in the higher life of the Christian world.
It is not as enlightened Gnostics that they are to be regarded, though the Gospel soon came to be regarded as a
higher theory of life; and esoteric truth came in no long
time to be one of its most impressive appeals to the keen
and enquiring minds of the Græco-Roman world. Much
as they did and much as they were, in the higher life of
the soul, one hardly dares to call the disciples creators
even of a new type of piety. Using a word which has infinite varieties of meaning, according to the character of
each individual, we must call them simply "Believers,"
Believers in Jesus.

It is a new ordering of life which constitutes the originality of the Gospel. A special coördination of the functions of the soul has been part of the immense force and
vitality, the creative activity, of Christian history. The

early Christians themselves came soon to call their new
spiritual orientation by the word "Faith."

THE SYNOPTIC GOSPELS

The first instance of the word "Pistis" in Matthew is in
VIII, 5-11:

"And when Jesus was entered into Capernaum, there came
unto him a centurion, beseeching him, and saying, Lord, my
servant lieth at home sick of the palsy, grievously tormented.
And Jesus saith unto him, I will come and heal him. The centurion answered and said, Lord, I am not worthy that thou
shouldest come under my roof: but speak the word only, and
my servant shall be healed. For I am a man under authority,
having soldiers under me: and I say to this man, Go, and he
goeth: and to another, Come, and he cometh: and to my servant,
Do this, and he doeth it. When Jesus heard it, he marvelled,
and said to them that followed, Verily I say unto you, I have
not found so great faith, no, not in Israel."

Here the essential meaning is undoubtedly the personal
confidence of the centurion in Jesus. Faith appears here
as fundamentally a relation between the human soul and
the being in whom it believes. It is the trust of the soul
not only in the power of Christ to help, but also in His
willingness to do so.

In many passages of Matthew faith does not mean
simply a trust in Jesus alone, but runs on farther and
implies a trust in God. For to those who have faith in
Him Jesus is, in the highest sense, a messenger of God.
Through Him God is exercising His power and expressing His love for mankind. The conception at last expresses that feeling which has struggled so long and so
hard in the hearts of men, that God is a loving Father
and that he will do good and not ill to the sons of men.
The idea is not yet clear, nor does it always appear in
distinct utterance; but, what is of more worth, it is to
be seen struggling in the hearts of those who crowd around

Jesus for help and strength. That Jesus Himself considered this faith of theirs not merely a belief in His miraculous power, or a trust in His personal character, is clear from His own words. Rather did it represent, at least to Jesus, a recognition of God's goodness, love and willingness to help. This is clear when we study one of the most difficult passages of the Gospel of Mark. In the eleventh chapter, twentieth to twenty-fourth verses, are the following words:

> "And in the morning as they passed by, they saw the fig tree dried up from the roots. And Peter calling to remembrance saith unto Him, Master, behold the fig tree which thou cursedst is withered away. And Jesus answering saith unto him, have faith in God. For verily I say unto you, That whosoever shall say unto this mountain, Be thou removed, and be thou cast into the sea: and shall not doubt in his heart, but shall believe that those things which he saith shall come to pass; he shall have whatsoever he saith. Therefore I say unto you, What things soever ye desire, when ye pray, believe that ye receive them, and ye shall have them."

Jesus turns their thoughts from Himself, and from the events which filled them with amazement and fear to reliance upon God. He declares the relation which exists between the souls of man and God to be such that there can be constant communion and fellowship between them. If this be true, we have reached the bottom not only of all theology, but of all the problems which have most deeply influenced man's thought of life: not only of all thinking, but of all doing. If this be *not* true, it makes little difference what else is true. But if this be true, then all other facts and experiences of life gain freshness, beauty, and higher meaning from the divine fellowship which lifts man above the earth and its dark clouds.

But much as such a state of soul involves (and it lies at the root of all that is noblest and strongest in human action and human thought), there is another aspect in which faith is represented or presented, which is as important as anything which we have touched upon, and is the source of what we call the distinctively Christian character of faith. We see it in that sadly memorable scene, so dear to every heart which has felt the burden and the darkness of sin, the weight and confusion of its own spiritual misery. Out of the lowest shame and degradation of human life goes up a silent appeal for help. Out of the sin and sorrow of a woman's soul rises the desire for purity and peace which Jesus saw, though no one else did, and to her the answer came: "Thy faith hath saved thee, go in peace." (Luke VII, 36 ff.) The deepest problem of life is to receive a new answer, an answer such as had scarcely been dreamed of before. That which moved the great agony to expression, Jesus calls faith. Let us not dare call it anything else or anything less; let us be immensely thankful that in spite of all the doctors and their definitions we have the words and the life of Jesus to set over against all the theories or definitions they may set up. These three illustrations taken from the life of our Lord are typical of all the rest. Nowhere else is there any use or application of the word which is really in conflict with them. The meanings vary slightly from each other, for the Gospels were not technical or scientific documents, and a large and vital word must necessarily have a breadth and elasticity which a purely technical or scientific word does not have. We may summarize the meanings of this word "Faith" in the Synoptic Gospels and divide them into three classes which include every given instance of its use.

I. A humble trust in a Heavenly Father who will hear and answer prayers.

II. A belief in Jesus as a Messenger and Revealer of the power and love of God manifested through acts which seem to be divine.

III. A confidence in Jesus Himself as an infinitely loving and forgiving Being who, in the power of his own supreme purity and love has the ability to cleanse man from sin and strengthen him to do the right.

The other documents of the New Testament do not pretend to be quoting the language of Jesus, but use "Pistis" as a term not only familiar to all but very significant to the writers themselves. Have we any right to expect to find the word used in precisely the same way and with exactly the same meaning by every writer in the New Testament? If we have any such expectation we shall be greatly disappointed. We must in each instance recognize certain fundamental facts, chiefly those of temperament, education, and surroundings. The times had changed somewhat and the conditions a great deal. The dispositions of men were often very different, and the speakers have far less authority and depth of soul. For example the central reality of Christianity to one group of early Christians was the conviction that salvation had come to the world, especially to the Jewish world, through Jesus who was the Messiah. One of the ideas therefore associated with the meaning of "Pistis" was a change of mind, from unbelief in this fact to an acceptance of it. The recognition of the Messianic character of Jesus was the condition of entrance into the Kingdom of God.

When we read the Book of Acts, which gives us the first simple and primitive statement of the methods and ideas of the little band which was not trying to understand itself but simply to live in the new joy and the new life which had its roots in the new spiritual confidence and delight, the word "Pistis" seems to have lost some of its most characteristic meaning as compared with the way in which Jesus used it. Faith is not so deep and personal an experience as in the Gospels. It is the kind of obedience which consists in recognizing as true the message which the first preachers of the Gospel felt themselves impelled to proclaim. Hence it is perfectly evident that the word "Pistis" does not refer to exactly the same thing as in the Synoptists. This is not to say, perhaps, all things considered, that one is of more or less value than the other. It is merely to state what is perfectly obvious, that they are not equivalents.

In the Epistles of St. Peter the word is used in the popular Jewish-Christian sense. That is, it is primarily conceived as trust in the Messiah. Yet the idea of faith, as directed toward God, is still preserved, and bound up with it is an element of hope which should not be ignored and cannot easily be separated from it. This hope is the hope of the future glory of the Messianic Kingdom. It is clear that this conception does not by any means involve a destruction of Judaism as a legal institution or a moral law, for it in no way contains an "ethical principle" which shall supersede the value or significance of "works."

In the Epistle of St. James we are dealing with a document which has produced a great deal of confusion and caused more or less bewilderment because of the assumption that in the use of the word "Pistis" St. James means just what St. Paul means; that is, in rejecting the adequacy of faith he is opposing himself to St. Paul with his conception of the sufficiency of faith. In James II, 14, 19, he declares not only the insufficiency of faith, but in the latter verse he gives a definition of it, or so states it, that we can readily see what he had in mind. Faith, in his view, is a faith purely of the understanding. The faith which the "Demons" have is the faith he condemns. This faith is simply the intellectual recognition of certain truths which are not a matter of the sense. It has no inner life; it stands in no relation to the spiritual growth or joy of the soul. Nothing can be more formal and nothing more unproductive. But in James II, 24, there seems to be an implication that, as justification cannot take place by faith alone, neither does it take place by works alone. St. Paul would reject quite as vigorously as St. James the purely historical view of faith and insist upon the organic relation with the inner life and the vital union of life and character or conduct and life. It is this same organic conception which St. James is contending for. The experience both writers have in mind is similar; they differ chiefly in that Paul would call the total Christian experience faith, while St. James restricts the term to a much narrower significance.

The Epistle of St. Jude accepts the very type of faith rejected by St. James, and in a form much more crystallized than St. James knew of it. For St. Jude, faith is the assent to a more or less formal body of doctrine or dogma. It is not said, nor is it implied, that these dogmas or doctrines are to be held in any unusual way. The idea associated with faith in this connection is simply that which would be regarded as characteristic of any school of philosophy. The contemporary Platonist had Pistis that the Platonic tenets were true, as contrasted with those of any other school. This emphasis upon a body of doctrine as essentially corresponding to the real meaning of faith is something new in the life of the church. So new, indeed, that we have to look far down in history to find parallels in expression and thought. It is for this reason, among others, and it is not the only one, that the vast majority of students from the very earliest times have been led to reject the Epistle of Jude and deny its representative character for the Christianity of the first century. Yet nevertheless a very learned attempt has been made to restore Jude to the first century and give him a canonical and apostolic authority. Dr. Bigg says of this Epistle:

"Jude's language about faith is highly dogmatic, highly orthodox, highly zealous. His tone is that of a bishop of the fourth century. The character may be differently estimated, but its appearance at this early date, before Montanism and before

Gnosticism, is of great historical significance. Men who used such phrases believed passionately in a creed." [2]

The facts could not be better stated. It is the language of a later age and it is far easier to believe that the document in which this language appears belongs to a later age than it is to believe that in the earlier years of the young church there was a Jewish writer who had completely passed beyond the thought of his own time and his own people.

We have one document written by a Jew who was either an Alexandrian or was familiar with the line of thought taken by the cultivated Jew of Alexandria. In reading the Epistle to the Hebrews we feel that we have entered an atmosphere which, in many respects, is singularly different from any other in the New Testament. We feel the air of another intellectual life than that which surrounded any other of the Apostles, not excepting St. Paul.

Before the mind of the Alexandrian Greek, steeped in the thought of Plato, hovered an ideal world and a life not realized. Above this world of pain and shadows and hopes unfulfilled was a world of life, reality, and truth. The mind of the Alexandrian Jew was a fruitful soil for the dreams of the Alexandrian Greek. His ancestors had dreamed of a great revelation of God, of a world of righteousness and peace. Sad as this world was to the most earnest Jew and pagan alike, it would have been infinitely coarser and viler if this dream, this passionate longing, had never existed. When the Jew who had been thinking in these terms became converted to Christianity, the veil between the seen and the unseen seemed torn away in the revelation of Jesus Christ. That other world with its infinite beauty was brought close to every man when Jesus entered earthly life. The ideal world which had

[2] Charles Bigg, *The Critical and Exegetical Commentary of St. Peter and St. Jude.* Reprinted by permission of Charles Scribner's Sons.

haunted so many mighty minds and filled them with such majestic thoughts was a reality. As the two worlds touched and blended in Jesus Christ, the soul of the writer to the Hebrews was stirred to solemn utterance: "Now faith is the assurance of things hoped for, the proving of things unseen." He uses the old language of his fore-fathers, but with a new passion and a new power. Here is what Schleiermacher calls: "The word moulding power of Christianity."

That which is here called faith is, in its essence, really hope—the hope of an unknown future which is stead-fastly held before the mind, giving power and vitality to the life. The reference is not to the person of Christ, nor to His death and resurrection. When Jesus is spoken of in the beginning of the next chapter it is as "the author and perfector of our faith, who, for the joy which was set before Him endured the cross, despising the shame, and hath sat down at the right hand of God" (Heb. XII, 2). He is the greatest and chiefest example for mankind, the great forerunner who has confidently taken hold of this invisible world which is the object of Christian hope. This faith which the Christian has at-tained bears a striking resemblance to that of the great heroes and prophets of the past. It differs from theirs chiefly, however, as hope realized differs from hope un-attained, as the fulfillment differs from the anticipa-tion.

Patience also is a necessary element of this faith, for the hope which was held was never realized during the long past of Jewish history. This visible world by no means expresses the fullness of God's thought of human society or of man's capacities. There is another world related to this as substance to shadow, as type to anti-type, as the ideal to the real. God has meanwhile been giving assurances and promises which correspond entirely with man's hopes. The fulfillment of these indestructible yearnings and these divine promises is the substance of faith, the essence of that which is involved in trust in God and His promises. The senses cannot grasp this other world, but it is there in the very presence of God Himself, and he who waits patiently upon Him shall have his heart's desire. The important point in Hebrews is not the believer's relation to Christ so much as to God and an ideal salvation. It is also obedience which is made the means by which through long-suffering and trial the faith which is hope and trust is made perfect.

THE PAULINE EPISTLES

The earliest literature of the Apostolic Church of which we have any clear knowledge is, in point of time, the Epistles of St. Paul. From the point of view of the nature and the development of Christian thought it is among the latest. With reference to the subject of faith it is by far the most significant and most profound. The word "Pistis" occurs in the New Testament 205 times and of these 104 occur in St. Paul, not including the Pastoral Epistles. This alone would be suggestive; but inasmuch as it also indicates that St. Paul placed the greatest emphasis upon the psychological factor which was represented by it, its importance is greatly increased.

St. Paul was one of the great geniuses of religion, and, as such, he touched life on such an immense number of points that it is extremely difficult to see, not what he means, but what were the various elements in his thought and whence they sprang. For, like every man of genius, he was not only keenly sensitive to all that was most influential in his own age, but he was also immensely receptive of ideas and emotions which had their roots in the great religious forces in the world around him. He has been described as a rabbinical theologian, on account of his inheritance and the direct influence of his education. He is also said to be representative of the Hellenic spirit which moved so strongly through the life of the Diaspora. Both statements are undoubtedly true, but they are not all the truth, nor even in the way in which they are usually described, are they entirely true. The rabbinism is perfectly apparent, but much which was absorbed by what is called Jewish theology has not been traced to its earliest sources in the historic influences which played so great a part in the passage of Jewish history. There are ideas in St. Paul which might have been taken from Philo, as in his conception of Abraham as the father of the faithful. (Philo, De Abra. II, 39) His treatment of the story of Sarah and Hagar (Gal. IV, 21-31), and his attitude toward the "spiritually-minded" heathen is quite in harmony with the ideas of the Hellenic Diaspora. But, since Rabbinism and Hellenism are not defined by the mere terms, we have not compassed the sweep of St. Paul's receptivity nor understood how widespread and sympathetic his religious interest was. His language and style also show an original spirit which assimilated and reshaped all that entered his mind or rose out of his experience. He belongs to no school because he belongs to so many. Yet one finds in St. Paul's style an originality and power, a compression and character which are all his own.

The terminology which he uses presents difficulties of its own. A change was taking place in the value and significance of old, familiar words, but there is a stamp upon much of his language which shows he gave to it the color of his own personal religious experience. It is one of the most fundamental truths of religion that religious thought seldom or never creates new forms of its own in the way that science does. Religion adopts those already in use, and we may be reasonably certain that St. Paul used forms which were neither unknown nor unusual. They must have been quite familiar to the mass of his hearers, though they may have failed, as we know they did, perfectly to reveal the vast world of emotions, thoughts, and experiences which he was trying to set forth.

St. Paul was a Jew of the Diaspora, with a rabbinical training. He was a citizen of a town which was not only a center of Greek philosophy, but which had also been profoundly influenced by one of the most austere and powerful religions of the East. Even in the time of Julian, the last great pagan Emperor, Tarsus was a great, if not the greatest, center of Mithraic worship. In spite of its reputation as a city where Greek culture was highly thought of and which possessed a distinguished philosophical school, the earlier oriental influences were too deep and firm to be displaced. Dion Chrysostom was struck by the non-Hellenic character of Tarsus. Considering then the various elements which entered into the life of St. Paul, we see that, underlying them all, there were some which were original and characteristic and which would necessarily give a somewhat different character to his faith or at least to his statement and expression of it. The Evangelists who were disciples of Jesus rose into faith by a slow process of education. In them it had its roots in the action and reaction of His life on theirs. It was the natural and unconscious way. They grew into it without in the least realizing what the process was or the change which was taking place in them. They were in immediate and personal contact with their Master and His life worked upon theirs through the unknown channels of daily intercourse. With St. Paul it was profoundly different. Great spiritual changes, which revolutionized his life, held his mind, and the whole energy of his intellect was bent upon reflection and the analysis of his experience. Hence we catch many glimpses into the way in which these new experiences appealed to him and the impressions and convictions which they wrought in his soul. It may be that the different conceptions of faith held by St. Paul and the Evan-

gelists rest upon the fact that theirs had its origin in an
objective historical Person and his in a subjective experience of an invisible spiritual Life which took possession of his own. When he endeavored to put these into
words, as he poured out his life for the saving of men,
the language is bathed and saturated with his own personal experience. The language is the language of the
common religious life of the world, and yet it has something in it which is peculiarly personal and wholly unique.
Faith to him, as to all the earliest Christians, is purely
subjective. It has been maintained by those who dispute
the Pauline authorship of the Pastoral Epistles, as well
as by some who admit it, that in them there is a purely
objective or historical use of the term. It is more than
questionable, however, whether the objective use which
characterizes this term in later centuries, where there were
such profoundly different underlying ideas, corresponds
in any degree with the use which St. Paul made of it.

Most, if not all, of the various ideas which we find
connected with the word in the New Testament, appear,
with some modifications, in St. Paul. Moreover, if we
examine them closely it can be seen that he developed all
these meanings for himself, at least the Christian meanings. For these stand related to each other as parts of a
great organic whole, the full expression of which is the
purely and distinctively Pauline thought which has taken
such deep roots in the Protestant Christianity of the last
four centuries and modified or influenced the best life of
the church in all ages.

What did St. Paul consider to be the origin of faith?
The disputes which have arisen on this matter deal with
logical refinements which seem not to have occurred to
the Apostle. In Phil. III, 12, it is distinctly asserted that
both man and God in Christ are the sources of the complete faith of the soul, and priority is assigned to neither.
Rather is it suggested or implied that they are concur-

rent. The love of God found man because man needed
God, and the chronological order did not impress him.
The sense of God's great love so overwhelmed him that
spiritually, it may be said to be the origin, but there were
shoots in his own soul which were dumbly seeking life and
light. This aspect of the spiritual problem was, however,
not developed or discussed by the Apostle who was a
Christian rather than a theologian, and the filial relation
of man involved not only the love of the Father but the
possibility of the love of the son.

When we come to the further question as to what the
psychological function was which is expressed through
faith, St. Paul is again indefinite. The psychological
terms which were current in the schools he seems to use,
but rarely, if ever, in a technical sense. He accepts and
uses the language which is at hand without discussing it.
His purpose was practical and personal, not theoretical
or academic. He evidently does not regard it as "Donum
Superadditum" in the crude, harsh way of the Latin theologians, but considers it as rooted in the whole spiritual
nature of man. It is not spoken of as an "Eye," in that
loose rhetorical way which has become so popular, but it
seems to involve the whole being as it responds to the
appeal of the Father to the son. It is concerned not with
the intellect alone, but also with the affections and will,
as the relation between faith and obedience shows.

Considering somewhat in detail the various uses of the
term, we find, in the first place, that theoretical kind of
faith in which the intellect is primarily involved. That is,
which consists in holding as true some fact or event which
has already taken place. Such is I Cor. XV, 12-15. He
stood, as every man must stand, upon some fact external
to his own life. Faith in the Resurrection as a bare historical fact is not sufficient to account for all that is included in the fullness of the Christian life. The merely
historical and intellectual conception of "Pistis" rises to

higher and deeper meanings as the relation of the historical events unfold themselves. Starting from the Resurrection of Jesus his soul turned to Him who had raised
Jesus from the dead. The thoughts which his Jewish
education had planted so deep in his soul were reënforced
by the flood of new emotions and convictions which were
born of his own spiritual experiences. The way in which
he turned to God is defined by this term, "Pistis"; but it
has in it now the common thought which pervaded the use
of the term all through the New Testament: that is,
Trust, Trust in God the Father. As his whole nature was
involved in this new life he could not look upon trust as a
mere matter of acknowledgment issuing from the certainty of definite historical or even metaphysical truths.
There was something more and to him something even
deeper. The full sweep of his life entered into faith, and
all the facts of God, hitherto somewhat cold and remote,
became living within him, and their burning flame shot
through the most potent activities of the soul. This
higher form of trust or faith he expresses in the vehe-
ment words of Romans X, 8-10. "But what saith it? The
word is nigh thee, even in thy mouth and in thy heart:
that is, the word of faith, which we preach; that if thou
shalt confess with thy mouth the Lord Jesus, and shalt
believe in thine heart that God hath raised Him from the
dead, thou shalt be saved. For with the heart man be-
lieveth unto righteousness: and with the mouth confession
is made unto salvation." Faith such as this far transcends
the meaning which the term has in St. James or St. Peter.
Moreover, it represents an exceedingly complex state inasmuch as it is no longer or chiefly a matter of the intellect or understanding but gathers into itself the whole
passion of life.

The revelation of the character of God in the Death
and Resurrection of Jesus Christ made a deeper and
more vivid impression than any revelation of the remote

past. It gave the assurance of a character, if not totally different from any previous one, as the Gnostics later affirmed, at least one vastly superior in weight of affection and intensity of feeling. In Gal. III, 23, St. Paul evidently conceives the Christian faith as a new thing because the facts upon which it was founded were new.

Faith of a certain kind might have existed and undoubtedly did exist before the revelation of Christ, but this special kind of faith could not exist, the peculiar trust could only be felt by virtue of the particular facts which called it forth and developed it. It was inseparably connected with the historic facts of Christ's Death and Resurrection. But behind these visible events stretched a series of spiritual revelations which exercised an immense influence over St. Paul. These acts which testified to God's power and love opened the way to a deeper insight into God's character than any that had ever before been attained. These were in his own inward experience. Behind these outward circumstances also lay the saving will of God, the wish that every man should bring his need to Him. St. Paul found in the nature of God revealed in Christ that which corresponds to man's need and so his trust was the supreme confidence of a lonely spirit in One who could be to it all that it could wish or think. It was not a conclusion reached by a long course of reasoning nor by fierce debate. The light of the Cross revealed to him the love of God through Jesus Christ. The faith thus inspired was not a theory but a life. All his words sprang from the living fountain of his own experience. His life was in immediate contact with God. Moreover, he believed in a growth in faith. This growth was not in an increase of knowledge mainly or chiefly, but a growth in fellowship and communion with God, with a consequent increase and growth in all the moral and spiritual elements of character.

Most intimately associated with this aspect of faith as

trust, is one which follows naturally from it: that is, "Obedience." It is expressed by the Greek word, "hupakoe," which is not found in classical Greek. It represents in the full strength of its meaning something which would not have found acceptance in the classical period of Greece. St. Paul does not refer to it often, but frequently enough to show that it occupied a very important place in his thought and is not to be confounded or identified with any other thought. In Romans I, 1-6, and 25-26, he refers to "Obedience of Faith." Does this obedience have regard to any outward act or to an inward character? If obedience has its roots in that trust in God which is faith, then it means fundamentally the surrender of the whole nature to God, and not a series of acts. For the ethical life of man is dependent upon his spiritual character. In it lie the roots of character and life. It is the surrender of the whole personality to the molding power of God to whom the soul has submitted itself in perfect trust, which constitutes that essential obedience which is the obedience of faith and the result of faith. The whole unity of life is preserved by this central union of the life with God. For even in the loftiest spiritual experiences the Apostle never lost the vivid consciousness of his own being in the wider ocean of the divine life, which has always been one of the chief dangers of the deepest spiritual natures.

There is one aspect of the subject of faith which is peculiarly and characteristically St. Paul's. Whatever its social meanings and values may be, the beginning of it all is the human soul and this human soul in the most singular and original relations with Jesus Christ. In Col. I, 27, "Christ in you, the hope of glory," St. Paul affirms a relation with Christ which had never been so directly and explicitly set forth. For this statement his authority is his own Christian experience and his guide is the spirit of Christ. He conceived such a relation between the soul of the Christian and his Lord not as an accident, but as the law of the spiritual life.

In Gal. I, 15, "He revealed his Son in me," we see how great the change was from both the traditional Jewish and the heathen view of life. The seat and source of authority are shifted from the outside to the soul's own center. The Apostle has within him a guide more authoritative than any which can be found elsewhere. More than that, this living energy within the life is transforming the entire character and molding it into the likeness of itself. His new life, under the inspiration of the Christ within him was one so full of moral possibilities and spiritual splendors that at times it seemed as if his possible life was so blended with the life of Christ that he was unable to discriminate between them. He could not decide which was his and which was the life not his own, which made his own so beautiful and strong to him. Gal. II, 20, "I live, yet no longer I, but Christ liveth in me," expresses vividly the same experience. Yet he interpreted his own experience as simply the manifestation of the universal law of the higher life. The secret of history was to him this spiritual gravitation by which each man was drawn to his own best life, which was the life of a son of God. The moral chaos which fronts each man, not only without but within, is due to the revolt or refusal of each soul to yield to this higher self, this Christ within the soul. The universal application of the new law of life, the principle of faith, he sets forth in all its breadth in Gal. III, 26-29. Here it becomes clear that St. Paul does not look upon faith as a merely personal, private matter. It is not something individual and isolated, to be attained by a few here and there, but is a deep, radical, penetrating force which is to transform society and build up a new life for the world. By faith in Christ, by union with Him, men are to become actually and really sons of God. Sonship is not simply theoretical and titular, but is the expression in man's spiritual character and moral life of the characteristics and essential qualities of Christ's life. The glow of this great revolutionary vision shines through all his language, for a new era seemed to have dawned in Christ, in whom are all and who is all. Hereafter each man can become a "new man," a new spiritual creature begotten by faith, or through faith in Christ. This faith, the living power of the soul, was also the transforming energy of the daily life and the common tasks. St. Paul was charged with antinomianism and with ethical indifference because he felt that the beginning of things was in the soul. He contrasted faith and works and rejected works, but it was "The works of the Law," as a means of achieving holiness, which he repudiated. The new spiritual relation into which the believer entered in Christ involved in it the highest moral manifestation, as in Christ Himself. The contrast in his mind is not a contrast of acts or conduct, but of character and spirit. In opposition to a mere reckless antinomianism he had a distinct conception of the Gospel as an ethical principle which shapes for itself a new moral life. If the path of human conduct has been already clearly and distinctly marked out there is no possibility of spiritual development or originality. The mere automatic repetition and fulfillment of the law is all that is left. But if the life of the soul is fired by new moral and spiritual ideals, it is free to rise to whatever visions of grace and truth unfold themselves through the swift-moving years. It is this ever-expanding quality, this power of an endless life which has made the Gospel of Christ the wellspring from which the stream of progress has flowed through all these centuries. The moral life springs out of the life of faith, not the reverse. If we live in the spirit let us walk in the spirit. This new ethical spirit of the Apostle has well been called "A landmark in the history of morality."

When, however, we turn to the scientific problem of the genesis of St. Paul's thought and the reason for the use of the language, we are beset with difficulties. The first question opens up great problems in psychology and also demands a clearer knowledge of St. Paul's actual historical experiences than we are ever likely to possess. The further question as to why the Apostle used the old word "Pistis" to represent this larger, more complex, and incomparably higher spiritual condition, we do not know. Whether he saw new hints and suggestions in the popular uses and ideas with which he was familiar and pushed them to a larger meaning and thus gave them a new value, it is quite impossible to affirm. The fragmentary and scattered glimpses which we have of the inner life of the man himself and the world around him, are so indefinite that even inferences, much less conclusions can hardly be drawn from anything we at present know. All through St. Paul's writings we hear dim echoes from the distant past of man's spiritual history reverberating in such a way that when we listen closely we realize that they tell us something of the man's own thoughts and the familiar and habitual attitude of the world around him.

In a man's life there are two main factors: first, his own spiritual experience, his thought and his passion, the play and power of the spiritual forces within the soul; and, secondly, the character of his environment. The latter shapes at least the expression of the life. It furnishes the man with a vocabulary not only vocal but mental. It reacts upon him and throws the light of its knowledge across his pathway. It does not make him what he is, but he would not be what he is or use the language and ideas he does unless it had furnished him with the clothing for his most vivid and living experiences.

Our literary sources for the life of St. Paul are practically a unit. There does not seem to be much change in his thought or expression except what is due to the varying circumstances and purposes which were the cause of his writing. The man is made, in all the essential elements of his character and thought, and we know him only as the swift and mighty spirit which flung itself into the great struggle of which Alexander's dream was but a shadow. The man is there, all of him that we know, in those few short years we see him.

There is a long period in the life and activity of St. Paul of which twe know nothing, and that period might be, and, we are almost compelled to say, must be, the most important in his history. From the time of his conversion to the time when he went with Barnabas to Antioch we know practically nothing. We scarcely know where he had been, and we certainly do not know what he was doing or what he was learning. We know that he was at Damascus and that he came into the region of Syria and Cilicia, and at the time he went to Antioch he was at Tarsus. During these long years he had many experiences which produced the profoundest effects upon him but to which we have only incidental and casual references. The region in which those years were passed was one in which the oldest and most powerful religions of antiquity were still exerting a deep influence. It is noteworthy that the three countries in which the first and greatest gains were made by the young Church, Asia Minor, Syria, and Egypt, the homes of the Semites, Phrygians, and Egyptians, were also the countries where the old oriental religions were most active. We see also in the language of the young Christian community many traces of the ideas and sentiments which had stimulated the spiritual interest of the peoples. The strong cosmological character of the eastern religions, especially the Babylonian, which was so closely associated with magic and astrology, had spread like a flood through all western Asia. The whole soil of the lands in which the Apostle lived through those unknown years was saturated with these ideas and with the sentiment of the primitive and indigenous religions of the country. This astrology which shaped so much of the religious thought and feeling of the times was profoundly fatalistic. And we seem to see this conception as the background against which the Apostle conceives the subject of redemption. (Ephes. I, 19 ff.; II, 2, 3; III, 10, 19; VI, 12.)

This universe, which was under the government of the stars, had also beneath it a mass of spirits, hostile or friendly, who came in time to fill the first place in men's thoughts. There seems to be no doubt that St. Paul shared the common belief in them, though he may have inherited this belief from his Jewish ancestors instead of having absorbed it from the surrounding paganism. These "Dunameis" or angelic powers play a great part in his conception of the universe in which he lived. (Rom. VIII, 38; XVI, 20; I Cor. II, 6, 8; IV, 9; X, 19-21; XI, 10; XV, 24, 26; II Cor. II, 11; IV, 4; VI, 15; XI, 14.)

The doctrine of "Aeons" which appears in St. Paul was also oriental in its origin and was now widely diffused through the western world. (Gal. IV, 10 ff.; Col. II, 16 ff.) The "Elements" which play such a part in St. Paul's thought were also largely a combination of oriental ideas of an astrological character mingled with the angelology of the East.

The new world-order which appears in the Book of Daniel and formed part of the permanent hope of Judaism, thence passing over into Christianity, was doubtless derived from or through Babylon. Yet it may have reached St. Paul more easily through his Jewish inheritance than by direct contact with the heathen circle in which he lived. Many of the facts and ideas which are familiar to St. Paul do not appear to be purely Christian in their uses or in their origin. The Charisma of

the Glosalalia which he describes does not seem to have
been confined to the Church. The working of the Spirit
as seen under this form appears to have been a characteristic of the mystic ecstasy of Hellenism as well, and
was apparently widespread during this period. Reitzenstein thinks there are echoes of Egyptian-Grecian mysticism in Rom. XI, 38, but the origin of this faith may
well be in the deep religious nature of the Apostle as in
some of the phases of religious feeling in the thought of
his day. The term "Euangelos" and the related words
were in frequent use among the Greeks of Asia Minor.

When we attempt to enter into the meaning of many
of the mysteries and cults which were so deeply and
widely influencing Western Asia at this time, we see that
the essence of the mystery was that the mystic or believer
was in some way united to the divinity. The union of
man and god in some way was the object of all of them.
"Enthusiasmos" and "Ekstasis" represent the opposite
sides of this divine experience. Eating is one of the oldest
forms of union with the divine, and the idea of marriage
as a means of union with the god prevailed in many of
the primitive religions. Both of these conceptions, however, seem to be repugnant to the Judaism of this period
at least. The idea of sonship which is involved in the
mysteries is united to that of a new birth; the old man
becomes a new man. The new life comes, also, through
Death. This idea of death and a new birth is the fundamental one in the cult of Isis, Attys, Dionysus, and
Mithra. There were certain social changes which, in a
way, intensified and sharpened the language of inner experience or desire. As the national spirit sank and traditional loyalty and patriotism disappeared there sprang
up a personal and individual loyalty which found its
object in the leader or ruler. On the awful height upon
which the oriental king stood he was surrounded with
an atmosphere half divine. Submission to him was not

merely the devotion of a soldier to his leader, it became religious and was the root out of which the worship of the emperor sprang. It involved a total abandonment, not only of acts, words, and thoughts, but even of the personality itself in favor of the monarch who was the equal of a god. This sentiment possibly shaped the language of St. Paul in II Cor. X, 5. The impression which the genius of Alexander made upon the Hellenistic world shows the blending of all these sentiments and it was out of this temper of mind that the thought of Apotheosis seems naturally to have arisen since we find it widespread in the period of the Diadochi. Yet it is to be noted that the apotheosis of emperors, philosophers and others did not bring with it either the honor, the reverence, or the divine power and qualities which the Christian attributed to Christ.

As an integral element in this new religious attitude of the world was the idea of salvation or redemption. This, however, was material and not moral in its operation, and was wrought through physical and not spiritual agencies. To enter into a study of this widespread view at this time would take us too far afield. But the figure of the god had become intensely vivid and personal, filled with some of the qualities which human life demanded. In almost all the mystery cults of later antiquity a god stands at the central point of faith. It is a god who has died and has risen again, who has journeyed through the kingdom of Death and returned again to the world of the living, who, as their leader, became the type of all his followers: Hercules, Theseus, Orpheus, Osiris, all have a common experience. In the mystery of Attys the death of the god is followed by his resurrection on the third day. According to the Dionysian Mystery the life power of the god must be transferred to the worshiper through personal union with him. The Mandeans knew a vicarious or representative anointing and communion of the

living for the dead. This representative character is
hinted at in that very obscure passage in I Cor. XV, 29.
Speaking broadly, the two ideas of the East and the West
were Incarnation and Apotheosis and some have thought
that these were shadowed in the language of St. Paul,
"Christ in you the hope of glory," and "Our citizenship
is in heaven"; but such inferences seem somewhat far-
fetched, to say nothing else. The popular life was too
deeply saturated with these ideas and conceptions not to
have had a definite and deciding part in forming the
language, or, at least, its uses. Yet in spite of all these
efforts to reach a conception of salvation which would
meet the deepest necessities of human life all these religions were tainted with the materialism of their primitive origin which seems invariably to dog religion as a
shadow. There are, however, certain facts in the use of
language which are at least striking, if not convincing;
such as the antithesis between Πνεῦμα and Ψυχή, Σάρξ
and Σῶμα, Πνευματικός and Ψυχικός; the opposition of
the earthly and heavenly bodies; the desire for putting
on "the heavenly body; the μεταμορφοῦσθαι and
μετασχηματίζεσθαι.

All these were terms used in the mysteries as well as
by St. Paul, and in the mysteries they had a definite and
technical value. There are, however, certain parts of St.
Paul's writings which seem to some to leave no doubt
about his own attitude toward the central idea of the
mysteries. Of late much has been said about the tenth
and twelfth chapters of I Corinthians, and one of the
most capable of recent scholars is convinced that in all
essentials St. Paul believed that Christianity was a mystery religion. Dr. Lake says: [2] "Christianity has not borrowed from the Mystery Religions, because it always was,
at least in Europe, a Mystery Religion itself." How
European Christianity inevitably became a mystery re-

[2] Kersopp Lake, *The Earlier Epistles of St. Paul.*

ligion he explains by saying: "This conception was in the air of Hellenistic thought, and a Greek, when he became a Christian, naturally continued to think along the lines already familiar to him. The spiritual experience of Christianity was no doubt the same among Jew and Greeks, but when it was a question of translating this experience into the language of the intellect, and stating its connection with the historical fact of Jesus, His life and death, each thought in the manner familiar to him." Even admitting the correctness of these statements or at least their intrinsic possibility, the question of St. Paul's attitude toward the problem is by no means settled.

If St. Paul adopted the mystery view of the Gospel, why does it appear in one passage only of his writings? The mere use of terms unfortunately does not always mean the same thing in different individuals and one of the most difficult things to determine is whether a writer is using language in a loose and popular way or with a definite, scientific and technical intention. The difficulty is a permanent one and is one of the characteristics of all literature in all ages. It might be easier to accept the view that St. Paul believed in the sacramental character of Christianity, if, in the second place, it were not in absolute contradiction with the whole burden of his teaching and preaching. Or, if not in contradiction, it is at least an inconsistency or incongruity which is very difficult to explain. The whole spirit of his preaching is personal, individual, ethical, spiritual. The absolute necessity for each soul of being in conscious spiritual relations with God through faith in Christ is in entire opposition to any conception which is found in the mystery religions. There does not seem to be the slightest possibility of reconciling these different attitudes, and the only escape is to assume that in his use of language he avoided raising new difficulties by adopting phrases familiar to all. It was inevitable that it should be so, for we all use language in a non-technical way and do not expect to be taken scientifically. More than that, the mystery religions always asserted that the practice of their rites was a protection against the enemies of the soul, but in I Cor. X, St. Paul distinctly rejects that idea both as to the Jewish and the Christian rites. Whatever authority there may be for interpreting Christianity as a mystery religion there does not seem to be any ground for it in the teaching and preaching of St. Paul. It is hardly possible that any of the facts above stated should have escaped the attention of St. Paul, or have failed to affect, in some degree, the mode of his expression. When he sets forth the union of the believer with Christ, or his death and resurrection with Christ, we are far away from any of the thoughts which influenced either the ideas or statements of his Jewish ancestors. One can hardly escape the feeling that these terms referring to spiritual experiences were adopted from the world in which he lived, from the religious mood which prevailed around him. Yet they were not mere copies. They are so irradiated by his inner personal experience that they are entirely different in their meanings. The union with the god, which was in the mind of the pagan, was a physical and not a moral or spiritual union. Or, if this seems to ignore some of the higher forms of pagan thought, one can say that it was psycho-physical. With St. Paul it was purely spiritual and ethical. It assumed a deep inward change represented by the word "Metanoia." This involved something scarcely even recognized by paganism, at least as expressed in the popular cults. This profound mysticism of St. Paul undoubtedly had its roots in his own religious experience, but no religious experience can express itself except in the words and forms congruous with the highest aspirations of its own day and generation. His forms of statement are simply the expression of the unconscious processes of his own mind and spring out of the influence of the oriental ideas which were floating in the spiritual atmosphere of the times. The ultimate fact of his own life, the molding influence of Christ upon his own soul, he attempts to describe in all the forms which contemporaneous religious life set before him in order to find an approach to the souls of those for whom he cared. When the completeness of this spiritual fact is asserted he sums it all up in one word, "Faith." We know what he means. It is the moral and spiritual union of the soul with God through the inner control of his life by Christ. It is a fellowship which is dependent upon nothing but the soul's inward fitness, built up through love and worship, for this fellowship. It is spiritual, and, because spiritual, it is beyond words. It is moral and therefore it is living and acting and submits to no definitions. The fact itself makes the language unsatisfactory, but the long history of the Christian Church has found no substitute for his language. We can see what he means by it, and thus the most important question is answered.

When we come to the further question: Why did he use this particular word? there seems to be no answer. There is nothing in the past use of it which offers the slightest hint or suggestion. He raises it out of its intellectual or theological interpretation and loads it with the weight of the loftiest religious experience. The supreme genius of the man has stamped a new meaning on it forever. Had the centuries which followed held fast to his spiritual definition the history of the Church would have been different.

ST. JOHN

In concluding the study of the New Testament we must consider the teaching of a book which has exercised as much influence over the higher thought of the Christian Church as the writings of St. Paul, and, at some periods no doubt, more. There are some facts which ought to be

recognized in connection with the Gospel of John even
if they present difficulties which cannot easily be answered. The vast majority of competent critics are in
relative agreement as to the age and authorship of the
Pauline literature. About the Fourth Gospel there is,
and always has been, a great diversity of opinion on both
these points. The present tendency is to deny the authorship of the Apostle John and attribute the Gospel to
some other writer whose name, however, is not known.
Its composition, too, has been assigned to dates varying
from one to two generations. If we find in St. Paul the
presence of ideas which were widely diffused through the
religious atmosphere of Western Asia, we see in the
Fourth Gospel evidences of a sympathy and syncretism
which point to influences which show few traces of a Palestinian source. The theology phrases itself in quite other
terms, and the Christology seems to owe its existence to
ideas which were not native to Western Asia. Without,
however, entering into any discussion of these problems,
the effort must be made to ascertain the special significance and value of Pistis, or Faith, in the mind of the
writer of the Fourth Gospel.

In the first place, it must be noted that the noun
"Pistis" does not occur in this Gospel at all. The verb
"Pisteuo," however, is found more frequently than in any
other writing in the New Testament. It is easy to exaggerate the importance of such differences; yet, on the
other hand, they are significant; they are not accidents.
Looked at from the psychological point of view, there
seems to be a shifting of the emphasis from the subjective
side to the objective, from the person believing and the
attitude of soul which the word implies, to the object of
this faith and what He is. In reality, the subjective faith
is inevitably conditioned by its object. Its value and
importance, therefore, depend wholly upon this object.
It may be that this change was due to the emphasis

which some who believed they were followers of St. Paul laid upon the value of their own spiritual condition or state without appreciating the value of its origin. Complaint was made in his own day, and has been made ever since, to the distortion of the real meaning of St. Paul.

However this may be, the fact of the shifted emphasis is patent even to the most casual reader of the New Testament. This act of faith, this believing, is not a merely or purely intellectual activity on the part of the believer. It does not depend upon the mental capacity of the individual to enter into and apprehend the truth set before it. If this were so, if "the knowing" which seems to constitute the act of faith were only or chiefly an intellectual operation, then the world and even evil men could "Know Him," for they have often had higher intellectual qualifications and powers than the Christian disciples. This "knowing" did not consist in holding certain intellectually related propositions which were united to the historical facts of Judaism or to the Person of Christ. It had a psychological value and significance of its own which distinguishes it from all other and earlier concepts and expressions which had been associated with the word "Faith."

For the existence of Jesus as an object of adoration and love obviously made possible for the human soul a relation which had never existed before. It also implied an experience of a spiritual character so wonderful and so vital that old terms might be used, but they could not adequately express this new condition, or state the psychological changes with accuracy and precision. This knowing or believing has reference to a Person and therefore cannot be merely an act of the mind, an historical apprehension, but must involve, as the object itself does, the whole realm of personality. It moves through the affections which recognize all the elements of personal being, as well as through the ethical nature which apprehends the moral and spiritual value of His Character. It is therefore as in St. Paul, not a simple but a complex act, not a particular activity but a complete movement of man's entire nature. It involves likewise a surrender of the will which expresses itself in conduct which reveals the inner state of faith. On one side it is the human soul with all its capacities of love, loyalty, and service, and, on the other, Jesus, with all the beauties and sanctities which draw forth these human powers. Between these two beings flows a steady stream of vital energy, demanding and supplying, needing and giving, until they become, so to speak, mutually dependent upon each other: the man upon Jesus for the strength and life to make him a real child of God, and Jesus upon the man through whom He reveals the wealth and power of His nature.

If we examine some of the passages in this Gospel in which man's relations with Jesus are set forth, we shall get a more living realization of the truth than from any merely abstract statements. Here, as in the Synoptists, there is the same variety of grounds assigned to faith, and it is likewise described in the same broad and unscientific way. In John II, 11, and elsewhere, the word "Sameion" (Sign) is mentioned as a ground for Faith. An act of Jesus stirred the souls of men and led them to Him. In John IV, 39-42. "His words" are made the basis of the faith which men felt in Him. The word "faith" here seems to cover even the slightest interest or confidence in Him, however aroused. Its characteristic is that it is entirely and purely personal.

As the writer has indicated two grounds of faith, so, also, he states two forms of faith: (1) A loving of Jesus (John III, 19; VIII, 42; XVI, 27); (2) An honoring of Jesus (John V, 23). A third form should doubtless be added here and that is "to receive" (John I, 12; V, 43; XIII, 20). This means the inward acceptance and obedience of the nature of man to the nature of Christ. The very extent of the language shows how important the writer felt the essential and common meaning of all his phrases to be. Having no technical purpose in mind, but only the interpretation of Christian experience, he pictures life with all that freedom and breadth which man's spiritual attitudes display. Yet the most impressive, if not the most important passage in this connection seems to suggest, or to imply, a more purely intellectual and limited interpretation of man's relations with God, the establishment of which is the end and purpose of Christ's revelation. In John XVII, 3, it is definitely stated that knowledge of God is eternal life. The phrase has been seized upon ever since it was written and interpreted in a gnostic, dogmatic, and philosophical sense. Theoretical knowledge, from this point of view, would be not only the beginning but the end of the highest efforts of the soul in its attempt to find God. The mystical element which is as characteristic of St. John as of St. Paul stands in the way of any such narrow and purely intellectual interpretation. For the purpose of Christ, as the writer describes it, is to give life to the world: to meet man on all sides of his nature and unite him in the closest and most vital union with Himself, and through Him with God. A knowledge which is co-extensive with man's nature must involve something more than an intellectual recognition of God. It *may* justify the philosopher: it *must* justify the saint. And the knowledge of God which a man believes he has acquired through Jesus Christ is not a knowledge which comes to him from the mind of Christ alone, but issues from the totality of His nature. Even an intellectual knowledge of God must be partial and weak, for He is something more (in the Gospel at least) than a First Cause, A Postulate for Being, or an Abstract Definition, upon which to base a process of

reasoning. The gnosticism of Clement and the later Neo-
Platonists, has no basis in the Gospel. The logic of the
intellect is not the knowledge of God to which St. John
refers. It is a Being, a Father, who is to be known; and
the organ of knowledge is the whole breadth of man's
nature meeting the life of God on all sides. When St.
John turns to the expression of the inner meaning of the
soul's experience as manifest in conduct, he does not use
any of the terms so common in all religious phraseology,
but, with true poetic instinct, interprets life as a tender
relation of love and obedience. The Good Shepherd leads
the way and the sheep follow him. There is no suggestion
of law and compulsion. The mystical hymn of Newman
is but a modern statement of St. John's view of the Christian disciple.

This form of faith which we have been considering
seems to imply a passive attitude, submission, obedience,
receptivity; but there is another and more active form
in which this knowledge or faith becomes energizing in
the spirit of man. The term "Lambano" and its com-
pounds have the most active meaning, signifying to seize,
or lay hold of something. Though translated "receive,"
this receiving has something of the meaning of a personal appropriation of Jesus after He has been recognized as the truth the soul has longed for. Blindness and
ignorance have been destroyed by knowledge, and
through the process of knowledge or faith, the sinfulness
which is manifest in refusal or opposition, is in turn destroyed. The result is the Sonship of man in God which
is formally and impressively stated. This receiving or
apprehending, this active state of faith, is also expressed
by "Akouein," "to hear." This hearing implies both an
intellectual understanding or knowledge and a moral disposition. We see, therefore, that though St. John does
not use the word "Faith" he attaches more real impor-

tance to the fact as a spiritual condition than any other
writer in the New Testament, save only St. Paul. He
gives also the widest and most varied meanings to the
truth, but each of them has as its root and center Jesus
Christ on Whom alone the different activities of the Christian soul in the most vital way depend.

CHAPTER III

CHRISTIANITY AND PAGANISM IN THE SECOND CENTURY

THE second century has been thought by many to be obscure and uninteresting. In its earlier days it is undoubtedly more or less obscure, but it is not uninteresting, for it was the century in which was developed the ecclesiastical system which has remained that of the largest part of Christendom ever since. It saw, also, toward the end, the formation of the Canon of the New Testament, the growth and development of Gnosticism, and the beginnings of Christian theology. And last, but not least, it saw the end of paganism, or the beginning of the end. The Roman eagles for the first time turned back from their forward march in A.D. 118 under Hadrian and evidence is thus offered that the energy and progress of the imperial spirit was weakened. Viewed historically, the second century is therefore one of the most important and interesting in the story of the western world. The old order was changing and the outward sign of the new era was the establishment and consolidation of the Empire. The social changes which such profound political modifications involve came gradually into view. Of far deeper interest, however, is the change in the inner life of men.

The old world of classical antiquity was dying and before the end of this century the mind and mood which had characterized it were profoundly altered. In many important respects they had passed away forever. The

old skepticism of the early empire had disappeared and
the world was filled with spiritual cravings which grew
ever stronger and stronger. By the beginning of the second century a great wave of religious interest was moving all classes, even the most intelligent and cultivated.
Even a century earlier Augustus had felt it necessary to
begin a reform in the religious institutions of Rome. In
the beginning of the century the feeling was to a great
extent vague and restless, without definition or direction, but before the end we feel that the religious destiny
of the Empire was being decided. At first, we are conscious of the breath of a new life moving unseen over the
souls of men. Deep anxiety and hidden unrest are everywhere stirring. When, however, the gates of the third
century open, the great forces of the future are already
gathering for the mighty struggle which is to decide the
history of civilization.

All through the Age of the Antonines the revival in
religion was growing more and more pronounced. The
cold and somewhat poverty-stricken abstractions of the
old Roman religion made no appeal to the new instincts
and emotions which were awakening, and the new spiritual
needs demanded other and wider satisfactions.

The relation between the East and the West, always
a problem of profound interest, was before the minds of
the men of the old world. Alternately attracting and
repelling each other as they have always done, it is impossible to determine which is more dependent upon the
other. It is easy enough, however, to say which has received the most from the other. Three times the West
has flung itself upon the East. The Greek, the Roman,
and the Teuton have each tried to pierce the heart of the
Orient and plant western culture and western civilization
in those far homes of the race. But of each attempt save
the first, we may say, as the modern poet has said:

"The East bowed low before the blast,
In patient, deep disdain;
She let the legions thunder past,
Then plunged in thought again."

Three times during the early years of Christian history
the East, in turn, hurled itself upon the West. In
Mithraism, Manichæism, and Mohammedanism it strove
for conquest, and though it failed, it produced effects
which have never been forgotten or erased. Mithra itself,
however, represents but the highest and purest of many
contemporary religious invaders from the Orient. Against
these foes the West was but poorly equipped. The nar-
rowness and rigidity of the Roman religion was not
strengthened or reënforced by the power and breadth of
the religions of Greece. For as Cumont said: "No people
so advanced in culture as the Greeks ever had so infantile
a religion." This Eastern invasion was conditioned, however, by two facts: one, the nature of polytheism itself;
the other, the new political situation which was the result
of the spread of Roman power.

The gods of heathenism, the moment they passed beyond the bounds of their original local influence, tended
to become identified with the gods of the new land into
which they were introduced. National hostility was never
strong enough to exclude, for any long time, the deities of
other peoples which, either because of national influence
or by virtue of the qualities ascribed to them, were rec-
ommended to the peoples of the new countries brought
in contact with them. This syncretistic tendency is manifest through the whole history of paganism and advanced
with increasing rapidity as the social intercourse and
political unity of the western world became more and
more manifest through the evolution of the Græco-
Roman civilization. The political factor worked in harmony with the natural tendencies of paganism and we

find that, as intercourse increased, the movement in this direction became stronger and stronger.

The foreign religions were not always popular with the authorities because they did not concern themselves with public affairs but with the interior life. They set a new stamp upon human personality and brought forward as the two great objects of life, Purification and Immortality. Official opposition was based upon the fear which was felt, perhaps unconsciously, that these religions exercised a disintegrating effect upon the established religions of the West. The spread of oriental religions, together with the development of Neo-platonism, are the capital facts in the moral history of paganism.

Yet these would not have exercised such influence or been so eagerly sought had there not been a great change in the spiritual attitude and consciousness of men. Certain new conceptions, ideas, ways of regarding life, ethical sentiments, and religious feelings were in the air and widespread. These not only shaped the language of religion, but filled it with new meaning. The influences which shattered the power of the old gods were widely different. The spread of Epicureanism, with its materialistic conception of life, had weakened the faith of men in the activity and influence of the gods. When astrology came from the East, with its dark shadow of an inscrutable and inexorable destiny ruling inflexibly the life of man, faith in the gods became more and more useless, hopeless, and meaningless. Stoicism, on the other hand, turned the thoughts of man toward himself and his solitude. To the Stoic, the national gods were but aspects of the Eternal Spirit. God and the human soul were the two poles of Stoic thought and, while there was much which was touched by the vague pantheism which lay at the root of this type of thought, Stoicism could not and did not escape the influence of the long course of Hellenic thought. The transcendental conception of God which was the basis of it was itself the result of centuries of Greek thinking. The mournful note of man's sense of loneliness sounds again and again from many a Stoic teacher who felt he represented the tranquil conclusions of his predecessors, although his soul was haunted by a sorrow quite unknown to the eager and hopeful days of Greek speculation.

Speaking broadly and roughly, from the point of view not of theory but of practice, there have been two general types of ethics which still influence, far more widely than is recognized, the lives of men, though as theories they may be rejected. They may be called the theory of Naturalism and the theory of Dualism. Primitive ethics was naturalistic; that is, the world-harmony or order was also the human harmony or order. Man's natural instincts were right because they were in correspondence with the laws of nature, and were his natural endowment from the beginning. This instinctive feeling is the source of that bewilderment which falls upon the soul in its first stages of self-consciousness.

Yet there was a sense of evil, or a something which filled the soul with an unknown alarm, as life revealed its mysterious experiences. Very early in his development, though sooner with some races than others, man began to sense a profound distinction between good and evil, and to feel each in some way represented in himself. What the beginning was of this first dualistic conception is a problem for the philosopher and the psychologist, and for the historical student only as he follows in their footsteps. To enter into the various theories which have attempted the solution of this question would be to write the history not only of ethics but of philosophy.

Philosophy is not the whole of life and the movement of the ethical consciousness has an influence, never completely defined, over the wide life of history. As the moral instincts of man find a clearer and finer expression, and as the majesty of their authority more vigorously asserts itself, so do we find a deep and reflex action upon both religion and what is accepted as authoritative. To all the naturalistic religions of antiquity what is defined as sin seems to be but a natural though melancholy necessity. The failure to reach the ideal is a consequence of, and involved in, the physical and material side of life. When the ethical sentiment and the spiritual impulse in man's nature insist upon freedom, the way out of this bondage or limitation is sought through physical means: through rites and ceremonies which are believed to have an effect upon man's life entirely apart from the nature of his character. Elevation or purification of the soul is attained by purely external, objective, and material means, which have an origin and history far back in the dawn of man's moral self-consciousness. The power these rites exert is a purely magical one and leaves the moral craving for the dimly apprehended righteousness imperfectly satisfied. In the Asiatic religions which, during the second century, spread with such rapidity through the Roman Empire the idea of Purification was almost, if not altogether, universal. Each religion appealed to the individual as such, and a hope purely personal began to fill the heart of the worshiper. Man was finding his way out of the mass in which he had hitherto been lost. The ancient ideals which had held sway through so many centuries began to fade before this more living and vivid personal consciousness whose coming was attended by such strange transformations in many lives. The inner changes reacted silently and unconsciously upon the outer life of man and the historic bonds of the past fell from the hands which were stretched out for another and different prize. As Cumont has said, "Oriental civilizations are all sacerdotal civilizations"; Western civilizations, on the other hand, were all political civilizations and one of the great forces which was at work transforming the Western world came through the presence of this different way of regarding life. Religion and not the state became the center of the individual history. The old national and political unity which had been shattered through the Mediterranean world by the state-power of Rome was to undergo further modifications and transformations. The Empire seized in its iron grasp the rule of the world, but with a wonderful insight felt, though it did not understand that a new force was moving through its wide dominions which was and would always be its undying foe. It was three centuries before it recognized the face of its enemy in all its power and then only to surrender. The time, however, had not yet come even for that recognition, but already the great changes in spiritual outlook and psychological conditions brought about by and expressed through the oriental religions, at least in part, foreshadowed the doom of the past. Already antiquity was perishing and a new era was being born. The absence of truthfulness and sincerity in the old religions and their gods weakened the entire character of ancient life. This weakness was felt and its causes in part recognized, and thus became one of the most powerful forces working in favor of the oriental religions which revealed and expressed a deeper sense of man's nature and needs.

Among the many results of these various currents of new thought and feeling was a change in "The Tables of Values." The deeper the sense of need became, and the greater the desire for purification and salvation, the more the limitations of this earthly life became apparent. A readjustment along the old lines of naturalism was now impossible, and the purely intellectual conceptions of philosophy had already revealed their weakness. Not "Now and Here," but "Then and There" express the new mood. A present realization of happiness no longer

lifted the soul to larger efforts, but beyond the rim of
time the vision lay of a salvation whose ultimate meaning
was spiritual and whose aim was the redemption of the
soul of man. This was a new element in paganism and
though mingled with the strangest inheritances from the
remotest past was full of life and force. The waking
thoughts, the distant recollections, the endless emotions
of men of the most diverse races and representing the
widest differences in culture and tradition flowed in and
mingled with each other. There was an endless shifting
and changing, borrowing and lending, sinking in some
to hopeless despair and rising in others to the most intense and enthusiastic conviction. Probably in no country in the Empire was this fusion and syncretism so great
or so powerful in the second century as in Asia Minor.
Long before the appearance of Christianity some of the
pagan cults in Asia Minor seem to have been influenced
by and borrowed from the religious ideas and phrases of
the Jewish Diaspora which had been settled there during
the era of the Diadochi. In Asia Minor also the influence
of Greece over oriental religion and thought was greater
than in any other part of the East, and it was in the second century that the Greek Orient sprang into new life
and its schools became again prominent and influential.

Antioch, while geographically not in the district of
Asia Minor, was yet in the circle of the same intellectual
and religious forces. And it was in this seething life that
Christianity was first planted in the outside world. It is
a matter of deep significance, too, that it was in Asia
Minor that it made its first and widest conquests. There,
too, for three centuries lay the heart and life of the great
Christian propaganda and there also it received its pre-
dominantly pagan-Christian tone and color, the largest
ingredient of which was Hellenic. But the Hellenism of
the second century was not the Hellenism of the great
days of the "Master of those that know," nor even of

the Alexandrian period, but a Hellenism, which, while it had not forgotten the glory of the past, had now lost its early joy. Across the sky once so clear and bright, rolled somber clouds and the soul was filled with new hopes and also new fears. The lucidity of Greek thought, the charm of Greek imagination and the Greek instinct for beauty never died, but they were charged with new thoughts and new emotions. In this world so vivid in its apprehension, so eager in its emotion, so intense in its earnestness, the Gospel appeared as a new religious influence side by side with the other religions coming from that mysterious home of all religions—the East. For Christianity entered the West in the same century and into the same territory in which the oriental religions began their march of conquest. Regarded from a strictly historical point of view it is part of that great movement by which the West was more and more orientalized. It found a language already formed for it, each word of which had a long history in the life and thought of those who used it. Each hearer also brought with him a complex body of ideas and conceptions with which to interpret the words he heard.

All the great writers and teachers of the first century were Jews who had behind them the background of their own nation and education as well as their own individual culture. All the great writers and teachers of the second century were pagans and had behind them the special experiences, national influences, and hopes which belonged to their races. As pagans, too, they represented all the diversities of the Empire. They were Asiatics and Greeks, Romans and Egyptians, and their endless varieties of sentiment and feeling were gathered into that huge mass which was the final expression of ancient life. The same variety of motives which is characteristic of our modern world must have existed then. The Messianic Hope and the Monotheistic Faith were the primary elements in the conversion of the Jew to the Gospel; but in the wide sea of human life, where so many emotions, ideas, and vague yearnings moved within it, the motives which led men to the Gospel differed considerably in each individual case. The Christianity of the second century is no more a repetition of the first than the twentieth is a repetition of the eighteenth or the sixteenth. Whether it was on the same level, whether it was higher or lower will depend upon the standpoint of the student and the standard he has set for himself.

To St. Paul and St. John the Gospel meant the transformation of life through the presence in the soul of the vital energy of the Savior of the world who lived with them and within them. God was revealed as present here on this earth, and life had a sacredness which told not only of a redeemed humanity, but of a world whose very being was divine. Union with God was not a far-off event to be realized in some unknown future, but life itself was touched with a sense of the Divine Presence, and man could toil and think, content with the companionship and power of his Master. This supreme fellowship, this complete and present union was expressed in one phrase— "The Life of Faith."

When we turn to the writers of the second century, who, whether perfectly or imperfectly, expressed something of the general Christian consciousness of the generation to which they belonged, we find some wide divergences, at least in the use of language. From this we infer something concerning the spiritual state of the men themselves. In all these men we recognize the influence of their previous history, the effect of the culture which had shaped the past and was still shaping the life of the present. Whether we are dealing with the calm and affectionate Roman Clement or listening to the burning words which flowed from the ardent soul of the Asiatic Ignatius, we see there are differences of the profoundest impor-

tance. Clement does not see anything fundamental in
the word "Faith" and to Ignatius it seems chiefly the
conviction of the truth of Christianity, the belief in the
reality of the human birth of Christ, His death and resurrection. Faith is, however, not a belief in some merely
historical or objective facts, but it has an ethical and
spiritual value, since it implies or involves confidence in
Christ, though it does not mean that deep and inner
union with Him which is so powerfully felt and expressed
by St. Paul.

Clement of Rome speaks of faith as directed exclusively toward God, and he regards God rather from the
Jewish than the Christian standpoint. It is God's om-
nipotence which is the especial object of faith. As a
consequence he attributes faith, and therefore justification by faith, to all who from the very beginning of the
world have spoken rightly of, and felt deeply, the omnip-
otence of God. There appears also in the mind of Clement
the influence of the same thought which is so strongly
marked in the Epistle to the Hebrews: that is, the idea
of faith as hope in the divine promises. Thus faith is
considered a spur to obedience to the will of God. We
find continuously the old language, as was inevitable, but
the feeling and the point of view are different.

In the Epistle to Barnabas the writer wishes to advance his readers on the high road to perfection, by add-
ing to faith the higher virtue of wisdom. When faith is
subordinated to anything else as a means of spiritual
growth, it is manifest that we are in a new atmosphere.
The element of hope is still attributed to faith as one of
its chief characteristics, but yet it is inferior to wisdom.
Faith is not the only subjective means of realizing salvation, but one of them. This is a decided variation from
the language of St. Paul and also from the New Testament.

In the Didache the term is still used in what may be

called the Jewish sense of the word, that is, as signifying belief in God the Father; tending, as in the case of Irenæus, to make it syonymous with obedience. "Credere Deo est facere ejus voluntatem."

In the writings of Justin Martyr, who represents the higher intelligence of the Church at this period, we find that faith is simply the holding for true of that which is believed. It is never used in the sense of confidence in Christ or surrender to God. For faith was not, with him, organically related to the life of the soul. Nor does his conception of the life of the Christian seem to share in the great spiritual and religious ideas of the New Testament. The general sentiments in regard to life which were the common possession of the cultivated and intelligent classes of the Empire influenced Justin, and inevitably shaped at least his expression of what he considered fundamental in Christianity. His conception of God is philosophical and ethical rather than religious, and the language he uses is borrowed from the prevailing theories of the age. God is unknown in His essence. No direct and present communion with God is possible for man here and now. The divine fellowship dreamed of by the apostles is placed in the future. Fellowship with God is therefore not the ground and beginning of righteousness, the only root and spring of the spiritual life, but the end which is the reward, or the result, of a life of obedience to the moral law here upon earth. The doctrine of rewards and punishments which has so often superseded and displaced the spiritual union with God takes a place in the foreground of Christian teaching, not primarily because it represented the teaching of the New Testament, but because it expressed the general conviction of the mass of earnest men at that day.

As a consequence, the spiritual relation of man to God in faith falls into the background and the relation established with Him through good works was emphasized in a one-sided and irreligious way. The great factors or facts of the religious life are all treated in this shallow and unsatisfactory manner and show a falling off in the depth with which the soul had felt the meaning of Christ in its spiritual history. Salvation is not the soul's rest in God, or the possession of man's nature by the spiritual energy and vitality of the spirit of Christ, but something far, far different. It is freedom from the power of the demons who haunted the mind of the pagan world with such horror, that relief was one of the most anxious and desperate needs of the time. One should not depreciate the real joy which the Christian felt in the sense of Christ's deliverance, and it did change the world for many devil-ridden souls. But such salvation does not imply nor did it involve a deliverance of souls from the forces through which and by which the demons were begotten and held their sway: the passions, the lusts, the unbeliefs. It is true, this salvation also meant freedom from the power of death and the promise of immortality, but these were, as we may say, outside the actual present history of the soul and were not felt as the dynamic working of the divine life within.

When we turn from a study of the spiritual phenomena of this age of the Church to the language which was used, we are struck by the appearance of a new phrase which was destined to play a great part in all subsequent history and represents the Gospel in a way widely different from that of the New Testament. Turning back to the generation before Justin we find in the Epistle of Barnabas a new term (Cap. 2, 6). The Gospel is called the "New Law" (Nova Lex). Here, no doubt, it meant chiefly that the Jews had not understood the will of God and had consequently forfeited His guidance. It did not mean primarily the legalizing of the Gospel, but it was a term destined to a long history and a powerful influence upon the view of the Gospel which the Church ultimately set forth. How shall we understand this phrase and what were the causes which first led to its use? The first question can no doubt be answered more satisfactorily after the second has been considered. It may not be possible to state all the causes, and the limits of our knowledge preclude it. But there are some facts, at least, which throw a strong light upon the subject and offer a reasonable explanation of one of the most significant phenomena in the growth of the early Christian Church.

One of the strongest influences which led the minds of the men of this age to turn to the East for light upon the great problems of their spiritual life was the feeling that the Orient was the home of the earliest and the oldest religions which men knew. In that dim and distant age when the dew of the morning was still upon the earth and the bright dawn had not yet faded into the light of common day, God had revealed to those souls who were as yet untouched and unworn by the fierce ravages of a world plunged in sin the secrets which were so soon to be forgotten by a self-seeking world. So the older a religion was the more authority it had. Therefore priority in age and origin became of supreme importance. When the pagan turned to listen to the words of the Gospel this sentiment was already in his mind and this craving in his heart.

Side by side with this feeling was an objective fact whose significance it is hard to realize at the present day. The one and only book which the Church possessed and to which it appealed as to an infallible authority was the Jewish Scriptures. At first they were used chiefly to vindicate, by means of the prevailing methods of interpretation, the faith the Church had in Jesus Christ. The Old Testament was not a history nor yet primarily a body of laws, but a book of Prophecy whose end and aim was to authenticate the message and person of Christ. Its value, however, lay largely in its age, and here again

the Pagan-Christian followed the path of his contemporaries and echoed the proud boast of the great Jewish
teachers who found in "Holy Plato" a borrower from the
books whose writers lived ages before Greece had risen
from the obscurity of its primitive beginnings. The Jew
believed his religion to be older than any in existence, and
the Christian accepted and rejoiced in this assumption.
But the time came when the Christian denied any Jewish
meaning whatever and declared it to be in every sense of
the word a Christian book. According to Justin, the antiquity of the Gospel was greater than that of any other
religion (Apol. i, 23, 44, 59).

A metaphysical dualism was the unconscious assumption or the conscious basis of all writers and thinkers
both Jew and pagan. A transcendent God hidden in some
abyss, far removed from contact with this world of matter, required some mediating agency or agencies to account for the world of matter and of life. In the Oriental
religions a theory of emanations had become the means
of explaining the existing order of things. This theory
played a large part on the Christian stage in the various
schools of Gnostics who were one of the great forces
through this and the next century. In the West the
Stoics had developed a theory of Logoi, which was, to a
large extent, a materialistic philosophy. In Alexandria
all streams met, and there in the great Jew Philo we find
the union of many elements taken from the various
schools or currents of thought of his age. Among these
the transcendence of God and the opposition of God and
the World were cardinal features, which caused Philo to
feel the need of a mediator. Instead, however, of turning
to the Eastern theory of emanations to explain the world,
he adopted, at least in part, the Stoic teaching. He set
forth in many forms and without much logical consistency his theory of "The Logos." This new conception
or new form and definition of an older conception was

adopted by the writer of the Fourth Gospel and became
the fundamental doctrine of the great successors of Philo,
the leaders of the Christian Church in Alexandria. So
closely did the later generations of Alexandrian teachers
and writers follow Philo that so great a scholar as Baur
has said: "From the pages of the Neo-Platonists as
well as from the writings of Philo we can construct a
system of dogma quite similar to that of the Church
Fathers."

In the hands of the Christian teachers the Logos became the explanation of history, and its unity was preserved by making the universe the work of this mediating
agency. Applying this principle to the historical Covenant of Judaism they insisted that it was the work of the
Logos, though St. Paul and the Epistle to the Hebrews
asserted that it had been established through the media-
tion of angels (Gal. III, 19. Heb. II, 2). Holding with
unflinching firmness, as the mass of Christians did, to the
identity of the God of the Old Testament and that of the
Gospel, as against the theories of the Gnostics: asserting
the unity of history through the operation of the Logos,
and having no conception of historical development, they
destroyed all those distinctions which exist between the
temporary and the permanent in the Old Testament, and
transferred the cardinal idea of the Law from the Old
Covenant to the New. So was the conception of the Gospel as the New Law validated for men of that age and
for many subsequent ages, with results from which the
Church has suffered ever since. In practice, no doubt,
the harshness and rigidity of this new conception was
much softened by the new spirit which was the essence of
the Gospel, but it was forever confusing the higher efforts
of the Christian spirit to reach that freedom which was
the spiritual birthright of the sons of God through faith.

Coöperating with this new conception which had its
origin in the Christian attempt to explain and to use the

Old Testament, as well as to explain human history, were elements which sprang out of the very heart of paganism itself and were the natural inheritance from those who had most seriously faced the problems of life in that age as well as in ages more remote. The paganism of the day with all its passion and its power still fell back instinctively and unconsciously upon the naturalism, the basis of all old religions. The fact most fundamental to all the heathen religions was that religious experience was conceived of as ordinarily the concomitant of a corresponding physical change or act of a purely objective character. This was the heart of the Mysteries, and the Mysteries were at this time the center of the religious life of paganism. How absolutely physical and material were the benefits derived through these cults we can see in the Mysteries of Eleusis. No moral effects seem to be associated with them or even expected. No demand was made upon men for a change of life, for no new disposition or character was required. The religious ends were accomplished through purely physical means.

These material means employed in the Mysteries were stamped with the physical experiences of man. Eating is the oldest form by which man conceives of his life nourishment. It is also one of the oldest forms of representing the union of man with the life of the Power above him. It is the means by which he gains spiritual qualities, though in the earlier stages of man's history these qualities are regarded as semi-physical. The act of eating is not a symbol but represents the actual manner of the union with the god.

Though this idea does not seem to have been an element in later Jewish religion there is a noteworthy passage in Ecclesiasticus XXIV, 20 f. which suggests the presence of foreign influences. The Jewish Apocalypse has its bread of life in connection with the Tree of Life (Enoch XXIV, XXV). The bread of life was found among the

Chaldeans, Mazdeans, and the worshipers of Mithra.
Water too had a power in itself. Among the Mandeans
baptism was an effort to become one with the divine element itself—water. This baptism, as among the Gnostics,
brings the forgiveness of sins and freedom from the power
of the Demons. Water was regarded also by both the
Babylonians and the Persians as having a divine quality
and the same feeling seems to have existed throughout
all of Western Asia. The objective factors in the Mysteries were considered as the essential conditions for the
effects, and these were the new birth and the divine life.
These "Means of Grace" were absolutely necessary. The
moral character of the individual, as has been stated, was
more or less a matter of indifference. The important
thing was conformity to the ritual and the ceremonial
requirements for regeneration.

One particularly repulsive ceremony, the "Taurobolium," adopted by the worshipers of Mithra from the
cult of Cybele, was a bath of blood. Through it the new-
born convert received a cleansing which made him
"Renatus in Æternam." The indelible character which
the initiate thus received was independent of his own character. He was a passive recipient, and the ceremony was
a kind of "Opus Operatum." Through it he came "sacra-
tus, renatus, tauroboliatus." Among the Gnostics baptism was regarded as absolutely necessary. And by the
Valentinians, the most intelligent and nearest the Church,
it was supposed to operate in a manner which we can
only describe as magical. The Taurobolium, too, was
often applied to a substitute for one who knew nothing
of the proposed act, and hence it was, in this case, regarded somewhat as a "Mass with Intention."

In some of the Gnostic sects the forgiveness of sins was
associated with a visible act. The destruction of the
"hylic" portion of the man was accomplished by the im-
partation to him of the powers of the Pleroma through

certain rites. Sin was thus conceived of as a real material existence and was associated with the physical organism. Release from it was therefore necessarily associated with physical or material means. The religious experience thus became closely united with the physical or material condition of the man. Other agencies were sometimes employed for the same purpose as honey in the worship of Mithra, and milk and honey in the Mystery of Dionysus.

Among the Gnostics, whoever had the right sign, formula, name, could exert power over the earthly forces and gain a portion of the eternal powers. Since the simple and correct performance of the mystery was enough, if it were spoken over the dead, they too could become partakers in its benefits and could be delivered from the bitter pains of captivity to the world-ruler and raised into the eternal Fulness.

Among the primitive religions of antiquity and the mysteries which had their origin in them the rites of purification therefore had no moral object whatever. In their very nature and quality also they had no moral basis, for it was not spiritual, but legal or religious purification, that they aimed to accomplish. The chief assumption at the base of them was that the impure had fallen into the power of hostile gods or demons from whose control these rites would release them. It is true, a peculiar state of the soul seems to have been implied as necessary to a full and proper appropriation of salvation, but this pathological condition had no moral character or moral significance. We see this in the meaning of the terms which were in use to describe the union of the soul with the divine—Enthusiasm and Ecstasy. The first implies that the god enters bodily into the believer; and the second that the believer enters bodily into the god. The essence of the sacrament which is the embodiment of these conceptions is that the heavenly descends through it to the earthly and the earthly is raised to the heavenly. The

old, undying Dualism still remains untouched and unchanged by all these efforts to escape it.

In connection with all the Mysteries there seems to
have been a liturgy which already had a long history
before we find it in later times. The numerous writings
of a ritualistic or theological character which belong to
the Orphic sects laid claim to be regarded as a revelation.
These liturgies were of signal importance and were handed
down secretly from generation to generation. The essential meaning of "Litourgia" is, that the believer in and
through it, by means of a sacramental act, and definite
sacramental formulæ, comes into relation with his god.
The secret formula of the Mysteries was called Σύμβολον
and the mystics were described in the Orphic mysteries as
οἱ ὅσιοι (Plato, *Republic*, II, 363c). The emphasis
which was laid upon these formulæ is testified throughout
the whole range of antiquity both East and West. The
unconscious pressure of this attitude of mind, begotten
of centuries of religious experience, was, in the case of
the heathen Christians, a matter of great importance.
It worked in every direction and while it transformed the
Christian Sacraments, by applying to them terms and
ideas borrowed from the heathen Mysteries it also affected
the root conception of the Gospel itself.

The moral and spiritual character of the Gospel was
not destroyed by this inherited Naturalism, but it was
turned in many ways away from the simple and central
fact of union with God in heart and mind to obedience
to the divine will as revealed in the moral and spiritual
requirements of Christianity. The evidence for this we
can see in Justin Martyr. For instance, the root of all
his thinking is the conception of God. This seems to have
been the popular, philosophical attitude which was prevalent among the cultivated heathen of his day. God was
to Justin Abstract and Transcendent, Whose existence is
authenticated by the Christian revelation. Justin never

refers to the love of God for man, as does the New Testament, nor of the love of man for God. Nor does he find in this mutual affection the basis or manifestation of a union with God. The doctrine of rewards and punishments is fundamental with Justin. The idea of service and obedience stands in the first place, for the root of Christian morality is not in love to God but in the fulfillment of certain definite commands. The conception of the "Nova Lex" is implied and involved in this position. For though the New Law is religious and may be Christian also, inasmuch as it asserts the revelation of God through Christ, it does not appreciate nor does it stand upon the central fact of that revelation as related to the soul. Other influences also were in operation which led still further along this same path until the legal conception of the Gospel became for the organized Church one of its most characteristic affirmations.

One of the most striking of these forces was undoubtedly what is called Gnosticism. The phenomena which are included in this term are so various that attempts at definition have nearly always failed by reason of their lack of inclusion. One can only gather up results and suggest points of view. For the various forms of Gnosticism are as manifold as are those of the religious life of the period. Harnack in his study of Gnosticism calls it "The acute Hellenising of Christianity." The motive and the method are Greek but the material and many of the fundamental ideas are not Greek in their origin. Some later investigators are disposed, if not to reverse this judgment, at least to modify it greatly. The definition of the word "Gnosis" is not primarily intellectual knowledge. It is rather a mood ("Stimmung," a feeling, or a contemplation, a condition of the soul itself). It suggests knowledge of secret means by which this state is produced. There is in it a union of magic and philosophy which is a preparation for the religious practices through which the end is achieved. Instead of discussing or disputing about the real origin or special character of Gnosticism we may regard it as a product of the age, in which both East and West played their part. It was one of the characteristic religious and philosophical phenomena of a period in which the two met and were united often in a very confused and confusing way.

The chief interest of Gnosticism for the student of Christianity lies in its relations to, and effects upon, the Christian Church and Christian thought. Here some of its peculiar forms, no doubt, had greater influence than others. The dualistic element in Gnosticism was so strong that among what we may call Christian Gnostics, or those who appropriated the main points of the Christian revelation, the Old Testament was rejected and the unity of history was broken into two parts, each of which had a different origin. Marcion emphasized this point of view and practically based his Gospel upon St. Paul. There was a moral and not a philosophical motive in his effort. Marcion felt that the declension in the spiritual life of the Church resulted from the belief that the Gospel was after all in harmony with the inherited thought from the past, while he declared it to be primarily a new thing, a revelation which had as its object and essence a new moral and spiritual life. Yet his logic left the Gospel suspended in the air, and the spiritual history of man as related in the Old Testament, without any connection with the Gospel whatever. The reply to his position affirmed the great truth of the unity of revelation past and present, but it did not recognize or assert the originality of the spiritual character and purpose of the Gospel, or did so only in a very unsatisfactory manner. In order to protect itself against the intellectual confusion and moral inroads of Gnosticism the Church felt it to be necessary and sufficient to define the contents of the Christian teaching.

Hence arose the Christian Creeds. Their purpose was

to give stability and definition to the Christian Church,
but in defining its claims it presented Faith under a new
aspect. Irenæus, and even Ignatius, made Faith a purely
objective thing, or else considered it chiefly from the
intellectual point of view as an assent of the mind. Form-
ulation itself implies a legal conception and tended to
further the adoption of the Gospel as a "Nova Lex."

Working as Christianity did with the universal movement of the times toward the realization of new hopes and
new emotions it was inevitable that many experiments
should be made. These are, however, the signs of life.
No soil which is fertile excludes by any process of selec-
tion seeds good or bad. They grow together and often
in their blending produce new forms and new species
hitherto unknown. One of the most interesting of these
early experiments was Montanism. It has been said that
"The history of the Christian Church may be described
as a history of continual Reformations." Measured by
this standard Montanism must be considered as one of the
first, if not the first, of these reformations. When it
sprang from its home in Asia Minor with its passionate
abhorrence of a merely formal and conventional religion,
it was uttering a true protest against the life which was
too prevalent, a life of worldliness and spiritual indifference. Considered from the ethical point of view, Phrygian
Montanism was but the revival or the survival, under a
Christian form, of the old ecstatic, religious feeling which
was endemic in that country. This was an element of
strength, in a way, but was also an element of weakness.
Montanism was greeted with enthusiasm by some of the
noblest and most earnest spirits in the Church. It was a
protest against worldliness and unspirituality and yet
strange and paradoxical as it may seem it seized upon the
old, familiar term, "The New Law," and interpreted it
with the bitterest rigor. The noble moral life it wished
to see realized was the sincere aim of its best spirits, and

yet the method adopted was not a larger and fuller acceptance of Christ and his Spirit but the enforcement of a stern and narrow code of conduct. It failed, and it deserved to fail, for in spite of its emphasis upon its visions, ecstasies, and revelations, these were but the gifts of the few and the mass was under the dominion of guides who claimed, by the authority of divine revelations, to direct the actions and thoughts of men.

The aim which Montanism had in view was defeated by its own weapons, and the foe which it hoped to vanquish was really strengthened. For the condition of the spiritual and moral life of the Church against which it protested was but a result, not cause, and the cause lay in the interpretation of the Gospel then so largely prevailing. By emphasizing the legal conception of the Gospel the idea of the "New Law" in which lay so many seeds destined to bring confusion and disaster to the Christian life, was strengthened. In claiming divine authority for their leaders the Montanists made an appeal to which the reply of the Church could not be doubtful. The value and ability of the organization of the Church under the authority of its bishops had been, and were being, fully demonstrated in the clash with the Gnostics. If now Montanists claimed to have inspired leaders, the Church claimed in answer that its leaders too were directed by the Spirit in the way of the true faith, and the Church's type of derivation of authority proved much sounder for producing capable organizers than the ecstasy of the Montanists. So the bishops were forced into becoming the recognized preservers and teachers of the new faith, while the Church adopted more and more the point of view of some of its most dangerous enemies.

The Gnostics had been the first to make a study of the truths of Christianity and to give the results the form of intellectual propositions. More and more they laid stress upon definite doctrines, and more and more did the

"Gnosis" become a system of speculation which the ignorant mass was unable to understand. As a result they
destroyed not only the primacy of faith and its claims
to universality, but they destroyed also its real meaning.
It was no longer a free spiritual act of the soul by which,
through Christ, the believer became united to God in a
conscious filial relation, but was reduced to a mere blind
assent. There were a great many Christians who adopted
this view and we know how irritated Celsus was with those
Christians who cried out, "Only believe." What was
meant by this was a mere repetition of theological formulæ or an absolute obedience to ecclesiastical authority.
Faith in consequence sank from its high estate and became a purely objective matter in which the moral and
spiritual life had little or no part. The study of these
dogmas became the chief occupation of Christian teachers.
The Gospel was reduced to a system of philosophy in
which accuracy of thought and subtlety of definition are
the chief concern. As a matter of fact, dogmas are a
product and not a cause of the Christian life. In the long
history of the Church the creeds have been passionately
professed by some of the basest as well as some of the
noblest of its members. This is such a commonplace of
history that it is difficult to understand, unless one is
familiar with the history of their growth, how they could
have been able to hold such a prominent place in the conception or understanding of the Gospel. Piety, not orthodoxy, is the aim of the Christian life, but in many Christian ages it has been subordinated to orthodoxy, and we
see the fatal beginning of this change in the very earliest
period of the Church.

There were many, however, even in the second century
who felt, unconsciously perhaps, that faith was not an
objective body of doctrine nor the Gospel a "New Law."
The word faith itself occupied too prominent a place in
those writings which were studied so earnestly by the

most thoughtful and intelligent scholars of the day. These men were anxious to grasp, so far as they were able, the central and spiritual meaning of the language in which the earliest Christian teachers had told how the Gospel had found them, and what it meant to them. Alexandria was, at this time, the great spiritual metropolis of the Ancient World. The rapid growth of the Church in Alexandria had brought into it many who had little or no real appreciation of the Gospel, nor of the spiritual significance of faith. They found in the prevalent idea of it, as the mere acceptance of the truth, sufficient justification for their membership. On the other hand there were earnest and serious persons who reacted from this reckless and ignorant dogmatism in which was neither spiritual life nor moral excellence. Men like Clement of Alexandria, trained in Greek philosophy and steeped in the ancient spirit of the Hellenic world, were unwilling to accept blind orthodoxy as of real spiritual value, and yet, without really grasping the fundamental New Testament truth, sought for a solution in definitions and interpretations of their own.

As a true Gnostic Clement felt that to know was more than to believe (Strom. B. II, c. 14). And in view of what was coming to be called belief, he was undoubtedly right. Yet, if knowledge is more than faith, and is the principal thing for the Gnostic, the inference is inevitable. For, comparing the type of character which was associated with that of the popular faith and that of the more earnest and intelligent Gnostics like Clement, it could not be denied that the rewards of faith were not so high or so many as those of knowledge (Strom. B. IV. c. 17). The identification of knowledge with salvation was then not simply the survival of the old philosophical theories which Clement had imbibed from his Greek teachers, it was also in a way an attempt to assert a higher meaning for the Gospel than that which the popu-

lar expression suggested. Theoretically the difference
between the higher paganism and the Gospel was only a
matter of degree (Strom. VI. c. 8). There are, however,
endless variations in use of the different terms by Clement and others which show that these terms did not
always stand for clearly apprehended truths or represent
well-understood spiritual experiences. Faith had its motive in fear, but love was the inspiration of the Gnostic.
Faith is the minimum condition of admittance into the
kingdom of Heaven, but it is not the full spiritual life.
Clement nowhere uses language which would indicate any
recognition of the deep meaning of faith to St. Paul, but
he is far too spiritual a man to be content with the mere
dogmatic definition. His soul is athirst for God and he
often speaks in a way which sounds like echoes or memories of St. John. Christ is, after all, the center of his
thought and life, though not perhaps in the way he was
to St. Paul or St. John. But Clement did feel that all
true knowledge is in knowing Jesus Christ, and, through
Him, the Father. The final object of faith is the Supreme
God raised above the world, who cannot be known by the
intellect. Though he understands the meaning of the
Gospel only in relation to certain personal and intellectual
needs of his own, as most of us do, no one can deny the
Christian spirit of Clement. His high character and personal culture, his wide sympathy and earnest appreciation of the best in the past helped pave the way for the
presentation of the Gospel to the cultivated world into
which it had not hitherto found its way. The Gospel
meant a great deal to him, but had it not meant more
than he seems to think one might doubt whether it would
have become that radical and revolutionary force which
has made it the creative element in all the higher and
nobler development of history.

When we turn to another Greek with a far wider experience of life and a more active and practical spirit we

find the same limitations and the same inadequacy of understanding. According to Irenæus, man is justified through faith and works. That is, faith is obedience to the moral law and this obedience is the evidence or manifestation of faith. Like Justin, Irenæus seems to regard faith as simply "holding for true," in the intellectual sense, of what can be accepted on satisfactory subjective grounds. The promises and declarations of God are the basis of faith, and it means, generally speaking, the hope and the expectation that God will fulfill what He has promised. He will reward the righteous and punish the wicked. Ultimately the fulfillment of the promises is completely identified with faith. Faith is thus not regarded as an act of God in man, by which man is moved by the revelation of the Gospel, but as a work of man toward God. It is true Irenæus speaks of love as a fulfilling of the law which, after all, makes man righteous. This is, no doubt, a great advance upon the harsh and narrow legalism, with its spiritual sterility, which characterizes his rather shallow attempts to state the meaning of the Gospel. Yet this love itself is not a response to, or an effect of, the Spirit of God, but is primarily a work or act of man. We can appreciate the value of this language when we examine some of the spiritual facts with which Irenæus organically correlated faith. The forgiveness of sins, which brought a cry of gratitude from the souls of the first Christian believers meant to them and for them the removal of the sense of personal guilt. To Irenæus and the men of his age the sense of loss or injury as an effect of sin occupied the first place in their minds. The thought of personal guilt, of a separation and alienation of the soul from God, remained more or less in the background. The heavy and oppressive weight which burdened the soul was but the old thought of antiquity transferred to the new Christian territory. For to Irenæus it was not through a selfish or evil inclination, but

through a tragic deception that Adam was led into disobedience. Forgiveness, therefore, does not involve a
change of heart or at all require it, but a removal of the
burden which oppressed men. The taking away of this
consciousness of oppression does not produce any spiritual renovation but simply a restoration of the original
freedom of choice of which sin had robbed man. This
new or renewed freedom gives one the liberty to select
either salvation or death, for freedom is not salvation but
only the pre-condition or opportunity for it. The positive side, the spiritual meaning of salvation, consists in
the loving confidence of the heart of the child in the
Father and also in a kind of hyperphysical recreation
of human nature as a preparation for immortality. More
or less has been made of what has been called the mysticism of Irenæus, but it is the mysticism of paganism and
not the mysticism of Christianity. The consciousness of
sin nowhere expresses itself in that passionate cry of the
soul for peace with God, which has been the mark of the
highest Christian devotion, but in a moan for the lost
Paradise.

If, however, we turn from the intellectual principles
and theological statements to the practical life of the
Church we shall reach a firmer basis for judgment than
can be attained in any other way. It is in the world of
moral motives and ethical ideals that the true reach and
force of the spiritual life are realized. It is often, if not
generally, assumed, that a strict theory, a clear-cut and
definite moral creed represents, as applied to life a far
higher appreciation of moral values and spiritual truth
than the mere power of an ideal without the rigid demand
of code or theory. This is an error which is confined to
no age or class, and has been one of the fundamental
mistakes of all moral evolution and history. A high
standard of conduct and a clear appreciation and apprehension of moral values in society are often supposed to

represent the supreme achievement of the ethical instinct.
Yet there is a great difference between an ethical ideal
or spirit and loyalty to a moral code. A code is definite,
fixed, and final. Obedience to it constitutes the chief aim
of the moral life. Its very rigidity gives it strength and
its definiteness inspired confidence. But it admits of no
extension or expansion except by way of addition. The
mind and the spirit move always within the limits which
it prescribes. The moral growth of man never surpasses
the measure of his conformity. The development of the
individual sense of moral values is dependent upon some
outer law or ordinance and not upon an inward inspiration. The type created by such an interpretation of the
ethics of society is so perfectly well defined, has so much
social value, and is so appealing in its quality that its
real mediocrity and its spiritual limitations are hardly
recognized. Its root is not in the soul of man, but in
tradition, and the most perfect expression of it is in the
moral pedantry of the appeal to unbroken custom and
religious antiquity. It is not expansive nor is it creative.
It is so external that it has no vital relations with the
soul any more than that which springs out of the daily
pressure of environment. Real ethics have their roots
within and spring from the living forces which are inspiring and energizing the soul of man, together with the
attraction of a great ideal.

In the Gospel we find no theory of morals as understood by the schools. The fundamental idea is not of a
system of conduct in which acts were ranged in the order
of their worth. Such statements may seem to be in conflict with much of the language of the New Testament,
especially of the Epistles. Yet all virtues and acts,
whether they be helpful or injurious, whether they be
good or evil, virtuous or vicious, are regarded throughout the New Testament as relative to a central condition
or spiritual state. The ideal is not virtue but righteous-

ness. This righteousness issues out of a relation with God, and all worth is in this fellowship. Expressed in the language of spiritual relation, it is the love of the child for the parent, and out of this true love flows all the immense stream of conduct and life.

The Gospel emphasized the sense of personality which had been growing through all of later antiquity, and in the great field of human action and conduct it took a sudden leap from the outer to the inner. The center of gravity was shifted from the universe without to the spirit within. The principles of conduct were to be found not in the laws of the universe or in the order of nature, but in the springs of action within the soul, the motives and the ideals which occupied the ground left hitherto without inner stability or authority. Regarded from the ethical point of view this change from the metaphysical to the psychological basis of ethics is the supreme fact in the new moral history of mankind. Moral values were no longer to be found primarily in their social worth or their historical correctness or their philosophical validity, but in the inner meaning which men found in the new life of sonship. It was necessarily involved in the great conception or recognition of the meaning of faith as union through Christ with God Himself. The soul was open to the movement of a new spirit and the world was seen as the field of human action, the theater of human conduct and not the source of moral law.

The first ethical expression of the new consciousness was the great cry for freedom. A new sense of liberty, so large and so wide, must and did involve reaction, and where it was not seen in its organic spiritual relations it seemed to imply a complete destruction of all the efforts of the race to find a ground upon which a stable civilization could rest. As the whole of ancient society rested upon the idea of the state and not of the individual, the new moral ideal seemed absolutely revolutionary, as indeed it was, and the social duties upon which society had hitherto laid stress were suddenly left without their traditional foundations. The prescriptions and ordinances of religion too had to submit to the same sudden decrease in values, and the great Apostle to the Gentiles was hounded as a renegade from land to land. The new problem of life itself, as it presented itself in the soul of the Christian, had no precedents. It stood upon its own feet and rested neither upon philosophy nor tradition. It was to be the life of Christ repeating itself in a new world. The seat of authority was in neither religion nor law, but in the new inspiration and the spiritual nature of man. Modern debates as to the relative value of liberty and law had no place in the first spiritual fervor with which the new inspiration filled men. The act of redemption was a total one. It involved and included the outer as well as the inner, and the outer because first the inner. The obedience of Christ was at the same time, and first, the freedom of Christ, for the Christian recognized no law as authoritative over the soul, in its inner development, save the spirit of Christ Himself. It is not in the least surprising that the splendor of this new moral ideal should fail to be fully or fairly recognized. Authority always has the basis of precedent to rest upon. Hence the fear aroused by Christianity. The new Christian freedom seemed about to sweep away all the institutions of the past, all the traditions and customs of ages and even the very ground upon which that ancient and majestic civilization had rested.

As a consequence, we find very early in the history of the Church, especially after it had reached a stage in which organized forms could express its real life, the survival and action of many of the old conceptions. The principle of authority became and has remained, the dominant force in shaping popular ethics. The whole story of the Christian Church as organized Christianity has been the effort to legalize ethics and give the weight of outward authority to establish or reënforce the inward spiritual foundation of the soul's life. The process has not been so satisfactory as one might assume, even though the claim has been made and conceded that the voice which speaks is divine.

Roman civilization in its splendor and its pride passed away forever, but the authority which it claimed was seized by an even stronger hand and the moral history of mankind for centuries still told the same old story, whose somber shadows had darkened the last ages of antiquity. It was in the second century that those ideas and institutions were shaped which ruled so long and with such mixed results. For it was in the second century that the Gospel first became a power and an influence in the wide life of the Empire.

The new life meant freedom, but to those into whom the true spirit of that life had not entered it meant many other things besides. The flexible syncretism, the easy hospitality of men's minds blended together pagan and Christian, old and new, liberty and license. The very wildness of Gnosticism strengthened the instinct for authority and built up the walls of the new Catholic Church which were slowly rising above the spiritual welter and religious chaos. The growth of episcopal power, which in the beginning had its origin, not in prescription, but in character, fortified the legalistic motive. And when the externalizing tendencies laid the stress upon the profession of faith as the most important thing, the earlier conception still existing, of faith as an inner state, led to a confusion which has not yet disappeared. The dangers of freedom are always haunting the minds of earnest and conservative men, but in matters of religion the dangers of law are greater. By and through the expression and exercise of authority an outward conformity and social order seems to be attained, but the inward

spirit with its loneliness and its doubts is often buried in
a slumber hard to be distinguished from that of death.

The vital and disturbing energy of the original Christian impulse was still too powerful in the second century
to permit that outward peace which was the boast of later
centuries, and the very activity of the new ferment produced some violent aberrations. In spite of every misunderstanding, and more than misunderstanding, perversion, the sum total of the Christian life was a revelation
of the most impressive kind to the world about it. The
sternest and keenest critics, and there were many, felt
its superiority though they could not explain its cause.
There was no philosophy here except that with which
they were familiar, there was no theology, in the metaphysical sense, with which they had not some acquaintance, but there was a life, springing from an inner source
which they could not fathom, and the beauty and devotion of many a human soul filled them with wonder. New
streams of emotion, new impulses of affection, a wealth of
devotion and unselfishness everywhere, to a greater or less
degree gave a new tone and richness to human life.

Something divine was in the air and living in the souls
of men. A hideous mass of ignorance, vice and shame-
lessness had made the world hopeless. But the immense
energy and hope of the new race were impressive facts,
though there seemed no way to explain them. To some
Christianity seemed like madness, and they were appalled
as they saw it spread. Yet the moral force, the spiritual
splendor shone brighter and brighter the less they could
be explained. It was the moral beauty and the moral
power of the Christian character which justified the declaration that a new life had come into the world. Behind
and beneath the various forms in which the Christian
Church expressed its manifold activity, in spite of the
secularizing and legalizing of the Christian faith, this life
flowed on in secret channels, testifying to the spirit which

had found its own, and to which the souls of men were yielding though they had no voice to tell the story except the silent yet convincing expression of life and character.

In the last years of Marcus Aurelius there broke out a furious persecution of the Christians in Southern Gaul. The prisons were crowded with victims who were later either beheaded or tortured in the arena. Day after day the maddened crowd was infuriated and astonished by the fortitude and patience of the martyrs. One young woman endured inconceivable suffering in a spirit of humility and tenderness which left even the most brutal oppressed with a sense of shame and awe. Her persecutors were never mentioned with resentment nor were her friends ever able to see any pride or self-esteem in her heroism. On the last day of this horrible exhibition she met her end in the same spirit which had shown itself in all those which had gone before. Her name was Blandina and she was a slave.

Some years later in North Africa a little band of unknown Christians were called upon to prove their faith in the same way. A young woman about to become a mother was dragged before the judgment seat and declared her faith in Christ. When she was flung into prison the hour of her maternity was at hand. The jailer said to her: "If thy present sufferings are so great, what wilt thou do when thou art thrown to the wild beasts?" She answered: "I now suffer myself all that I suffer; but then there will be another who shall suffer for me, because I also will suffer for Him." Her name was Felicitas and she was a Montanist.

CHAPTER IV

THE CRISIS OF THE THIRD CENTURY

In the last half of the third century took place the final struggle of the various forces in the Empire for the spiritual possession of the world. Over against expiring Paganism Christianity had raised new and higher ideals and had drawn to itself all the moral and religious forces which finally gave it the victory. Change and decay were on every hand. The political influence of the East was already evident and when, in the early part of this century, an Oriental, and a Syrian, sat upon the throne of the Cæsars the old Roman knew the world had changed for him forever. "The walls of Sparta are the breasts of her sons," was the reply of the proud Lacedæmonian to the question of the surprised visitors. So too would Cato or Scipio have spoken in the days of the Republic. But when in the middle of this century the ablest soldier Rome had had in more than a generation threw a wall around the city it is manifest that the once mighty people had fearfully declined. The day had passed when the very name of Rome inspired terror in the breasts of the remotest barbarians and filled her neighbors with awe. The wall of Aurelian is something which might escape the eye of the casual visitor, but the condition of the city and the Empire during these terrible years of the third century can have but one meaning. The half century from 235 to 284 was a perfect hell, and into this hideous abyss sank all philosophy, refinement, and grace. The soldiers were the masters of the Empire and sold the imperial mantle at public auction. At one time there were ten

115

pretenders to the throne and the barbarians were entering through every fissure.

Yet it was under just such conditions that the greatest religious movement of the ancient world advanced toward its crisis. The political influence of the East, which strengthened the despotic tendencies and instincts of the rulers of the Empire, were sustained by, and, in reality, in many cases sprang out of the religious forces which lay behind them. There was a great oriental Diaspora in the whole of the Latin world, composed of Jews, Syrian slaves and merchants, which were modifying not only the material civilization of Europe, but also its religious conceptions and beliefs. Not even during the epoch of the Mohammedan invasion was Europe nearer becoming Asiatic than in the third century of our era when the oriental influence was at its height.

The Greek religions had no longer any deep influence upon the spiritual life and the ancient Roman cults were dead. In the East religion represented almost every stage of culture, from the primitive naturalism, which was, so to speak, unmoral or a-moral, and which expressed itself in the forms and ceremonies of the different cults, up to the point where it was associated with some of the deepest and most poignant experiences of the human spirit. The crude and soul-less religions of the West had no chance in an encounter with those from the East, throbbing as they were with some of the most vivid emotions which have ever stirred the heart of man. Their swift progress from their distant homes on the banks of the Euphrates or the Nile, to the banks of the Tiber and the shores of the Western Sea, is one of the most remarkable and significant events in history.

No one has more clearly set before us the true character of this period than Cumont. In his brilliant description of the oriental religions and their influence in the Empire he says:

"The spiritual condition of the western world in the early part of third century was much like what it would be if we today were to see in modern Europe the faithful desert the Christian Churches to worship Allah or Brahma or to follow the precepts of Confucius or Buddha or adopt the maxims of Shinto. Let us also imagine a great mingling of all the races of the world, where Arabian Mullahs, learned Chinese, Japanese bonzes, Llamas from Thibet and Hindu pundits were preaching at the same time fatalism and predestination, the worship of ancestors and devotion to the deified sovereign, pessimism and deliverance through annihilation; all the priests building in our cities temples of exotic architecture in which were celebrated all their different rites: thus we would gain a picture of the religious incoherence and chaos into which the ancient world had fallen." [1]

The paganism of the third century, so different from that of the first, was due not merely to the adoption of new and foreign religions with their strange cults, but was itself the expression of a new consciousness. It adopted and absorbed these foreign cults not for the sake of their novelty or their antiquity, but because in and through them were manifest certain instincts and emotions which were part of the life and the spiritual experience of the man of this age. The very confusion of ideas and emotions, the monstrous and grotesque elements so repugnant to the man of the present, did not affront the soul that felt another, different, and, as he thought, a higher life, striving for expression in these old religions.

The feeling became widespread that life on earth was a painful thing. The old springs of joy which had made life beautiful in the days of long ago were now dried up. Religion and philosophy were both preaching flight from the world. Help from God seemed the only thing which could save a dying world. All the more earnest and pious shared in the common desire for participation in and enjoyment of, the divine life. Communion with God was sought particularly through the Mysteries, for the out-

[1] Cumont, *Les Religions Orientales*. Reprinted by permission of The Open Court Publishing Company.

ward show of things seemed but a shadow while the eternal reality lay in the secrets of the Spirit.

The longing for a Savior became one of the deepest passions of men's souls, and though the feeling itself was not clearly defined, it meant, primarily at least, One who could help, One who would bring health and salvation to the sick spirit. The old problem of evil which had puzzled the ages and filled the soul with suffering, emerged in a new and pathetic form. Human nature and not the physical world is the source and seat of man's sorrow and tears. There is something inherent in the very nature of man which is the root of all the agonies which have shaken the soul. This root is evil but as such was not viewed as a positive force seated in the will, but rather as a loss whose shadow haunted every life.

The aim of life, then, was to regain this lost purity. This new consciousness marks one of the principal stages in the history of European ethical speculation. Although with this sense of want and emptiness there went the consciousness of weakness and impurity these were regarded as the effect of spiritual loss rather than of wilful choice. Hence earthly life became abhorrent to the spirit. For this life itself stained the soul. The old longing for immortality was quickened into the most intense passion. Pessimism undoubtedly clung to many souls and filled them with despair, but the inexhaustible vitality and the spiritual energies of man, in most cases led him to leap, "beyond the shining ramparts," and claim the future as the only hope of realizing man's deepest instincts.

The appeal of the mystery religions was at once stimulating and meeting the longings of the man of the third century to invigorate a greater and purer life, even more than in the century before. Three of these Mysteries had now become oustanding in recognition, the Mysteries of Cybele or the Great Mother, Isis, and Mithra.

Cybele offered the savage but gratifying rite of the

Taurobolium, the baptism in bull's blood, as well as a spiritual meal in which the initiate partook of the spiritual food and drink consecrated to Attys. The myth on which the mystery was based also had great appeal. For the mystic learned of a divine youth who was mutilated and killed, but brought back to life by the yearning love of the Great Mother, herself Virgin. In his resurrection there was hope for a similar consummation for all who in the sacred rites identified themselves with him.

Isis shared with the Great Mother that devotion which in all ages seems to be inspired by the maternal instincts and the maternal character. The larger part of Christendom feels to-day toward the Virgin much as the men and women of the third century felt toward Cybele and Isis. In her was expressed the divine response to the need of sympathy and guidance on the part of the poor and helpless, the sorrowing and the sinning. For the first time perhaps in the ancient world the idea of the Divine Pity was set before the eyes of men. To the broken and the heart-sick, to the lonely and the oppressed, who had lost all sense of self-sufficiency this pity had been only an object of dumb desire in the hours of solitude and despair. Now, to all the world's unhappy is offered the sweet affection of a mother. She is the purest and the most perfect; she personifies in the most ideal type the tenderest and strongest sentiment which moves human nature. The need of all who call upon her is met by her strong and helping hand, and in so doing she inspires in the hearts of the unfortunate the desire to render help to all others of their fellow men who need it. The pity of the goddess enters into the soul of her worshiper so he too can assuage the sorrows of the miserable. The strange, new satisfaction of unselfishness became part of the divine life and a nobler aim than personal success was inspired by the new devotion.

Thus there grew up the feeling of a secret and hidden

relation between the common worshipers: the idea of a
higher brotherhood than the merely political or national
one: something which was entirely new in the West. The
ideas of Purification and Renunciation which were the
common possession of the higher minds of this age and
the root of so many of the more vital religions, come into
full and complete expression here. They were also unac-
companied by any of those brutal, cruel, ghastly, or
obscene rites which belonged to some of the most naturalistic religions of the East. The life which was demanded of one who would enter into communion with the
deity and share in the knowledge of the sacred doctrine,
was a life sober and temperate, free from all excesses of
the senses and the pleasures and excitements of passion.
Moreover, it was not accomplished by one merely formal
act of renunciation, like that which is made by many to-
day, but by a steady and persevering effort which was
often made stern and severe by the spiritual aspirations
of the worshiper. He always had a comforter, consoler,
and guide in the priest who initiated him and who afterwards stood toward him in a parental relation, with all
the sympathy and strength which are implied in the idea.
This was the ideal, and the surprising thing is that it
was so largely realized. The life and manners of the
priests of Isis were so pure that Tertullian considered
them models which should make Christians blush.[2]

The old Hellenic conception of immortality had found
a fertile soil in Alexandria and it reappears in the teaching of the Egyptian divinity, but to it there was also
added a new idea, that of the Resurrection. Following
this was a Last Judgment, and a reward after death to
the faithful servant of his god. These ideas were immensely strengthened by their association with the divine
drama of the Birth, Passion, Death and Resurrection of
Osiris, the anniversaries of which, beginning with the

[2] De exhortatione Cœlibat. XIII, c. Liber de Monag. XVIII, a.

twelfth of November, were the great festivals in this cult. That the actual facts did not realize the aim which was sought does not surprise those who have any acquaintance with religious history. Many fierce and bitter denunciations are to be found in the literature of the Church against the worshipers of all the non-Christian religions. We have no more reason, however, to accept the hostile statements of the Christian Fathers than we have to accept statements of the same character made by the pagans against the Christians, unless there is some other and more reliable evidence furnished to us. The attacks upon the Jews in our own day are in many respects exactly the same in kind.

The long account given by Apuleius in the "Metamorphosis," of the initiation of Lucius, has been so often referred to by others, that it is only necessary to say here that it indicates the great value which was felt to lie in the faith and worship of the goddess. The prayer of Lucius to Isis is full of religious feeling and deep devotion. In the inscription which has come down to us we are told that the Mother Goddess sympathizes with her worshipers and plants in the heart maternal instincts and maternal duties. She also punished unkind parents; she puts in the heart of man the love of woman and inspires the soul with a desire for beauty and purity. The moral and spiritual value of this worship must have been far greater than that of the old native religions with which it came in contact, and it at least reveals the fact that a new and different sense of the meaning of life was felt, even if it was not understood.

The religion of Mithra, in some form at least, was one of the oldest in the history of Western Asia. It had a long development and a most complex growth before it came into contact with European or Hellenic culture. Like all religions Mithraism found a home in the West first among the lower classes, and, being oriental, its worshipers were found chiefly among the vast hordes who flowed westward as soon as the way was opened, or who were taken there as slaves of their Roman conquerors. After the establishment of the Empire the Roman soldier was enlisted from all parts of the world and as the Latin ceased more and more to display the old Roman military spirit the army became more and more foreign. The Syrian element became increasingly important and the hardy natives of Asia Minor, especially of Cilicia and Commagene, furnished many recruits. It was here, too, that Mithra was most firmly established, and his worship advanced with the Roman legions into all the parts of the world where the eagles were displayed. It is along the military frontier of the Empire that most of the Mithraic monuments were found; along the Danube and the Rhine, and wherever the standards were planted there rose also the altar of Mithra.

For the military character of Mithra himself gave him an immense prestige in the army and the army in turn affected the social life around it, so that the spread of Mithraism in the West took place, after the second century, with relatively great rapidity. It was at its height during the third century, and was raised almost to the dignity of a state religion by the sympathy of the imperial house. Under Marcus Aurelius Mithra was established on the Vatican, on the site where now stands St. Peter's mighty dome. Commodus had been initiated into the mysteries of Mithra at the end of the second century and this event produced a great effect in Roman society, similar to that which took place when Constantine declared himself for Christianity. In the year 307 A.D. Diocletian, Galerius, and Licinius joined in the consecration of a sanctuary of Mithra, "The Protector of their Empire," at Carnutum on the Danube. It was at this period that Mithraism attained the highest point of its influence throughout the Roman world.

The chief appeal of Mithraism lay in the character it strove for and the ideas it set forth. It was primarily the character of the god himself, and the ideas associated with his worship which appealed so strongly to the Græco-Roman world of that day. Mithra was a god of Light. He had been born in a grotto. His whole career had been for the welfare of mankind. He was the "Soter," the pagan Savior, who would lead his followers through this mortal life to a glorious immortality which lay beyond. He was also the mediator between man and the unapproachable and unknown god. Much of the naturalism which was associated with the ancient gods of paganism was absent in Mithra. He was chaste, true, and holy, "Sanctus." Originally, no doubt, he was the sun god by whom the natural world was redeemed from darkness and made fruitful for the use of man. But he was now preeminently a spiritual guide who would bring light to the souls of men. According to the original myth, after the end of these earthly struggles which were necessary to redeem the earth, Mithra celebrates with Helios and his other companions a last repast, and then ascends to heaven where he watches over and protects the faithful who serve him. His service was severe, arduous, long. It appealed to the nobler side of life, to the power of self-restraint, to the spirit of sacrifice, to the faith in nobleness, to the hope of immortality. This religion, above all the others, was personal. It was the faith and hope of the individual which were fundamental. Its aim was moral and spiritual and it strove for purity and for immortality.

The place of worship was designed to represent the grotto in which the god was born. It was below the level of the earth and into it the worshipers descended. The heads of the cult were called "Fathers" and the members "Brethren." This new conception of the character of its members sprang out of the fact that the priest was no

longer or only the guardian of ancient traditions, the
intermediary between man and the state, or man and the
gods, but he was the director of the moral life of each
individual "brother." He taught the hearers the long
series of obligations and restrictions which were necessary
to protect their souls against the attacks of the evil
spirits, and in the new and paternal relation he had a
personal and individual interest in the spiritual welfare
of his flock. The grotto into which the candidate walked
was, in its gloom and darkness, an image of earthly life.
Light and life are in the presence of the god, not here.
All the rites of initiation were accompanied by lights and
music. The last act was the unveiling of the figure of
the hidden Mithra for which the mystic had waited. A
liturgy was one of the most important and conspicuous
features of this cult, as it was of most of the pagan religions, and one of the most important documents we have
of this worship is supposed to be a fragment of a Mithraic liturgy. The initiation was called a "Sacramentum."
Like the Roman soldier the soldier of Mithra was bound
by a solemn oath. Tertullian with his martial spirit introduced this Latin word into Christian use as a substitute for the Greek μυστήριον.

The soldier of Mithra was also branded on the forehead
with a red-hot iron as a visible sign of his membership.
There were seven degrees of initiation, corresponding to
the seven planets. The candidates took successively the
names: 1. The Raven; 2. The Veiled or the Secret One;
3. The Warrior; 4. The Lion; 5. The Persian; 6. The
Couriers of the Sun; 7. The Father. This latter was
called "Pater Patrum." They each wore garments or
disguises to mark their rank. The cult was so thoroughly
democratic that a slave might hold the highest position
in it. According to Tertullian Mithraism had its "Vir-
gins and Continents." Sunday was the chief holy day in
the week and the great feast was December twenty-fifth,

the "Dies Soli Invicti." Renan quotes Justin and Tertullian as calling Mithraism a satanic plagiarism for it had a baptism, eucharist, an agape, penance, expiation and unction. There was also a "Confirmation," and the Agape was a memorial of the love-feast of Mithra with his friends before his departure. Apparently there were seven sacraments of which we know little, and in the communion or supper, the priest pronounced a sacred formula over the elements. There were also seven heavens or spheres, associated with the planets, as in St. Paul. The world was to be consumed by fire (this was also the Stoic view of the universe), after which the blessed abode in the upper world. There was also a hell for the wicked, situated in the bowels of the earth. A last judgment decided the destiny of both good and evil. However much these and like beliefs influence men, either in the past or the present, the ultimate and decisive factors are not cosmological or eschatological, but ethical and personal, religious and spiritual.

Looked at from the strictly theological point of view Mithraism made its contribution to the great syncretism out of which grew the monotheistic conception which was now, with many limitations, becoming the prevailing one. Popular polytheism still survived, as it does yet, but it was as an expression or manifestation of an underlying monotheism. Each religion insisted upon, or implied, a divine unity, from which the subordinate and dependent divinities drew their life. These various religions were more and more blended with each other and out of these heterogeneous elements the conception of a solitary and supreme god rose with living and impressive power.

The evolution also of Greek philosophy had, in its effort to obtain a consistent and coherent system of thought, reached an ultimate unity which was defined in different terms in different schools, for the necessity of some principle controlling and coördinating the whole range of existence, was, we may say, universally recognized. Sometimes this unity was expressed in abstract and dialectic forms as a law or an ideal unity, sometimes in terms of materialistic pantheism, as by the Stoics.

The practical interest in life and the weakening of speculative activity no doubt contributed to the change which was taking place in Hellenic thought. The ethical interest, too, became more and more an element, either as cause or effect, perhaps both, in the change which was taking place whereby philosophy was moving more and more into a religious atmosphere and becoming charged with religious influences and a religious purpose. As a result of these inner changes the outer form was silently modified, not to the eye but to the mind, for the schools of philosophy had in them many of the elements out of which a religious congregation or Church might be developed. The growth of the oriental religions in the Latin world spread throughout the West the idea of a supreme, sovereign God, absolute, illimitable, transcendent. The limitations of the Stoic philosophy were too obvious not to be soon recognized, and while we cannot say that the substitution of a transcendent conception of deity for an immanent one was due to any one cause, there is hardly any doubt that the oriental religions were a large factor, at least so far as the intellectual expression is concerned.

The religious changes, on the other hand, were elements of far-reaching significance in this profound modification which took place in the theological mind of the West. The very language now used implies not only a different intellectual idea, but a distinctly different religious one. God is regarded as "The Most High," and wherever this became the prevailing conception the ineffable mystery of the Divine Existence was realized to the mind and eye through that which is, especially for the Oriental, the supreme expression of the cosmic energy—that is The Sun.

All the various cults tended toward unity under this common symbol. The individual deities more and more lost their earlier characteristics and became solar deities. It was true of Attys as well as of Mithra. The last religious formula of paganism is a divinity unique, all powerful, eternal, universal, unknown, who manifests himself in all that is visible, but of whom the sun is the most energetic and splendid expression. This solar pantheism was the central idea of Mithraism which was the last and highest expression of antique paganism.

Viewed from the moral side of life, Mithraism was the fullest expression of the old Persian religion in its ethical purpose. It introduced into religion a new principle, that of dualism. This dualism was not primarily materialistic but ethical, and was saved from pessimism by the part assigned to Mithra, that of mediator and redeemer. In this respect it was distinguished from all other pagan religions, and by this ethical dualism both the dogmatic as well as the moral statements were inspired. The philosophical dualism, which was latent as well as expressed in much Greek speculation, differed fundamentally from this, since it was not inspired by the same ethical interest or rooted in the same moral conception of the divine powers. The evil principle in the Persian religion was not Matter as opposed to Spirit, but a conscious, malignant force against which the Good struggled. This Iranian dualism did not exhaust itself in formulating a powerful metaphysical conception, but it had an immense practical value in laying the foundations of an efficient ethics and simplifying and developing the problems of the moral life as they presented themselves to that age and generation.

The entire Mazdean system was dominated by the ideas of purity and impurity; not the ritual purity of the Pharisee or the social purity of the caste, but an inward personal purity of character followed by its natural and

vital expression in the outward life. For life was a war-
fare without truce and without mercy. The end was that
supremacy in moral character which would fit the worshiper for association with his god. It is curious to re-
member in this connection, that as genuine a philosophic
spirit as John Stuart Mill found in ancient Manichæism
the best solution of the moral difficulties of the universe.
With Mithraism the hard, unredeemed pain of life was
met by a moral and martial appeal to the fundamental
human instinct for struggle, and this appeal was not in
vain. For character springs out of action, not acts, and
the energy and force of the striving moral nature of man
bring with them their own authentic valuation.

As to the extent and influence of this great Persian
religion in this the period of its widest sway, the utmost
variety of opinions prevails among the students and
critics. Reville says, "From the second to the fifth century Mithraism brought new life into the Roman Empire." Renan goes farther and says: "Had Christianity
been checked Mithraism would have become the religion
of the Western world." Cumont has repeated his words
with sympathy, if not with implied agreement. Yet others
have offered strong reasons for believing that it is easy
to exaggerate, if not the moral and spiritual value of
some of its elements, at least its extent and depth of
influence.

At bottom the spirit of Hellenism was profoundly
averse to the underlying metaphysics of the Persian religion. Fundamentally dualism is really an inverted naturalism. The old naturalism had brought its terrible
penalties in the grossness and materialism which degraded
life, and, though dualism seemed to be an advance, it was
not a solution of the problems of life in which the spirit
of man could finally rest. It is true it has haunted the
ages ever since and made its appeal to the unconscious
instincts which have led men upwards, but it was not and

could not be, the final synthesis of man's moral experiences or his spiritual aspirations. At bottom it meant pessimism for this present life and a gospel of despair to those whose fresh and virginal instincts were turning to the cradle of Bethlehem, the Galilean hills and the great Galilean dreams. It is true, Christianity did not wake into being the religious sense of man, but it offered to that sense the fullest opportunity for being satisfied. Paganism fell because the less perfect must give place to the more perfect, not because it was altogether sunken in sin and vice. It had of its own strength, we may say, marked out the ways by which it advanced until at last it lost itself in the arms of Christianity. To recognize this fact does not by any means imply a minimizing of the significance of Christianity.

Perhaps the most important fact of all in the disappearance of the mysteries before the advance of Christianity is that the foundations of these different religions, as contrasted with those of Christianity, were purely mythological. If we were to describe these different aspects we may say that Attys was an idea, Isis was an inspiration, and Mithra but a myth, Jesus Christ was a historical character, no matter how described. All efforts to reduce Him to the level of the mythological characters of the past have failed. The reality of Jesus Christ as an historical being was the ultimate cause of the victory of Christianity. But this is not to say that in the history of the growing Christian life there were no relations whatever between the mind and the temper which found help and strength in the mysteries and the historical development of the Church.

One must ask one's self: Did the Christian Church in any way feel and respond to any of these various influences and practices which were so widespread and from whose votaries it received so many converts? Were the changes which took place within Christianity the result

merely of the development of its own inner and vital
power, a natural, necessary and real evolution of its own
inherent force? Or are those changes modifications produced, in some degree at least, by a different environment; by the action and reaction of new social, intellectual and spiritual influences? Are they to be accepted
as the true and inevitable expression of the growing
Christian consciousness, or are they the accretions or
accumulations, which are a characteristic feature of all
historical movements, and to be distinguished from the
essential spirit which is the ultimate expression of Christ
in life and history? Few questions are more important
and few more painfully difficult to answer.

The fundamental problem is, whether Christianity is,
or is not, a mystery or a sacramental religion. The word
sacrament is used here in its primitive, original and historic sense. It is a translation of μυστήριον, a word with
a very distinct and definite meaning, differing fundamentally from the modern use and meaning of sacrament or
sacramental. From the fourth century onward we know
that the term μυστήριον was the one used to designate the
Sacraments, especially the Lord's Supper. The word sacrament, too, is not an original Christian word, but was
an appropriation from pagan customs. The two words
Mystery and Sacrament stood for the same thing. The
idea which they contain is not clearly expressed in primitive Christianity. The circle of Judaism with which Jesus
was most closely associated gives no indication of having
any sacramental representations or ideas even if we assume that the Essenes were inclined in that direction. It
is generally admitted by all critics that Judaism is not a
sacramental religion and hence we must seek elsewhere
for the origin of the sacramental theory. Thus, in the
sense in which this word or idea was used in the Christian-
Pagan church we cannot derive it from Judaism, nor
directly and inevitably from either the words of Jesus

or those of the first Christian teachers, with the exception, perhaps, of St. Paul.

St. Paul's spiritual sensitiveness was extreme, and under the pressure of the tremendous emotional experiences through which he had passed, and which became the living energy of the whole of his history as a Christian, he interpreted the life around him from a different point of view and in a different spiritual attitude from that of the Palestinian Jew. Through all his language run reminiscences, echoes, suggestions which reveal the presence of a life, vivid, intense and powerful, which worked upon his imagination and brought him into sympathy with the spiritual mood of the mysteries. But to trace the sacramental theory to St. Paul is to place its origin where it would not easily enter into the common life of the Church. For the religious significance of the Gospel to St. Paul and the circle of ideas in which he lived differed in many striking ways from those of the chief and most representative writers of the Ante-Nicene period. The original description of the Lord's Supper in the primitive Church is: "The Breaking of Bread" (Acts II, 42). This simple designation does not in any way correspond to the elaborate and suggestive ritual which surrounded both baptism and the Lord's Supper in the third and fourth centuries, while St. Paul speaks of baptism in a way which is hard to reconcile with the theory that the mysteries had shaped his whole idea of the Christian rites.

In I Cor. XV, 29, St. Paul speaks of a practice which he found already established in Corinth, that of baptizing for the dead, which can in no way be derived from him as its author. This baptism "for the dead" can only imply a mystery which had sovereign and magical effects, and had its origin and justification in ceremonies and beliefs which existed outside the Church and had been early adopted by certain groups of Christians. There appear to be some obscure hints of such a baptism among the Mandæans. The Shepherd of Hermas speaks of the righteous of the Old Testament who were baptized by the Apostles in the underworld and with this Clement of Alexandria seems to agree. It was also a familiar idea in the heathen mysteries. The Lord's Supper is spoken of by Ignatius (Eph. XX, 8) as a medicine of immortality: the antidote of death. Irenæus is still stronger in his language. He says it has a life-begetting power and is the food of immortality. The same ideas and the same terms are associated with Baptism. Immortality is supposed to be the result of Baptism by both Irenæus and Tertullian.[3]

The idea of the physical resurrection which soon became so prominent in the popular mind of the Christian communities was closely connected with the magical effects of the sacraments. We find everywhere among the heathen religions a firm belief in a heavenly food which brought healing and strength to the soul, a faith which existed anterior to the appearance of Christianity and could not therefore have been adopted by heathenism from the Christian communities. That the reverse was the case is at least made probable by the evidence, and no other satisfactory explanation seems to meet the facts.

Most of the Church writers show a familiarity with the mysteries and some of them, as Cyprian of Antioch, had been initiated. Clement of Alexandria shows such a knowledge of them, though they were regarded as profound secrets, that it has been conjectured that possibly he too had passed through some of them at some period of his life.

The more the prevailing religious mood of the time found itself able to express itself through Christianity, so much the easier it was for the more elevated and serious-minded among the pagans to enter the Church. Hence in a way, the mysteries became a bridge by which men passed

[3] III, 18, 1. De Pæn, 6 *passim*.

from the old religions to the new. This shifting of ideas and terms was in a way inevitable, for no living force is ever able to preserve itself free from contact with, or assimilation of, the dominant elements of the spiritual life around it. Almost all the terms in common use in the mysteries were taken over into the Christian Church in connection with its various rites and ceremonies. This, however, is not surprising, for it was in most cases probably unconscious, since the ideas associated with the terms remained unchanged. (Παράδοσις, also Traditio [Lobeck Aglaophamus], Παραλαμβάνειν, accipere, acceptio.)

After the period of Constantine the number of those who simply changed their religion without changing their ideas or feelings was very great. The essence or nature, the attributes and qualities of the earlier divinities of paganism which they had worshiped were transferred to the Christian saints of the popular religion and they have retained their place ever since. As a consequence of the rapid spread of Christianity among the masses of heathenism it became with many simply a loose stratum overlying a deep heathen foundation.

Sacramentalism, as it appears in the pagan mysteries, represents a way of understanding and interpreting religion which is, historically and psychologically, midway between the ancient naturalism and the higher and more spiritual meaning. It is associated, and always has been, with a greater or less amount of mythology. As a confirmation of this we find that the vast mass of mythology which grew up around and within the Christian Church entered into it at the very time when the sacramental conception first became prevailing and primary in Christianity. The striking manner in which Christianity was affected by the modes of thought and life existing outside of it shows how slight the difference between them. Philostorgias relates that Christians offered sacrifices to the image of Constantine and honored it with lighted candles and burning incense. And it should not be forgotten that in the beginning the people among whom the Gospel was first preached were the very classes among which the mysteries had a large, if not the largest, following. They were also the most uneducated and the least discriminating and critical.

It would seem then that Christianity in its original environment was not a mystery religion, but that as it expanded into pagan countries it quickly became so, though we are now unable to retrace the steps of the transition. There is no more illuminating way to describe the change in Christianity from the fearless Jesus in the synoptic Gospels to the Christianity of the Fourth Century than to say that the inspired religion of a Galilean peasant had become the greatest mystery-religion of history.

So far as the social or organized expression of the Christian life is concerned we may say that then, as now, it adapted itself to the conditions by which it was surrounded and to the prevailing ideas of administration and government which then existed. So long as its members were confined chiefly, if not entirely, to the lower classes, it appears to have been democratic, and largely what would now be called socialistic. It was preëminently in the primitive church a brotherhood or community of "Believers." The more it included the higher classes, and especially after its political importance and value became recognized, the more it conformed to the organization which ruled the political life of the epoch. Ultimately it superseded the Empire with its unlimited despotism and its official hierarchy, and the history of the Papacy is merely the extension of the later Empire which molded and shaped the ecclesiastical state which succeeded it.

The idea of political authority was perhaps the chief contribution to history and civilization which Rome made.

It was planted so deeply in the Roman mind that the impulse to organize the Church after the model of the Roman State was natural, instinctive, and inevitable. The working of this idea is stamped upon almost all the ecclesiastical institutions which arose during the centuries in which the organization of the Church was consolidating itself. The growth and development of ecclesiastical offices and powers were, however, conditioned not merely by the influence of existing institutions in the Græco-Roman world, but also by the operation of certain ideas and modes of thought which were characteristic of the religious outlook and point of view of the world of heathenism. Conjoined with these was the authority of the Old Testament, which presented strong claims for a priestly class; and as this Book was interpreted altogether in a Christian sense its influence in this direction was thereby increased. The heathen view of the priest as the dispenser of the knowledge concealed in the mysteries, coöperated to further the establishment of a Christian priesthood separate and apart from the laity. A hierarchy which corresponded to that of the state would be a natural analogy as a necessity of administration. But when, in addition to this, it was assumed that the possessors of these offices were, *per se*, endowed with special and peculiar spiritual gifts and powers which placed them apart from, and above, the body of believers, a great change was introduced into the conception of the church.

It was the constitutional and historic tendency of the Greek to emphasize theoretical knowledge as the path to eternal life. This Greek tendency, in its senile form of wanting formulæ for metaphysical realities, also made its impression upon the church. As a consequence there was a confusion of theology with religion, and the latter was interpreted in terms of the former, greatly to the injury of real piety and Christian character. Much of the thinking in the religious sphere was based upon assumptions, both scientific and philosophical, which are no longer valid. While they gave a systematic and unified character to Christian theology, they transferred the center of interest from the real heart of the Gospel to the forms under which it was once understood and expressed.

It was on the ethical side of life that the confusion of theology with religion worked most disastrously. The assumption that hatred of evil meant practically hatred of the body, was almost universal at this period. The evil in man was a result of his connection with matter, or the body, and asceticism became the way of holiness. One must admit, however, that behind the asceticism which poured over the Church in a great wave and presented such a distorted and perverted conception of the Christian life lay oftentimes, as its inspiring motive, a very deep, tender and unselfish love of Christ. A love, it is true, which, according to our experience did not understand or recognize the true relations which existed between Christ and the soul of the believer.

The real standpoint often almost vanished in the conflict of views and emotions which were struggling to control the spiritual and moral forces of life. The widespread feeling both within and without the Church, was that redemption and salvation meant a separation of the soul from conditions which were natural and injurious. If one could escape the world and the flesh the consequence, or the fact itself, would be salvation. Fellowship with God was a result of this escape from the world. The meaning of the Incarnation, or the life of Jesus, was the union of the soul with God through Christ *here*. The difference is the difference between St. Anthony and St. Paul.

We have, as a result of three centuries of history, three things of supreme importance:

I. The Greek Spirit, contributing its intellectual energy to the estimate and formation of the creeds. In consequence of their primacy the conception of the personal faith of the individual undergoes a transformation. It is no longer the spiritual apprehension of Jesus Christ by the soul, the dwelling of His spirit in the hearts of the believers as the essence of the Christian faith. But it is a "holding for true" certain intellectual statements, certain theological propositions concerning the metaphysical character of God and the spiritual nature of Jesus Christ.

II. The Formation of a Powerful Ecclesiastical System, corresponding to the historical conditions surrounding it, and divided into various hierarchical grades of officers. A ceremonial and ritual so elaborate and splendid that it has maintained its power over the imagination and senses of men ever since. The center of this liturgical development and the cause of it was a sacramental theory which had its roots not in the mind of Jesus but in the religious sentiment of the Græco-Roman world.

III. The Ideal of the Moral Life. There was here the establishment of an ascetic ideal wholly unlike the life of the Lord whose servants they wished to be. The effect of this new ideal, which was, no doubt, largely Oriental in its origin and character, was to divide the body of members into two classes with different standards, a division which created two different types of character.

The wide differences between the Church of the Apostles and that of the third century are not simply those of number, nationality or class, but of moral values, and the way one estimates these differences will decide forever his ideal and the idea of the Gospel of Jesus Christ.

Science teaches us that in the development of many species of life there are some organs whose function is largely or purely protective. These vary in the course of evolution, or change from time to time as the conditions of life require, or as the environment changes. The

necessity of protection, however, requires at all times
some organs which shall fulfill this function, but these
protective elements are modified by the energy of the life
which seeks to express itself. They are subordinate to the
end of self-realization. They are not identical with the
life whose vitality they protect, nor are they permanent
in the form they take. The shell of the turtle and the
quills of the porcupine, though answering the same end,
are wholly dissimilar in character, and preserve the particular type with which they are associated. The origin
of all the species with which we are acquainted, is due
to the operation of certain physical laws, and changes in
environment, working through long periods of time. The
energy of the living germ adapts itself to, or is modified
by, the existing conditions in which it lives: and the protective coloration which we find in the tropics, for instance, may be of an entirely different character in the
arctic regions.

So in the history of the spiritual evolution of man we
find certain organs which play the protective part from
the very necessity of the situation. Language, laws, institutions, and the higher forms of art enclose within them
the living spirit of man and express his efforts or his
aspirations, as these seek to realize themselves in the world
of man's highest life. These forms of expression are dependent upon the intellectual and historic conditions out
of which they rose. They are protective, inasmuch as it
is only by and through them that the living spirit can
maintain itself at any given time and prevent dissipation
or disaster in the future. That these particular forms
of expression are final or controlling for all time, is contrary to the law of organic evolution. And however high
we estimate the protective value of any institutions or
formulæ these are not identical with the living energy
which works within them or through them. The whole
history of man reveals this process of modification and

change, or even of atrophy and decay. The failure to perceive the working of this principle and to discriminate between the life and its expression, has been the fruitful source of controversies which have troubled the whole history of the Christian Church. The triumph of Christianity was, in terms of science, only the survival of the fittest.

The energy of the Greek intellect which had worked for a thousand years completed the theological structure around the person of Christ in the Nicene period.

The powerful organizing spirit of the Latin race had been at work for more than two hundred years shaping the monarchical episcopacy and the ecclesiastical system which as a form of church government, with all its limitations, has never yet been surpassed. Whether the democratic spirit of the future will lead to new forms or modifications, time only will tell. This whole structure inspired by the life and history of the Ancient World was completed only when that world was passing away forever. But before that transition was achieved and the old classic spirit perished, the genius of antiquity and the spirit of the future met in one who stands among the greatest names of any age.

CHAPTER V

ST. AUGUSTINE AND THE END OF THE
CLASSIC WORLD

"At the hour of midnight, the Salarian gate was silently opened, and the inhabitants were awakened by the tremendous sound of the Gothic trumpet. Eleven hundred and sixty-three years after the foundation of Rome, the Imperial City, which had subdued and civilized so considerable a part of mankind, was delivered to the licentious fury of the tribes of Germany and Scythia." In these brief words the great Gibbon recounts what took place on August 24th, in the year 410 of the Birth of Christ. Nearly eight centuries had passed since the sword of Brennus had been thrown into the scales amid the ruins of the desolated city, yet in that long period of time it had never been forgotten. Many, too, of the wisest and best had foreseen the day when it would be repeated.

For vast as the power of Rome was, and wide as her sway, the dominion had been established upon the foundations of civilizations already declining. The Greek genius had spent its force before the Roman rule was established on Hellenic soil, and the mighty powers that had governed western Asia were already crumbling to decay when Rome snatched the scepter and the crown from Babylon and Egypt.

Yet no circumstance in the long history of Rome impressed itself upon the imaginations of men as this terrific event which stunned both pagan and Christian. The fear of it haunted all those who knew the worth of that old classic world, and when the news passed on from land to land a great terror fell upon the souls of men. The night of the gods had come. Golden Rome, Aurea Roma, had fallen. The end of the world was at hand. The end of a world had indeed come: a world so beautiful and so proud, so rich and so base that none had ever seen its like before. It had gathered under the name of Rome all that had grown up in the greatest races of antiquity. It represented the aims and thoughts of some of the greatest minds the world has ever known, and one at least of the highest cultures mankind has ever produced. But now the spell was broken and the light was passing from the world. A new age was at hand, an age so rude and chaotic, so fierce and brutal, that the last rays of the setting sun were hidden by the storm clouds that rolled century after century over western Europe. Long ages were to pass away before that light should arise again to kindle the thoughts and energies of men. Meanwhile generations were to puzzle over the fragments of that mighty past and strive to construct out of them a world in which men could live again.

At no time in its history had Rome been so splendid and imposing in appearance as in the hour of its capture. The Imperial City had gathered into it all the wealth and beauty of the past, and the sun which lightened the path of Alaric shone serene and calm upon the luxury and the vice, the art and the magnificence which were passing away forever. A change had come over the spirit of mankind though it might not itself be aware of it. The old confidence had perished and the old faiths had vanished. The gladness of life and the joy of the soul in its first vision had faded.

Against this background of gloom and disaster there arose one figure in the Christian Church whose voice was to sway the hearts of men and point the path for human thought for many long centuries. He had the soul of a

Roman, yet not a drop of Roman blood flowed in his veins.

Aurelius Augustinus was a native of Tagaste in Numidia. Here, on November 13th, in the year of Our Lord 354, was born of Patricius and Monica a son. Patricius was a Romanized African of some property and position. He appears have been shrewd, high-tempered, impulsive and rather rough: a loose liver, as were most of the pagans and many of the Christians. Monica, the mother, was a Christian and her name has gone out into all lands through the tender and loving picture of her painted by her son. There were two other children besides Augustine, his brother, Navigius, and a sister of whom we know almost nothing. Whether they were older or younger we do not know, but from certain hints it would seem they were probably older. The young boy early displayed such brilliant talents that his father, and also his mother, determined that he should have the advantages offered in preparation for the bar. This education included practically all the important branches of learning taught at that time, especially rhetoric. He tells us that he loved only to play, and paints in the blackest colors his boyish tastes and habits. He says he did not study: that, in fact, he hated study. He gives a picture of the children sitting round their teacher listlessly and monotonously repeating the old, old table every child has had to learn. "One and one make two, and two and two make four. "Jam vero unum et unum duo, duo et duo quattuor, odiosa cantio mihi erat." Every healthly child and almost every man will agree that it is indeed "odiosa."

His native town had its own attractions and interests. It was the meeting place of many roads and a distributing center where the men of the sea-coast and the men of the larger cities came in contact with the men of the country and the desert. It was charmingly situated, and, almost on the edge of the desert, presented a picture of flowers and fields and wooded hills. All the contrasts which North Africa presented were here sharpened by closest contact. In the town itself these same contrasts appeared. The civilized and polished Roman officer of Latin or Greek origin, here came face to face with the barbarian nomad from the far south. The fruit of the desert was for sale side by side with the importations from Bona or Carthage. Though not large it was a busy and active little city.

Here the boy grew up and here was stamped upon him the characteristics which made him a true son of Africa. He was full of passion for light. No modern writer has spoken of light with more rapture than he. Not only the immortal light of the blessed, but the actual light of the African sky he knew so well. All his senses were amazingly keen, and he loved beauty like a Greek. He loved music and wrote upon it too. He draws a comparison between the "Divine Word" and the nightingale. Long after his youth, when he was in Milan and heard for the first time the songs and chants which Ambrose had just introduced into his cathedral, he was overcome with emotion.

With his great gifts he was urged to the utmost and soon exhausted the resources of Tagaste and then went to Madaura, a larger city and one not too far away. Ultimately he went to Carthage and while there he probably stayed with Romanianus, the rich friend and patron who had furnished the means for continuing his studies.

Carthage was one of the five great capitals of the Empire, and here for the first time he came in contact with the old classic civilization, in all its power and in all its splendor, also in all its weakness and corruption. The hot African blood was heated to a fever and the young man, or growing boy was swept into the life which was led by almost every man in the great cities of the Empire. What happened he has told us with a frankness which permits of no disguise, and in fact he makes no apologies and offers no excuses. It was at this time too that he formed the union with the mother of his son which was to last so many years. And yet he was not all, or only, what he describes himself to be. It was at this period that he first read Cicero's "Hortensius," which roused his interest in philosophy and pointed it out to him as a pathway to truth. Everything which influenced him did so deeply, and he took up the different sides of life with an intensity which would have exhausted most men. He tried the Scriptures, but after Cicero their style seemed harsh and repellent. It was during this period, too, that he became a Manichæan. The reaction against pagan self-indulgence had produced a sense of the reality of evil which was, in many minds, the deepest and most profound conviction of the soul. After some years of wandering and hard study and many efforts to establish himself he at last found himself in Milan as a professor and was soon under the influence of Ambrose. Yet that influence has been much exaggerated. Augustine was in every way far the greater man, and such as he must always find his own path. And he did. It was in the little villa which had been lent him by a friend, near to Milan, that in 386 A.D. in his thirty-second year, the event took place which is called his conversion. From that time his life is part of the history of the Christian Church. He yearned for Africa, but returned only after his mother died, leaving him alone in the world.

The story of his life, at least of his spiritual life, has been told by him in that wonderful book which was the first of its kind and still stands at the head of all those self-revelations which the human soul has made of itself. Two things stand out clearly in that story: First, the immense spiritual energy and vital originality of the man. Nowhere else in all the history of the Church is there another like him. Yet, though he labored like a giant, he appears to have suffered from ill health all his life.

The second impression which we receive is, his dependence upon, and sensitiveness to, the influences and forces of his own age and civilization. He was a man supremely of his own day and generation. Three things above all others he said he desired to see: I. Rome in its glory; II. Cicero in the tribune; III. St. Paul preaching. Nothing better could be said to tell us the spirit of the man. He stands out clear and distinct above all the other figures of the western world, and yet as has been said of him: "He repeated in his own life the whole development through which the Church had passed up to this time."

The enormous difference between the intellectual resources, the philosophical, historical, and scientific knowledge of the past and the present is better seen in Augustine than in any other Christian writer or thinker, for he was far and away the ablest and most encyclopedic of them all. Yet again, it must be said that his greatness does not consist in his knowledge, but in his spiritual gifts and his moral intensity.

A study of the man himself is worth more than many generalizations. He was the last of the classics. His was the last mind for centuries which steeped itself in the intellectual wealth and culture of classic antiquity. His eagerness for knowledge was the quenchless passion of his youth, and all through the long and busy years his mind was forever advancing into new fields and searching out new problems. The orthodox view was largely then, as later, that pagan literature was unfit for Christian eyes, but the greatest of the Latins were ever in his mind and on his lips. It has been disputed whether he knew any other language than Latin, and his own Punic. Hebrew he did not know, but Greek he did. The question is only as to the extent of his acquaintance with it. He disparages his own knowledge, to be sure, but it is not likely that his acquaintance with Plato, Aristotle, and Plotinus were entirely through translations. The means for obtaining this knowledge had not as yet vanished from the West, especially in the great cities like Carthage, where he spent nine years of hard and faithful study. The results of these studies we see in later years. His knowledge of the classic philosophers, which were very much neglected at that time, made him so strong a dialectician in his theological controversies that after one experience his opponents shrank from the combat. It has been said of him that he was too sensuous for a thinker and too abstract for a poet. Yet in these very defects lay his power. His enormous appetite for impressions, sensations, ideas and experiences led him into the very heart of his age: and for good and for evil he knew it all as no other man of his generation. It was his intelligence, his sympathy and his power of interpreting human life in terms which were intelligible to his contemporaries which made him what he was. All which seems to us crude and allegorical in his interpretation of Scripture, for instance, was a source of particular satisfaction to the hearers or readers whom Augustine addressed. His history, science and philosophy were those with which all cultivated men were familiar, but they were used by a nature of extraordinary breadth and depth, and used too in the interest of the central and fundamental idea and purpose of his life—to bring men to God.

The spiritual nature of Augustine was by no means a simple one any more than that of any other great spirit. Three factors existed in the complex of Augustine's thought. First, his abstract philosophical theory: second, his moral experience: and third, his religious and Christian convictions. The unifying element, or that by which all these were blended and fused, was his consistent psychological method. It is true that inferences were drawn in each of these fields of expression which could not be harmonized with those in the others, but this was the inevitable result of his controversial method. His conclusions were not the result of a consistent, systematic theory wrought out in the field of experience, but the results which he reached through controversies at different times and also under varying conditions. He never attempted to harmonize them or reconcile them, and so we have a body of thought organized for particular controversial purposes only. They are not brought into organic relation with each other, but stand often violently opposed to each other and often mutually destructive. Taken separately, however, they are admirably suited to become the foundation of independent theories, but are incapable of being shaped into a unified system.

The world which this man faced was in some fundamental respects unlike that which the previous generations had known. Three great spiritual forces were contending for the mastery of the Roman world when Augustine reached his manhood: Manichæism, Neo-Platonism, and Christianity. I have given them in the reverse order of their historical manifestation, but in their order in the spiritual experience of Augustine. Their interest here is chiefly in their connection with his own personal experience and development.

Manichæism was named after its founder, Mani, who was born, according to the latest authorities, at Mardinu, a village in Babylonia, between the years 214 and 218 A.D. He is said to have been a Persian, and the basis of his system, or the principal sources of it, were the myths of old Babylonian, Chaldean, and Mandæan religions. The influence of Christianity upon it was practically nil, though some of its language seems to suggest the contrary. His system began to have prevalence about the end of the third century, but it spread in the course of the fourth not only through the Christian Orient, but also over every part of the Christian West: in Rome,

North Africa, and even in Gaul. The probable cause of
the wide and rapid spread of Manichæism was its union
of the ancient mythology with a rough, harsh, and materialistic dualism, a highly spiritual and simple culture
and a strict morality. For the problem of Good and Evil
was the problem of the second and third centuries. In
Manichæism, as in so many other religious systems, any
distinction between physics and ethics was neglected, and
so it became, at bottom, a fundamental materialism. Matter was in itself evil or The Evil. This being so, the
ethical conception of evil, or the conception of sin, is lost.
According to Manichæism the existence of sin is due to
the union of the soul with the material body. Sin is consequently not an ethical fact, but rather only a physical
condition. Morality, therefore, as well as religion, consists in asceticism, the absolute renunciation of the body
and the purification from all material associations. On
the other hand, the strictness of the asceticism involved
made it impossible that any successful propaganda could
be carried out and concessions became not only necessary
but inevitable.

Two classes therefore arose: The Elect (Perfecti) and
the Catechumens (Auditores). We have here practically
the same classification as in the Church, which in another
form became the theoretical distinction between the
clergy and the laity of later centuries. There was a wide
chasm between the two orders. The "Auditores" were
only partially instructed, while the deep and esoteric doctrines were reserved for the Elect.

Although Augustine was a member of the sect for nine
years he never became more than an auditor or catechu-
men. In consequence his direct and personal knowledge
of its inner teaching was very limited and he can hardly
be regarded as an authority upon its esoteric character
even though he wrote extensively upon it. Like all popular religious movements a great mass of superstitions and

of practices attached itself to the parent stem, and what was original and what parasitic is almost impossible to determine. Dealing with it broadly we may say that its two chief features were its dualism and its asceticism. Dualism was a crude but striking way of dealing with the moral experiences of mankind, and answered promptly the first question which rises in the anxious mind of one who is tormented by his own inner experience. Its materialistic character and its assertion of two great opposing powers, which to-day seem to be the chief objection to it from a philosophical point of view, were in fact, at this time, the actual sources of strength. For the dominant conception of matter was so positive that the monistic idea of Christianity appeared hopelessly vague and unreal. A spiritualistic interpretation of the universe seemed wholly incredible to the mass of men, and Augustine himself tells us how utterly impossible it was for him to conceive of God as immaterial and spiritual. Material conceptions influenced his thought of the divine nature, yet these ideas were not confined to the Manichæans but were, we may say, native to the thought of the mass of men of that day, the Neo-Platonists excepted.

Asceticism was the natural and inevitable reply to the problem when thus stated. This too was the general attitude of the Church. The weakness and insufficiency, the moral poverty and spiritual imperfection of such a thought of life seems not to have suggested itself to them, so far had men drifted from the earlier and apostolic interpretation of life. For hidden behind this austere form of rigid physical abstinence lay a gross and hideous perversion of nature itself. The origin and processes of life became instinct with evil, and concupiscence was regarded as the origin of all sin.

Sin from the Manichæan point of view, stripped of all evasions, was simply a physical necessity, and a necessity too, to which the mass of men were inevitably exposed. That it therefore could have any moral value or significance was out of the question, and the ethical struggles and inner problems of life received no light from this apparently so logical interpretation of life. Such a theory might do for the many who ask no questions, but not for the few who do, and it is the few the many in time invariably follow.

Augustine plunged below this materialistic conception of sin into the depths of his own soul, and showed not only to himself, but to others, that the problem of evil was a far deeper mystery even than that of matter. Yet he was and remained an ascetic all his life, and in spite of the acuteness of his psychological analysis he still shared to a greater or less extent in the common sentiment which has had such ghastly results in the history of Christianity. Eucken has said that he brought over from Manichæism the idea that procreation was sin, and thus tainted the whole subsequent life and thought of the Church by reducing evil to mere physical properties. And one of the greatest living authorities in church history has said: "It is one of the worst, at all events, the most hateful consequences of Augustinianism that the Christian religion in catholicism has been placed in an especially close connection with the sphere of sex." This may all be true in fact and yet it should be borne in mind that Augustine was not the author of asceticism, even if much of his teaching did lay the emphasis upon the physical side of life. Origen had castrated himself nearly two hundred years before Augustine was converted, and the great stream of ascetics to the desert had been flowing for at least a century when he was born.

All his life Augustine was moving from one position to another as the demands of the time or his own spiritual experience revealed new problems for thought. He was struggling to find himself, and he accepted any and every means which offered. Likewise he was ready to cast them aside when they had done their work or he had discovered their inadequacy. He had long ceased to be interested in Manichæism before he wholly broke with it and he broke away not through fear, but indifference.

It was his reading of Cicero's "Hortensius" in his nine-teenth year which roused his interest and his hope that in philosophy he might find the true path. It was this that led to his adoption of Manichæism, from which in the course of the next ten years he passed, through scep-ticism, by the way of the New Academy, to Neo-Platonism.

His Neo-Platonism came to him by the way of a trans-lation of Plotinus. According to his own account given in his "Confessions," the critical point of his history was his so-called conversion to Christianity. But any one who studies his life more objectively must feel that these ex-periences would not have occurred had he not come under the influence of the new Platonism. This was after all the real turning point in his spiritual history. He en-tered now into the higher sphere of speculation where thought was independent of sensuous representation. It was here the basis was laid upon which rested all his later speculations: the psychological and theological concep-tions which distinguish his contributions to the advance-ment of Christian thought.

For Augustine the passion of his life was, "Deum et animam scire cupio. Nihil ne plus? Nihil omnino." [1] To know God and his own soul were the main objects of his existence. And amid all the changes and chances of his stormy life these were ever the end. Plotinus brought before his mind a vision of God which appealed to his inmost soul. More than that it swept away forever any

[1] *Solil.*, 1, 7.

of the Manichæan materialism which had surrounded the being of God in his previous thought. In Plotinus he found a Being who was pure and simple spirit.

In attempting to define or describe more particularly this character or being he had recourse to Neo-Platonic language and ideas. God being simple, is and must be, immutable. For simplicity excludes every change. We have here the language and method of Plotinus. From this fact also there result three other qualities or attributes, to use a later theological phraseology: First, His immortality, or rather His eternity; second, His Ubiquity; third, His spirituality. In this order we see the same process repeated which we find in Plotinus. He does not start with the spirituality of God, nor does he find in the divine love a ground for his belief in a being of pure spirit, as the source of the paternal affection, but he takes an abstract term or quality and proceeds to draw from that all the elements which he thinks constitute the nature of pure being. He achieved this result in the true Neo-Platonic way, by a system of negations. Yet like Plotinus he finds himself unable to be satisfied with a description of God which is reached only by negations and passes on, as did Plotinus, to more positive definitions. In describing God as the highest and simplest being (Essentia), in distinction from the world of multiplicity and change, he ran the same risk that Plotinus did, and was in danger of leaving an impassable chasm between man and God. The idea of Revelation came to Augustine as necessary for the establishment of his argument for the divine existence.

To say that Plotinus saved Augustine for the Christian Church sounds rather startling in view of the traditional ideas. But it was Neo-Platonism which furnished Augustine with his most powerful weapons against Manichæism and helped him build up his own strong spiritual faith so that it was never again shaken.

If Augustine was dependent upon Plotinus for the means by which he attained a nobler conception of God than he had hitherto been able to reach, there was one field, psychology, in which he was supreme, and owed no man anything. In the beginning of the fourth century most of the doctors of the Church were inclined to think that the soul was material. It seemed to them that in declaring the materiality of the soul they were better able to understand how the soul could be rewarded and punished. Its condition in the future was analogous to its condition in the present. At the end of the fourth century, however, a revolution had taken place in the Church on this point, and the change is due, in the West at least, to Augustine.

The great phrase of Plotinus, "Matter cannot think," may have been the key to his own thought, but Augustine applied it to the soul itself as descriptive of its real character. The soul, he taught, is simple in its essence, though multiple in its operations. It is not corporeal though it moves in time as the body moves in space. The soul knows itself more clearly and more certainly than it knows anything outside itself. It is a reasonable substance charged with the government of the body. "Substantia quædem rationis particeps, regendo corpori accomodata." [2]

As to the question of the origin of the soul Augustine's path was beset by difficulties. It is true there were few questions which more deeply engaged his attention, and yet he was never able to come to a positive or definite conclusion. For the problem of evil, as he understood it, and as it was generally understood at the time, weighed so heavily upon him that he could attain no satisfactory results. Traducianism or Creationism seemed to be the only explanations which had anything to recommend

[2] De Quantitate, Animæ, Liber unus. Cap. XIII. De Trinitate, lib. III, c. lib. X, c. IX, c. V, VI, VII.

them to his mind. But on account of the difficulties attending both he was unable to accept either. He became so intense an idealist in many ways that it was easier for him to believe in spirit than in matter. That is, it was far more difficult to understand why a body was given to a soul than why a soul was given to a body. For to him the soul's knowledge of itself was the most sure and perfect which man can have. The soul knows itself better than it can know anything else. For nothing is so close to it as an object of knowledge as itself. That I think and live, and that I absolutely know that I think and live, are the most certain of all the elements of my consciousness. This knowledge is the very heart and essence of human knowledge. For the very fact that we think at all is an evidence, and the highest evidence, of our existence. To doubt this would in fact only prove it. For doubt itself is an act of the mind and proves its existence. This argument of Augustine has been regarded as the most important contribution made by him to philosophic thought. It is from this principle, though independently, that Descartes started the development of modern philosophy eleven centuries later.

Augustine regarded himself as a Platonist and held to the theory of ideas which owes its origin to Plato. But he did not hold to the strict Platonic view, that the ideas had an existence outside of and independent of God. He believed on the contrary that the ideas are contained in the Divine Intellect: in this way he followed Plotinus who unquestionably held the same view, and from whom in all probability he directly derived it. His Platonic or Neo-Platonic sympathies led him to believe in an intelligible world, a world of ideas and truths above the material world and beyond the historical data of faith. In this world the soul is brought into immediate contact with, and contemplation of, the truth. Contact of the soul with

truth is purely incorporeal and mystical and it has in it
nothing material or physical, a conception which suggests, in many ways, the thought of Plotinus in his ex-
hortation to be like God and fly to our dear country where
God is.

The capacity of the soul to enter into vital and personal relations with the truth or with God, is not only
the witness but the guarantee of its immortality. For as
truth is immortal, unchangeable, eternal, that which is
able to possess it must also be immortal. This was unquestionably also the view of Plotinus. Augustine's views
of the faculties and activities of the soul seem also to be
directly drawn from Plotinus: that is, that the soul is
active in sensation and not passive: that the body alone
suffers and that the soul views this experience, detached
from it and unaffected by it. Yet the soul in its experience of God does not come into instant and immediate
communion with Him. The progress is definite and gradual. In his statements upon this subject it seems clear
that Augustine owes to Plotinus the determination of the
different steps by which the advance is made. Sometimes
he gives three stages and sometimes seven. In his writing,
"De Quantitate Animae," Augustine goes into a classification of the various stages by which the soul ascends to
God. There is: I. the somatic life; II. the life of the
senses; III. the life of human activity; IV. the knowledge of the moral good; V. the attainment of the moral
height; VI. the calm and true contemplation of that which
is to be seen; VII. the height of the Vision of the Truth.
It would almost seem as if here there was an echo of the
orders of the mysteries. Augustine's mysticism · differs
essentially from that of Plotinus inasmuch as with the
latter the soul is absorbed in God as the goal and result
of its being. With Augustine, on the other hand, the distinction between God and man is, and remains, fixed.
This undoubtedly is because he started first from his

interrogations of the soul, thence to advance to the knowledge of God.

Augustine was more than a Neo-Platonic mystic. He had plunged too deeply into the mystery of his own self-consciousness and had realized too intensely the problem of human personality to lose himself in a spiritual or mystical absorption. The very heart of all his search was to enter into the core of personality, the meaning and worth of the conscience and will. Abstract metaphysics or philosophical speculation could not keep him for long from the investigation of the more immediate and pressing problem, that of his own self-consciousness. Because of his emphasis upon the conscience and the will all his thinking tended to move in the region of ethics, the direction of the moral life; and in the field of piety, the life of the soul in God. Still in his thinking on the problem of sin and evil we find the influence of Neo-Platonism of great importance. In his "Confessions" he emphasizes the hatefulness of sin in contrast with the beauty of God. This, no doubt, represents a true idea, but it is not taken from Scripture, nor primarily from Christian experience, but rather from a philosophical theory. The Scriptures represent the guilt of sin in opposition to the holiness of God. Augustine felt this, too, and stated it elsewhere. As a result we find these two alien factors appearing again and again in his writings, the Neo-Platonic influence and the Christian experience.

When Augustine accepted the Platonic influence his whole attitude toward any solution of the problem of evil was changed. Manichæism regarded evil as a substance, opposed to the good, another substance. Under the influence of Platonism Augustine conceived the good as the only real existence, and evil as the non-being, in opposition to being. Evil therefore was not an absolute but a relative conception and as a consequence had no fixed and positive character of its own. This metaphysical defi-

nition of evil as a loss or negation of being, which is
Neo-Platonic in its origin, cannot be reconciled with the
psychological theory which Augustine was the first to
advance. In this he places it in the will as a self-deter-
mination of the soul against God. The philosophical theories left no way out and the insolubility of the problem
arose from the fact that non-being, from the nature of
the case, could not be known.

In contrast with Hellenic thought, Augustine's psychological speculations led him to regard evil as a personal
choice, a deliberation of the will. He had accepted Manichæism because he believed in sin and evil. He did not
believe in sin and evil because he was a Manichæan. As a
result, the moment he entered more deeply into the path
marked out by his self-consciousness the more it became
impossible for him to remain a Manichæan. For the
metaphysical dualism of matter and spirit, of good and
evil gave way as he entered farther into his psychological
analysis. There was still a dualism, and the language he
used was dualistic, but it was an ethical and religious
dualism: a dualism of sin and grace, of inner disposition
and not of outer conduct and relations. It was not the
specific act, or the particular physical relation which constituted the nature of sin, but the human will, with its
intentions and purposes, which was the root and cause of
all moral qualities and values. This was such an immense
advance upon anything which had hitherto been attained
in the field of ethics, that even to this day it has not been
superseded. Yet even in the discussion of this problem
there does not seem to be an absolutely fixed determination on the part of Augustine. There are conflicting theories between which he wavers from time to time. What
the essence of the will is was not absolutely fixed for him.
According to him man is essentially "will." [3] By this

[3] De Civ. Dei, XIV, 6. Voluntas est quippe in omnibus, imo omnes
nihil aliud quam voluntas sunt.

declaration Augustine shows the difference between his position and that of the intellectualism of Plato and Plotinus, as well as that of the ancient philosophy and the modern idealism, according to which man is essentially a thinker. He thus becomes the creator of modern ethics and the philosophy of religion.

Against the Manichæans he asserted the doctrine of the freedom of the will in order to prove that evil was of human and not of divine origin. He declared that there was no evil nature or substance from which it could proceed. Evil was "defectus," "negatus," "privatio." He says, "That evil then which I sought to know whence it is, is not any substance: for were it a substance it should be good." [4] "And I enquired what iniquity should be: but I found it not to be a substance, but a swerving merely of the will, crooked quite away from thee, O God, (who art the Supreme Substance) towards these lower things: casting away its inward parts and puffed up outwardly." [5] He also asserts the freedom of the will in opposition to the fatalism of the astrologers. In his denial of evil as a substance he shows how he shared with all antiquity in the idea of its reality: he also reveals the fact that in spite of all his efforts he found himself moving in the field of natural and not moral philosophy, even though his moral intuitions were of the most positive character. The conception of evil as non-being involved a monistic conception, it is true, but it was a monism which was largely naturalistic, though more by inference and unconscious assumptions. His definition of evil as a "defection," or negation, was urged in opposition to the Manichæans, who asserted a duality of principles, a "summum malum," as well as a "summum bonum." He declared that evil was not a nature, but only a negation, privation, corruption. On the other hand he affirms the positive character of evil inasmuch as he considers it an

[4] Lib. VII, c. 12.   [5] Lib. VII, c. 16.

act of the will. Since it has this positive psychological stamp in his mind it is hard to see how Augustine can be classed with the Manichæans who regarded evil as a substance. It is, however, very easy to see how again and again he is inconsistent with himself. The confusion of thought which resulted from this conflict of statements can be relieved, at least to a degree, if we go beyond the language of the occasion and find the roots from which these different statements sprang. At bottom there were two different theories which remained, side by side, unreconciled and sometimes unrecognized, in his own mind. One of these Augustine inherited from his Neo-Platonic teachers and the other was a result of his own deep and anxious spiritual questioning.

The Neo-Platonist with his æsthetic idealism and his essential intellectualism left no ground for any facts which broke up the harmony of the universe as he conceived it. The facts which were called evil were merely the shadows in the landscape, and the dark tragedies of human history only brought out the interesting and dramatic qualities of life. The pain of the soul which could not be denied, was explained as hunger and want. The aspirations of the spirit of man for the First and Only Fair, brought with them sufferings so long as they were unsatisfied. But this pain was negative, it was the result of not being, of not possessing. It was a privation of the good, the absence of light, the emptiness of the soul. That evil does bring leanness into the soul is not the same as saying that the evil is the leanness.

Here the cause and the result were inextricably mixed. The Neo-Platonic view revealed its insufficiency so soon as one passed from the outer order of life to the spiritual experiences of the soul. For in the end the question of good and evil had unconsciously been reduced by Neo-Platonism to an almost mechanical basis, since character became a matter of more or less being. More than that, if evil in itself be nothing, there can be no responsibility for its existence, for what is nothing has no origin or cause; it is simply privation and non-existence. To claim then an actual reality for evil in any sense of the word whatever, is not possible. From the point of view of ethics and human experience a bad act is just as real as a good act, and the badness is as definite an element as the goodness. When Augustine was thinking out of his own experience and analyzing his own consciousness he instinctively and immediately recognized this. He then expressed himself not only with the greatest positiveness, but also with the greatest clearness.

The fact is that Augustine's doctrine of evil is composed of two elements radically distinct from each other. One is specifically Platonic and the other definitely and positively Christian. The Platonic element is that evil is nothing or the No-Thing. The Christian is that evil is the product of the free will. Perhaps it would be better to say the second element is the personal contribution of Augustine to Christian thinking. For he affirmed positively and categorically the causality of the human will. These two distinct conceptions of evil he tried, but tried in vain, to fuse into a system. Between these two radically different conceptions he hovered all his life. And it is the presence of these different conceptions in his discussion of the great problem of evil which introduced confusion not only into his own thinking, but also led his readers into the same perplexity. As late as his "City of God," he says: "Do not seek for an efficient cause for a bad will, for a bad will is not an action but a failure to act." [e]

If the bad will is only a defect of action we can understand how evil is nothing, but in that case how can evil be produced by a free will? The will is the power to act. It is the faculty or function which produces acts, but it

[e] De Civ. Dei, B XII, c. iii.

does not and cannot produce the want of action. The contradiction between these two theories is obvious and cannot be reconciled. One of the primary difficulties with Augustine was that he never seemed able to grasp the idea that a free being is a distinct cause, a creative power, which has received from God the ability to produce a real disorder, a positive opposition to the divine will. In spite of Augustine's vacillation on the nature of evil, it is his supreme merit that he marked a great advance in the interpretation of life, inasmuch as he asserted that the Gospel was related to the control of the world of will as well as the world of thought. For the will would and could be transformed by the inspiration of the spirit of Christ. So he laid the basis for an increasing sense of the meaning and worth of personality. Through the new moral self-consciousness the attitude of man toward God was changed. Instead of an intellectual acceptance of an objective dogma, that is faith as a body of doctrine, there was a new relation between man and God not only implied but asserted. As a moral personality man has a value in himself. He is not simply an instrument moved or directed by universal law or the will of God, but out of this real character he possesses the right to attain or the possibility of attaining, the highest good and a personal union with God. The relation between man and God was a relation between two personalities, and the root of this relation was the spiritual character or qualities which rose out of love and personal obedience to the nature of God as an ethical Personality.

When the great Pelagian controversy arose Augustine was face to face with an entirely different situation. The question of human responsibility was no longer challenged. But in a way the old problem appeared under new conditions. It was no longer a matter of personal responsibility or the origin of evil. In appearance at least the Pelagian controversy did not concern itself with the question of good and evil. The dualism of the Manichæans reappeared only indirectly. The real issue was as to the relation between God and man, the actual conditions of salvation.

Pelagius was a monk, and therefore an ascetic. Asceticism implied the worth and ability of human conduct. It meant that salvation could be attained, at least in part, by the individual activity. Augustine too was an ascetic and never renounced ascetic practice. Yet here is one of the paradoxes of his life, that he was adopting a mode of life and emphasizing its worth, both of which were by his own theory utterly denied. This denial did not spring out of any logical or theoretical consistency, but rather from the overwhelming conviction wrought by his own Christian experience.

Pelagius is said to have been a British monk, and some writers add, a eunuch. His was a cold and rather austere nature, with high ideals and a strong and impressive character, much averse to controversy. His monastic education and his monastic spirit led him to emphasize the power and worth of human effort. He was shocked, too, by the easy, indolent and morally low type of Christianity which then prevailed. The widespread acceptance of the magical character of the sacraments had produced a feeling that individual responsibility and individual initiative were unnecessary. One could depend upon and expect that this sacramental religion would operate, even if there was a slow and low valuation of the heights of character. Against this spiritual indolence he protested most earnestly and vigorously. He preached a noble life, with the profound conviction that it was possible for every man to attain it. His asceticism had its roots in this conviction and was also the expression of it. Apparently he knew nothing of those volcanic experiences through which such men as Augustine had passed, and must pass. The implications of his logic seemed to sweep away all that was characteristic of Christianity and reduce it to the plane of Stoic theology or philosophy. That he intended any such thing is hardly to be believed.

He came to Rome and all the most earnest men felt that here was a new moral appeal. It was sincere and it was also true. If individual effort is to be eliminated there is no possibility of moral and spiritual progress. But many of his own phrases and more of those of his disciples seemed contrary to the deepest Christian inspirations. Rumors of the new movement came to Augustine and had the effect of stirring him to greater efforts than he had ever made before. It seemed to Augustine that this easy moral optimism had no place in the dark world he knew. Indirectly also the statements of Pelagius involved the whole question of the Gospel revelation. If the highest life could be attained by the personal initiative there was no real necessity for a revelation. The position of Pelagius seemed more logical than that of Augustine, but with Augustine it was not a matter of speculation but of experience. His whole argument was inspired by his own religious history. Emotion flooded all his speech and led him to make statements which as propositions for universal acceptance have never been approved. Far below all his harsh and repulsive language lay the fundamental fact that he was emphasizing the divine element, the life and will of God, in the life of the believer as against the rational and logical solution which was set forth by his opponents. If we distinguish between the aim and the method of Augustine it will be more easily seen how high his purpose was and how deeply it lay at the heart of his own spiritual history.

Against what he felt to be the easy-going optimism of Pelagius, Augustine had two great arguments, history and the Scriptures. The historical evidence as he read it gave little ground for the theory that man could or would attain a noble and holy life without the direct action and

aid of God. When he came to give the reasons for this
he turned to Scripture. He took the story of Genesis and
found there, as he thought, an account from God Himself
which showed that man had been created in righteousness
and holiness, but had fallen into disobedience and sin and
lost his original inheritance. When Augustine came to
develop or explain this fallen state, he affirmed it to be
a condition of total and hopeless depravity, which cor-
rupted all the powers and faculties of man, leaving him
hopeless and helpless before the indignant wrath of God.
He did not see that moral responsibility cannot be expected or required of one incapable of either seeing or
following the light.

His theory of total depravity also involved the loss of
all spiritual freedom through the corruption of the will.
Here again he seems to have contradicted himself, when
he declared that all power for good was lost, and yet
asserted that the freedom of choice, the decision for or
against good or evil, was still man's possession. In his
discussion he involves himself in almost endless contradictions, for, in order to explain the continuance of the
state produced by the Fall, he had to introduce a theory
of inheritance which raised the whole problem of hered-
ity in an age when there were none competent even to
approach the subject. If sin is in the will, how is it
inherited? There is a permanent difficulty, however, in
determining what Augustine really thought, arising from
the fact that his definition of the freedom of the will
varies, or seems to vary, from time to time. It is certain
that in his argument against the Manichæans he affirms
it explicitly and fully, but in his debate with the Pelagians
he seems to deny it, at least by implication. In order,
however, to insure salvation or to establish the possibility
of it, he introduced a new factor into Christian thought,
that of grace. He attributes to grace what the Scriptures
ascribe to the direct influence and work of Christ, upon

the soul or in the soul. The simplicity of the fellowship with Christ is lost and the mind is plunged into a dialectic dispute which leaves no savor of life behind it. If, instead of struggling against Pelagius with a theory of grace which made no appeal to the filial instincts of the soul; if, instead of trying to prove the precedence of this grace over the free will of man, he had simply thrown himself back upon the truths of his own Christian experience, and had regarded the problem not as a philosophical one which he must solve, but as a religious one; if as a child of God he had started from the Fatherhood of God the solution would have been reached at once. For the parent always loves first and most. The whole process of grace, in spite of its spiritual ends, takes upon itself a semi-physical or mechanical mode of operation.

In order to assure the results of the activity and end of Grace Augustine added a theory of election and pre-destination. To his critics then and now, this seems to destroy all incentive for personal interest or coöperation in the work of salvation. In order to meet the objection that predestination would lead either to pride or despair Augustine affirms that the predestination and election are secret and unknown and therefore there can be no ground for either state of mind. If this is so, what evidence is there possible that there is any truth whatever in this doctrine save only the language of Scripture itself? Here Augustine ultimately rests his argument. He admits that election is an insoluble mystery, not only as to its exist-ence, but also as to its reason for existence. The reason for doubting the validity of Augustine's argument arises from the fact that at bottom, it proceeds from a deistic and not a Christian thought of God. There is no room here for the yearning for a spiritual Father, nor is there any place for an historic Christ, with his personal appeal and personal passion for the salvation of man. God is reduced to a blind force which works through unknown

causes for unknown effects, impelled by unknown reasons.
At least so it appears to those who do not realize how the
limitations of existing thought bound Augustine to a
method of argument which was in conflict with his own
spiritual experience and inward faith.

When, in his doctrine of election Augustine asserted
that God chose to save some and allow others to perish,
and that since all were sinners and therefore condemned,
there could be no charge of injustice against this decree,
he seemed to himself to be declaring only what all would
admit. But the moral repulsion felt by the Christian
conscience had a root deeper than the logic of the schools,
and that was the instinctive, though perhaps unconscious,
recognition, that such an affirmation concealed a real
partiality on the part of God. If all were guilty, why
were some chosen and not others? Augustine again takes
refuge in the plea of a great mystery, and asserts that to
this question there is no answer, or at least that he finds
none. In all his thinking Augustine really started from
his Christian experience in which he found the power of
the divine love as the root and source of his life. He
converted this faith into a dogma of philosophy as defined in the doctrines of Grace and Predestination. He
thus overwhelmed human personality, and practically denied any participation of the soul in salvation. The whole
problem was dealt with as a matter of dialectics and not
as the outcome of the nature of the component elements
of the problem. The soul's union with God consists in the
fact that God alone is active in it. Thus any idea of the
independent activity of the creature is excluded. Yet the
very depth of his religious life had its roots in the growing consciousness of his own being as a person.

To judge Augustine by the Pelagian controversy alone
would be wholly unfair. As a controversialist he always
puts forth his whole strength and is absolutely indifferent
about reconciling his statements with any other, or pre-

vious, views put forth by him. Behind the anti-Pelagian logic lay two tremendous facts. First he knew the world as few men of his age knew it. It was a world almost dead to nobility, a society corrupt beyond words, and a race which seemed to have forgotten all the greatness of the past. Here in this huge welter there were a few elect souls who bore an undying witness to the greatness and the goodness of God. Augustine had a terrible insight, and to him human nature often seemed a wholly and hopelessly depraved thing. Leaving mere words, theories, and conjectures out of the case and starting from the world as he knew it, what other conclusion could he come to? The problem of human nature was grasped now for the first time not by an historian or a metaphysician, but by a psychologist of the first rank.

Along with his knowledge of the world was his own personal experience. This he believed in absolutely. He knew as a fact that God had saved him. There had taken place in his soul a change in which he felt he had played but a minor, if not a passive, part. In trying to reconcile the world he knew with God's work within himself he was face to face with the greatest problem of human life. We assert that Augustine did not solve it. He himself often felt that he had not, but who has?

It was in Augustine's age and through his teaching, more than that of any other, that the conception of Catholicism as a great historic reality was completed. The Church was called the "Kingdom of God" first by Augustine. Whether we are entitled to say that he identified the Church and the Kingdom, is a harder question. Some of his language would suggest it, and other phrases would seem to deny it. He did set the phrase free to move in the minds of men and associated it with the great historic fellowship or organization known as the Catholic Church. It is in his language about the Church that we find the greatest confusion of all. The correlation of

Church and Kingdom was so new, or so largely new as an idea, that one can easily believe he had not thought it out.

Another and even more important point in the developing theory of the Church was the fact that Augustine represents the turning point in the conception of holiness in relation to the individual and the institution. The Donatists had emphasized the holiness of the individual and denied the worth or validity of the offices of the Church when performed by unworthy individuals.

To escape this difficulty Augustine declared the holiness of the institution. The holiness of the individual was merely derivative and dependent upon membership in the body of the Church. The organization became therefore of primary importance, and the salvation of the individual was made dependent upon union with the same. There is no doubt this line of argument cut away the ground under the feet of the Donatists, but it also cut away the very foundations of the personal relations of the soul with God. These were subsequent to membership in the body of the Church and not necessarily part of the Christian consciousness of salvation. A further development of his theory in opposition to the criticisms of the Donatists upon the character of the clergy was that the clerical validity depended not upon the personal character of the clergymen but in the nature of Holy Orders and in the Grace which these conferred. It may be contended that for the common practical life of the Church the theory of the Donatists was entirely too subjective. But on the other hand that of Augustine was too objective. The moment it was applied, two results ensued which were disastrous both for the Church and the individual.

The Church was divided into two classes: The Clergy and the People, or Laity. There was a priestly and sacerdotal class over against the vast mass of believers. With the ascetic practices which were adopted by the so-called "religious" two types of piety were set before the world, a higher and a lower, with the lower tending always to become still lower. The immediately personal results were inconceivably injurious. The ideal of holiness ceased to be spiritual, and became not only official but purely conventional. To fulfill the particular or peculiar official obligations of the class to which one belonged was the highest aim. Later a theory of sacramental activity extending over the whole span of life, came to supersede that personal, self-conscious dedication of the soul to, and communion of the soul with, God. However definitely and clearly Augustine set forth this theory, the evidence of its power over him personally is very feeble. Indeed there is practical evidence that for him it was never much more than a theory which was used as an instrument against the unreasonable attitude of the Donatists. The proof of this lies in the fact that later, when he was engaged in his great struggle, that with the Pelagians, he seems to ignore all his anti-Donatist arguments, and to sweep the whole theory into the scrap-heap by his doctrine of Election. He does not even attempt any readjustment or reconciliation. He does not verbally limit the elect to the members of the Church. There are those of the elect who were never members of the Church, and there are elect now who are not at present members of the visible Catholic Church. By inference there will be elect who will never be recognized or numbered with the Church as an historic body. Of course this implies what he explicitly asserts, the existence of an invisible church. It was from Augustine that all those evangelical writers drew who contended against the mere external organization and pleaded for a higher and more spiritual conception of the Christian Church.

The historical relation of the Old and the New Testament was never clearly grasped by either Augustine or any other man of the Ancient Church. Yet Augustine does realize the difference between them far better than any of his predecessors. The Gospel is for him the "New Law," the "Nova Lex," in opposition to the "Old Law," the "Vetus Lex," but the fundamental conception of legality prevails in both. His conception of Faith, Pistis, Fides, approaches here more nearly that of St. Paul than any that had hitherto been attained by any of the ancient writers. In spite, however, of this approximation there are great differences, due to the presence of ideas, not of Christian origin, which exercised great power upon him through his entire life. In addition to that they so molded the expression of his religious consciousness that they became characteristic elements in the entire feeling and thinking of the Western Church for centuries.

Having accepted, even in a modified form, the legalistic conception of the Gospel, it almost inevitably followed that the idea of faith as a body of dogma which had developed in the Greek intellectualism, should furnish the natural mold for his thought. The original personal and subjective idea was necessarily weakened even when he spoke of it as an individual and personal experience. When Augustine describes faith he does not appeal directly to the Scriptures for its true expression nor even to history, of which he had quite a different idea from the modern one, but to psychology. He attempts to analyze the subjective state as he finds it already existing. Owing to his theory of sin, he assumes man's incapacity, and therefore postulates faith as a gift of God, a "Donum Dei," but not in the Scriptural sense. It is an endowment bestowed upon man in order that he may enter into the knowledge of truth and of God. It is the foundation of the Christian life, but principally in this way, that it enables one to "hold as true" that which is presented upon the authority of the Church and the Scriptures. But this faith, or fides, is merely preliminary. It is not an historical truth or an objective creed, but a psychological state or stage, through and by which man passes on into ultimate knowledge and conviction. It has the character of a speculative and philosophical assumption, which is based more upon Plato than upon Scripture or personal experience. He insists emphatically upon its necessity. Apparently, however, faith is for him necessary not as an ultimate in itself, but as the condition of knowledge, which is the end held before the soul. He is thus led to introduce another element as necessary to safeguard the acceptance of truth by faith, and that is the will. "The will to believe," appears already centuries before its modern revival, and is applied with a vigor which leaves nothing to be required by even its most ardent advocates. Faith then seems to resolve itself into an acceptance, which is caused by the will, of certain definite facts or truths which are guaranteed and commanded by external authority. As a consequence it is not complete as an experience in itself, but only as a step in the spiritual progress upon which the soul has entered.

If we try to enter into the method of faith as Augustine conceives it we may state it somewhat as follows. Before our sensuous or spiritual eyes, something objective and external appears. In so far as we accept its reality and recognize it as existing, we believe in it. According to the Platonic theory the human mind was able, through the reason, to accept and appropriate the divine ideas. True to his Platonic training, Augustine believed that it was to the reason and through the reason that God revealed Himself. Thus in its essence faith is the subjective appropriation of an object or truth into the consciousness, really a primitive or elementary knowledge. As the aim and goal of life lay that knowledge which was only mediated through faith, that is, the knowledge of God.

Roughly classified, we may say there are three stages in the spiritual progress of the soul as indicated by

Augustine. I. Faith, this, too, understood as a psychological condition. II. Knowledge of the historical contents of faith as revealed truth. III. Knowledge of the eternal truth as revealed in God, or the contemplation of God. In this last stage the historical element of the Gospel loses its significance, and fades away before the splendor of the Absolute. We here see traces of Neo-Platonic influences which were to pass from Augustine into the whole later history of the Church and become the source of all the mysticism which represented the higher spiritual life of many centuries. Yet Augustine does not, and dares not, discard faith as the mere holding of historic truth and we have as a consequence a confused mingling of historical Christianity and Neo-Platonic mysticism, from which neither he nor the Church ever escaped.

There are, however, some students of Augustine who believe that they find in his conception of faith something fuller than either a psychological state of receptivity or an acceptance of historic truth. M. Naville believes that for Augustine faith is a confidence, not primarily or exclusively of the intelligence, but of the entire human personality. That is, that it is a personal relation, a complete surrender of the man to God or Christ. In this submission the intellectual element does not occupy the first place. The acceptance of the truth is a result of the confidence in the person. Whether this be or be not so, it in no way affects the ultimate conclusions of Augustine. According to him, the supreme act and aim of life, is to see God. But the eye of the soul by which it sees God is the reason, and thus an act of intelligence becomes the highest effort of man. We are here breathing the air of mysticism, both medieval and modern. For John, for Paul, as well as for Jesus, the highest act is that of love. In this form of statement we see the survival of the old Hellenic spirit and especially of the later expression of it in which it found utterance in the Neo-Pythagoreanism, Neo-Platonism, and the mysteries.

The very asceticism of Augustine had as its characteristic note, not merit and reward as the end, but rather such freedom from earthly entanglements and interests as should enable one to realize the higher life. The ideal aim, of perfect detachment from the world, has its roots in mysticism and not Manichæism, and forms part of that conception of life in which the theory of disinterested love played such a large part in the subsequent history of the Church. That Augustine was a mystic in the fuller sense of the term as later understood, can hardly be affirmed, for the mystical experience had not yet found any vocabulary or form. But it can be most positively affirmed that the very essence and heart of his being was the passionate desire for God, which is the source of all mystical utterance. Great as was his influence as a theologian and ecclesiastic his highest influence was in the spiritual life and the shaping of the spiritual history of the Church. One of the greatest of modern critics has called him "The Restorer of Piety," and this he was to an extent which has been more or less obscured by the controversial matter, both theological and ecclesiastical, which is found in his writings. No mere polemical theologian or ecclesiastic has ever deeply affected the spiritual springs of man's higher life. Into this higher life as he conceived it in God Augustine earnestly strove to enter. This entrance into the higher life is the ascent of the soul to God, while at the same time it is a sinking deeper and deeper into one's own soul. "Thy God is the life of thy life unto thee." "Deus autem tuus etiam tibi vitæ vita est." "By this very soul I will ascend unto Him." ("Per ipsam animam meam ascendam ad illum.")

Yet Augustine never loses himself in the Absolute Being of Plotinus nor in the divine heart of things, as did many of the later mystics both philosophical and emotional. "It is one thing to be God, another thing to be partaker of God." [7] This vision of God which is the ultimate aim of his pious fervor is, in its attainment, thoroughly mystical according to the accepted meaning of the terms. It is not an act, thought, feeling or willing, but rather a having, a possessing, an enjoying, which is the reward of faith. It is a being in and with God, of which no closer definition can be given, and for whose reality the man contributes nothing. It was an existence in God which he desired. "Nor did I desire as not to be made more certain of thee, but to stand firmer in thee." [8] It is this profound spiritual absorption of his soul in the being and presence of God which gives such a thrilling intensity to many passages of his writings, and which has made his "Confessions" a living book for all ages and all types of piety.

The question as to how much of this language is original and how much derived from his great Neo-Platonic teachers, even though answered, after all settles nothing. Many phrases like the "return to God," and the "ascent of the soul," have a Neo-Platonic sound and remind one of the mysteries, but the heart of the matter is not in words and phrases. It was the inmost desire of his soul which adopted and used these phrases to express its own great passion and purpose. In that remarkable passage in his "Confessions," [9] where he gives an account of his last interview with his mother at Ostia, before her illness and death, while he does not use the Neo-Platonic term "Ecstasy," the idea is there and it is hard to understand how he could have expressed himself as he did if he had not already been familiar, not only with the teaching, but with the aim of the Neo-Platonist.

He opened up before the eyes of men the possibility

[7] De Civit. Dei. XXII, 30.

[8] Nec certive de te, sed stabilior in te esse cupiabam. Conf., Lib. VIII, c. 1.

[9] Lib. IX, c. 10.

of the soul of man coming into such intimate and personal communion with God that the soul of the man would be immediately conscious of God. He turned this possibility into a certainty by his own life and conviction, and the faith in this relationship has never passed from the life of the Church. He restored the "faith" of the Apostle Paul, though in a different form of statement, and with a very considerable weakening of the original significance of the soul's filial relation with God. Through the inner life of Christ in the soul of the believer as St. Paul had declared it there was not only forgiveness of sins, but peace and power as a present source of life and strength. With Augustine there was always a wistful yearning for a realization which was more or less postponed and a longing for the infinite fruition of the soul in the future. It is this vision of the far-away and hoped-for realization of their dream which is the pathetic charm of all the mystics, standing as it does in strange contrast with the vivid and energetic passion of the actual life already possessed.

Augustine broke through the prevailing intellectualism of the Greek Church and transcended the magical sacramental system of both East and West so that for centuries there were in the Church pious mystics who kept the vision of the Eternal before the eyes of men and yet lived entirely apart from the ecclesiastical system. Nevertheless these were held by all to be the saints and saviors of the Church. This resulted from the fact that Augustine asserted, as no one had done it since the Apostles and the Master himself, that goodness and blessedness consist in the absolute dependence of the soul upon God, and the union of the human will with the divine. He thus translated, unconsciously it may be, all those conventional and officially accredited institutions by which the soul was to be saved.

Had it not been for Augustine the Latin Church could

not have ruled the Germanic races as long as it did. He was read and studied by all the students and saints in all the monasteries and schools of the West. He held up before the aspiring souls of the new men to whom the Church was but a great political institution a dream of another life and another history to be lived in God. With their eyes filled with these visions they went far and wide preaching the great hope and the great vision, and gathered around their names and their dreams the reverence and loyalty of mankind.

CHAPTER VI

THE MIDDLE AGES AND THOMAS AQUINAS

FROM the death of Augustine to the Fall of Constantinople is a period of a little more than a thousand years. The changes wrought by the movements of these centuries produced a world wholly unlike either the one which preceded it or the one which followed it. The old world was bathed in the rich and tranquil light of Hellenic culture. The modern world stands out clear and sharp in the bright light of scientific knowledge; but the world of the Middle Ages was a moonlit world in whose deep shadows and pale light all things took upon themselves an unreal and fantastic character. It was the age of feudalism and chivalry, of mythology and miracle. The depths of the forest and the dim mountain-tops were peopled with spirits both good and bad. Wonders were on every hand and the imagination of mankind never revelled in such creations as rose during these strange and troubled years. The very figures whose names have come down to us have a character entirely unlike any we meet elsewhere. Dr. Arnold declared that the histories of Greece and Rome, in the highest stages of their development, were more truly modern than any before or since. So too with the individuals. There is more and better understanding of Plato and Aristotle than of Erigina and Aquinas. Cæsar is more a man to-day than Charlemagne. The men also differ among themselves as much as they differ from us. They stand out entirely alone, singular and enigmatic problems still for the historical student, as St. Francis with his delirium of joy and

177

Frederick the Second with his wide culture and cool skeptical temper. There seems to be no resemblance between Narses and the Blind Belsarius, and Karl the Great and William of Normandy.

It was an age of wonder and of romance. Peter the Hermit preached to a listening world, and all Europe flung itself in reckless enthusiasm upon the sword of the Saracen. It was a world of extremes: the wildest excesses followed by the most passionate renunciations. Kings gave up their crowns to die in a monastery, and the coarsest and most brutal soldiers were turned suddenly into the most devout saints.

That world has passed away, and passed away forever. The harsh contradictions, the brutal self-contempt, the gross animalism, and the ecstatic visions no longer mingle in the same souls. The men of the Middle Ages loved and hated, sacrificed, tortured and suffered as few before and none since have done. It is in this world we must find our way, if we can, realizing that the aims and the motives, the ambitions and the dreams, as well as the methods and the means, were different from our own.

In spite of the many dramatic features in the history of the Middle Ages and the profound changes wrought in the political institutions and the character of society, the most significant fact is the intellectual change which was brought about by the fall of the Western Empire. The character of this change was such that it can only be regarded as one of the greatest catastrophes which has ever happened to the human race. The late Mark Pattison regarded the "triumph of the Church organization over the wisdom and philosophy of the Hellenic world . . . as the saddest moment in the world," to the Humanist. In this judgment all those who are interested in the intellectual struggle and progress of the world must feel the strongest sympathy. For the change meant the destruction of the antique culture and all the intel-

lectual and artistic interests which were associated with
the ancient civilization, and which the world has ever
since been so painfully struggling to restore. The storm
of hatred and destruction which beat down that mighty
fabric was stirred up by theological animosity and ascetic fanaticism, which are, after all, only temporary
phases in the progress of history. The instincts of humanism, on the other hand, represent the unchangeable
and ineradicable instincts of the human mind.

There was something even more tragic than the destruction of the past and the rejection of its treasures,
and that was the changed attitude of the human mind
itself. The divine gift was reduced in scope and its cultivation became an abhorrent thing. Ignorance of all but
that which the Church taught was a virtue, and one of
the greatest sins was either the cultivation of, or the
desire for, what was called heathen learning. The penalty which was paid and the results which followed, are
some of the most characteristic features, especially of the
early Middle Ages. Humanism was trampled underfoot,
and the victory culminated in the popular apotheosis of
ignorance and dirt, the ascetic ideal of holiness in the
common mind. Prohibitions of all secular learning were
early in favor and ultimately, by force of concurring circumstances which resulted from the mingling of the barbarians in the Empire, ended in the destruction of all
forms of education except those carried on in the monasteries. The darkness of ignorance settled down upon
the world.

It has been said that for a thousand years no man in
Europe ever took a bath and it might also be said that
for a thousand years almost no laymen and few ecclesiastics or monks could read or write. Yet here appears one
of the strange paradoxes of history. The very monasteries which were the home and fountain of asceticism,
whose aim and object were not the cultivation of thought,

but the establishment and spread of the ascetic temper, became the home and nursery of learning. For in these stormy centuries when the world was falling to pieces, and brutality and strife were the law of life, all that was thoughtful and earnest, every soul that dreamed of a better and nobler world, looked for some refuge where peace and quiet might give it time to think of God and prepare for that life which lay beyond. Whether it were possible for such to have made a stand against things as they were, and out of the wreck to have built up in human society new institutions and created a new spirit, is one of the questions which it is fruitless to ask. The facts are that the best men left the world, some in sadness perhaps, and some in scorn and bitterness, but all with the feeling that the world was hopeless, and only in those silent places could the soul find rest and peace. But the very thoughts which came to them in the cloister's calm, the dreams which were dreamed by those young and ardent spirits, would inevitably tend to rouse questions and hungers which would not cease. Among them were some who had still in the soul traces of the old instincts and habits. More and more as they worked at their tasks or listened to the sacred words which recalled a long-ago past, the insatiable curiosity and hunger of the human mind were stirred into action.

Shortly after Justinian had closed the schools of Athens and the few teachers, thus cast out, had wandered away to Persia in the hope of being able to continue their rather futile and hopeless occupation, a distinguished member of Theodoric's court, after the victory of Belisarius, gave up public life and became a monk. He founded on his own ancestral estate two monasteries, in one of which he himself became an inmate. Cassiodorus was practically the last heir of the ancient humanism and in his monastic retreat he set himself to gathering together what fragments of the ancient literature he could secure. He seemed to anticipate the coming darkness and did what he could to preserve for the future the ancient heritage of the past. He taught his monks to collect and copy manuscripts and began a library which should include not only the Christian, but the pagan literature of the earlier ages. Monte Cassino, the original foundation of St. Benedict, continued the work begun by Cassiodorus, and the Benedictine order stood, so far as possible, in the dark centuries which followed, for the spirit of its earlier days. Amid all the changes and misfortunes which befell Monte Cassino, the torch was still kept burning. The monasteries of other orders shared, to some degree, in the spirit of the Benedictines, and, though dim and pale, the light never went out until as centuries passed, it grew in strength and won back the world to a recognition not only of the power but the purpose and nobility of human thought.

For though it seems at first glance as if there were in the early Middle Ages no longer any interests in the things of the mind, or in the deeper interests of the soul as a spiritual force; yet there was, and continued to be, progress. The steps were slow and groping, but at no time did the instinct cease to work even in the most hopeless centuries. Under the conditions which then prevailed the character of this new intellectual activity was, though perhaps not consciously so, a struggle of the mind for emancipation from the grasp of authority, as it was then expressed. Herein appears the relation of this period to the ages which followed. For from the very circumstances which surrounded the intellectual activity of the early Middle Ages there could be less control than might have been expected from the authorized powers. It was seated in the monasteries and later in the schools and universities, and notwithstanding the vigilance of the ecclesiastical authorities freedom of thought was not curbed so much as one might think.

Viewed from this standpoint, scholasticism in all its forms, from first to last, was, in its general results, the first insurrection of the modern spirit against authority. In spite of the pressure of authority against which the rising intelligence of the West was in constant conflict we must recognize even in it a certain compensation which reconciles one, in part at least, to the medieval method of seeking the truth. It was a dark and barbarous world, in which only the rule of the strong was recognized. The national consciousness of the various peoples now constituting the European states, was wholly undeveloped. The political sentiment was crude and immature, and in such a chaotic state a recognized authority like that of the Papacy, however arbitrary and unintelligent it might be, was of enormous importance and value. The mistake was to extend its sway into every corner of life and claim for itself an origin and a power practically divine. Yet claims of less breadth would doubtless have been treated with less respect.

The joy of thought, the sheer pleasure of mental activity in and for itself alone, this was one of the moving impulses of what grew to be scholasticism. For thought as an independent effort of the mind was a new thing in the world in those early centuries. Words have always exercised a mysterious power, wholly unlike any other agency. When first the mind begins to puzzle over the connection and relation between speech and thought a way in the darkness seems to be opening. Men feel they may enter here and find a solution of some of the great problems which already, in a vague way, the awakening intelligence was feeling. Rarely, if ever, in the history of the human mind, has there been such hard and continuous thinking, such strenuous effort made on such meager food as by the first, at least, of the Schoolmen. When the great ontological argument, which has divided metaphysicians and logicians ever since, first dawned upon the mind of Anselm he was torn with such a passion of thought that he could not sleep until the problem was solved. For sheer and splendid intellectual energy some of these men have never been surpassed.

We have other men to do our thinking, and we collect off the battlefields of the past our arms and armor. They entered the struggle practically barehanded and naked and did great things. They laid the foundations of modern European thought and shaped the language in which men have expressed themselves ever since. Their thought is forgotten and their names are to most men only names. But they were living men, and as much by their mistakes, perhaps more by them, they opened the way to a nobler world than any they ever saw; a world where freedom and science, truth and justice are the standards and the ideal for all. There is about many of them a great charm. A strange and almost childlike simplicity mingled with the most profound intellectual effort. They believed much we do not and cannot believe. They dared to solve and they thought they did solve, problems which are forever hidden. Laborious, patient, passionate, devoted, high-hearted and loyal to their great tasks, they scorned delights and lived laborious days, and went to their reward.

What had these men to work with? This is a question which will help us understand and appreciate better than perhaps any other question what these men were and what they did.

The vast array of literature which was the possession of the classic world had to a large degree perished, or was inaccessible on account of the language in which it was written. The great volume of ancient knowledge which is now in the possession of every real student was wholly unknown to the men who first began the work of bringing back to the human mind the stores of knowledge necessary for it to live and to grow in power. As

years passed this volume increased, but in the very beginning of the Middle Ages the list of works is relatively
small, though not unimportant. The following contains
practically all that we know of any value. 1. A part of
the "Timæus" of Plato translated by Chalcidius, and
accompanied by a comment. 2. Two treatises on "The
Categories" by Aristotle, and on the "Interpretation," in
the translation by Bœthius, with explanations, as well as
with two Commentaries. 3. The "Isagoge" of Porphyry,
in the translation of Victorinus and of Bœthius, together
with the commentaries of the latter on both translations.
4. The Writings of Bœthius, Cassiodorus, Macrobius,
Apuleius, Martianus Capella, Seneca's "Naturales Ques-
tiones," Lucretius, "The Topic of Cicero," The Pseudo-
Augustinian writings on "The Categories," finally the
writings of the Church Fathers which contained the His-
torico-Philosophical matter.

It can be readily seen that this is all in Latin, for at
the time Greek had practically become an unknown
tongue in the West. Indeed the knowledge of Greek had
been gradually disappearing from the West for some
centuries before the Empire had ceased to be the political
reality it once was. Aside from the Church Fathers,
probably the most important of all these works were
those of Bœthius and Aristotle, and the latter was chiefly
understood as Bœthius explained him.

It is upon Bœthius and his influence that the eye must
be fixed, if one is to grasp at all accurately the meaning
and movement of the new intellectual revival in the western world. Much misunderstanding existed then and to
some degree still remains, as to the real character and
mind of this most interesting and influential writer.

Anicius Manlius Severinus Bœthius was probably born
in the year 470 or 475 at Rome, and early became one
of the most cultivated and distinguished members of the
Roman aristocracy. His ability and intelligence soon

won him a place at the court and in the favor of Theodoric. Owing to his part in the protection of the natives
against the intrigues and exactions of the Gothic party
he became unpopular and was accused of plotting against
Theodoric. He was thrown into prison and after a time
executed. It was while he was in prison that he wrote the
work which was best known through the Middle Ages
and upon which his fame still largely rests: the "De Con-
solatione Philosophiæ." Gibbon speaks of it as, "A
golden volume, not unworthy of the leisure of Plato or
Tully, but which claims incomparable merit from the
barbarism of the times and the situation of the author."
On the strength of this volume he was regarded all
through the Middle Ages as a Christian, but modern
critics are almost unanimous in doubting this. He made
numerous translations from the Greek, and his highest
ambition was to hand down to the future as large a body
of the ancient literature as possible. It is upon these
translations that the first students of the Middle Ages
fixed their eyes, and it is from them that they drew the
material which furnished, in the beginning, the chief
problem which engaged their attention.

The doctrine of Ideas which formed such a central
place in the philosophy of Plato was contested by Aristotle, at least in its Platonic form, but the later Greek
writers never came to any positive settlement of the question. Involving as it did both metaphysics and psychology, it is not surprising that, in an age when the intellectual and philosophical interests had sunk so low, no
later writers were capable of treating it with any measure
of scientific accuracy or philosophical grasp. In the
"Isogoge" of Porphyry the problem was recognized but
was also evaded. Porphyry says that the matter was
one which involved such deep questions that it was not
possible to treat it briefly or in a casual way.

The first figure who, after the close of the Dark Ages,

impresses one with the sense of a new world beginning to rise out of the gloom and hideous disorder, ignorance and barbarism of the past, is that of the Irish monk, John Scotus Erigena. His birthplace is unknown, but he was educated in the Irish monasteries which still kept the lamp burning while all the rest of Europe seemed buried in darkness. He is the first one whom we meet who knew Greek, and he was the last one too for many a long day. Nothing of his early history is known and little of his later. Born during the lifetime of Charlemagne, about 800 or 810, he lived until 877 A.D. He was called by Charles the Bald to his court and came to France where he was placed at the head of the court school and occupied himself in making translations of the Pseudo-Dionysius and many of the Fathers. We know little or nothing of his personal character or life. If a story which has been preserved is authentic, he was not without a bold spirit and a somewhat daring humor. It is said that the king asked him what was the difference between a sot and a Scot, and his reply was: "The table." "Quid distat inter sottum et Scotum? Tabula." The same story, however, is also said to have been told at the court of Charlemagne.

Erigena is chiefly known for his work called, "De Divisione Naturæ." It is an astonishing intellectual feat. Its maturity, originality and independence of view were such as to leave it entirely without influence upon the thought of his own age. He stands alone and apart from all the currents of his time and had to wait for generations for a real appreciation of either his power or his performance. We, too, must leave him in his isolation with only this passing glance at one of the strangest and most original minds in the whole Middle Ages.

As has been said, Bœthius was the handbook of the Middle Ages and when in the eleventh century the minds of real power began to apply themselves to the problems of philosophy and theology they came in immediate contact with the questions which had already been the subject of debate in antiquity, but which had been left unsolved. The outstanding question was, the reality of Ideas, or of Universal Concepts. Two opposing tendencies manifested themselves at once. First, an extreme realism which saw the true nature of things in the universals conceived in the sense of the Platonic Ideas, and which ascribed to them an independent existence.

Over against this theory was that of a bold and crass nominalism, which attributed reality only to the Individual and saw in the Universals simply names. These as instruments of human thought exist, not in objectivity, but only in the human spirit itself. In the long controversy modifications ensued between these extreme views. Finally the theory was formed and accepted, which assumed or acknowledged the Universals, but only as realized in the Individual. Independent of their individual expression they exist simply as thought or ideas in the mind.

The chief interest of the Schoolmen was metaphysics, though logic and philosophy were studied with passionate enthusiasm. These, however, were only a means to an end. The outer world of nature and man was subordinate to the central motive of thought which was God. In God theology and philosophy seemed to harmonize. For from the beginning the scholastic was convinced that he could reach Being through thought. In this respect, at least, his efforts resembled and repeated those of the Greek schools.

To the thinker of the Middle Ages philosophy did not present itself as it does to the modern man. To the man of to-day philosophy is an instrument, it is a working theory or hypothesis by means of which he is to go on into the wider realm of facts and through them gain insight into the meaning of the world. Looked at on the

psychological side it is the way the world is reflected in
the souls of the most earnest and vigorous thinkers: the
interpretation which they give or find for the objective
world outside of them. To the Schoolman philosophy
was an actual increase or extension of objective truths.
For truth was a fixed fact, a body of reality outside and
above mankind which the individual is to strive to attain.
Philosophy is that sum of matter which is knowledge,
and in the study of it he gains a body of truth which is
ready for him to appropriate. Not the method, philoso-
phizing, but the matter philosophy, is the object to be
sought and learned.

In this respect the Schoolmen resembled Augustine for
whom there was a world above into which he sought entrance and which was ready for transmission to the seeking soul. In this attitude we find the old Platonic influence active to the very end of the age. The truth was
thus to be attained by a process of pure thinking, or
rather by inference from certain fixed premises by logical
methods of reasoning. As has been said of these thinkers,
"They do not observe, they argue." Truth as understood by them too often seems to be but a matter of pure
demonstration except in their psychological investigation
which oftentimes seem to be the result of personal preoccupation rather than the outcome of a conscious scientific principle. For their method was based upon abstract
logic, not observation. It could arrange and classify according to the categories by which it worked upon the
body of facts already known, but it was not suited to gain
new knowledge, especially in the very fields with which it
occupied itself.

After the short renaissance under Charles the Great
followed a period of disorder in the social and political
world, and a failure in the spiritual world to rise on the
wings of the new inspiration. This led to intellectual
decadence and to mental gloom which profoundly affected

the whole social order; then another change took place.
At the beginning of the eleventh century a spirit of depression and pessimism was widespread. The end of the
world was expected and awaited. But toward the end of
the century a change in temper and attitude was everywhere present. A strong and hopeful spirit filled with
a new passion for freedom and knowledge broke the
chains which had hitherto bound the souls of men, and
a new era began to dawn in the spiritual movement of
history. The great revival manifested itself in a variety
of forms, and in this movement France led the way. It
was then that Gothic architecture began its wonderful
development, and, according to one of the latest Roman
Catholic writers, it was the time when the tide of pulpit
eloquence reached its high-water mark in the Middle
Ages.

The beginning of the twelfth century marks a new era
in the history of Europe. The old world-struggle between
the East and the West entered on a new phase. Far
back in the past in the days of the Persian the East had
flung itself upon the West and the West had retaliated
by flinging itself upon the East in the time of Alexander.
The strife swept back and forth for centuries, ending as
it always has ended, in the situation remaining substan-
tially as in the beginning. The same struggle continued
in the Christian period. The Mohammedan Conquest regained not only all that had been lost by the earlier conflicts but swept with immense power into new territories.
It had flowed over the larger part of the East and much
of the West like a wave of fire. But unlike the later
Turkish conquest, unlike even the then existing European
civilization, it showed itself not only hospitable to but
eager for the ancient classic culture. Schools and universities sprang up all through the new Mohammedan
states. At Bagdad, at Cordova and wherever the Sara-
cenic power was established there was a revival of the old

Hellenic spirit and the old learning and science were received and studied with eager enthusiasm. The old literature had been preserved still in the East and the conquerors took over from the conquered the means to enter into the thought and spiritual world of the past. The Greek texts had in many instances been preserved and these were translated or transmitted by the Nestorians particularly, and soon filled the libraries of both their own people and those of their Arabian conquerors.

The new Arabic culture spread far and wide and in the possession of this new science, they felt themselves to be, as indeed they were, far in advance of their Christian neighbors. Again a new impulse seized the West and it flung itself upon the East as in the days of Alexander. The Crusades which began in this period were the old challenge and the old duel, and, so far as geographical conquests are concerned, were a failure. But the intellectual results were enormous.

It was by way of the Jewish and Mohammedan commentators that the study of Aristotle began to be pursued with a new interest. The world was on the threshold of a new age. While crusade after crusade swept away some of the noblest and the best and ended only in failure, the social and political changes, the immense growth in the spirit of individual freedom, are marked on every hand. The old schools of Charlemagne, which had begun a renaissance that ended in confusion and darkness, were succeeded by new and greater schools and universities, or what became universities, under the influence of the new spirit.

The first figure which we encounter as introducing this new and changing age and which still rises sharp and clear against the dark background of the past, is the lofty, tender, and humble Saint Anselm of Aosta. Less than any other great man of his age he seems to be under the yoke of the prevailing controversies. Born in the early part of the eleventh century (1030 A.D.) he lived on into the twelfth. His place is so high and his influence upon some of the profoundest questions ever presented to the human mind has been so great, that he has been called the Father of Scholasticism. Yet there was an independence of thought and a freedom of treatment which really separates him from the great mass of Schoolmen who succeeded him. He was, moreover, a man of genius and of the most profound and simple piety, facts which in themselves would create a wide difference between him and his contemporaries. He was the first to treat single problems in dogmatic theology in a new way and to lead theological science into new paths. In him appears very clearly stated what has been claimed to be the real and essential character of scholasticism, that is, the solution or statement of the relation between Faith and Knowledge, or Reason and Authority, which problem was also fundamental for the whole course of scholastic theology.

He chose as his motto: "Credo ut Intelligam," basing it, as he said, upon the passage from Isaiah 7. 9. "Nisi credideritis, non intelligitis." How he ever interpreted the passage in this manner is not easy to understand. In the Vulgate, and also in Jerome's own text, the reading is quite different and does not even suggest such a translation. The whole matter, therefore, is quite obscure. The recognition of authority as above reason is, however, very plain and yet he endeavors to show that the most profound truths, or the most mysterious, although above reason, are not contrary to it. His greatest works have the definite aim to try to prove that there is a fundamental rational basis which will enable the pious and humble soul to feel that what he accepts on the authority of the Church has its foundation in reason itself. The subjects he dealt with led him far away from most of the controversies which were engaging the schools at that time, though they aroused new and nobler ones. The titles of his greatest works are familiar to even the most careless student of theology, and form part of our great inheritance from the past. His ruling ideas governed theology down to the present day and still hold power over many minds. He left, however, no completed system and attempted none. His mind was not of that character. His soul was busy with God, in an intense absorption which finds few parallels in the history of piety.

The one who, however, is best known to the world through his misfortune and his fame is a younger man, though a contemporary of Anselm, Peter Abelard (1079-1142). The story of Abelard and Heloïse is one of the great romances and tragedies of the Middle Ages. The soft glow of sympathy has hidden from men's eyes the hard, stern fact that this was one of those natures to which tragedy was inevitable. It was not his fame as a lover which gave him his power and renown in his own age, but the fact that he was perhaps the most brilliant scholar, the keenest intellect and the most daring spirit of his times. He was by nature an Ishmaelite. His hand was against every man and every man's hand was against him. He destroyed for generations the influence of the old Platonic realism, of which Anselm was the most noted representative of his day. He overthrew both Roscellinus and William of Champeaux and brought the debate about the Universals to a new stage even if he did not end it. The difference between Abelard and his opponents was not merely a logical theory or a philosophical interpretation or speculation, but something even more radical and fundamental. He practically reversed the position of Anselm and regarded religious faith as primarily an acceptance of truth by the intellect, and asserted that this faith could be rationally conceived and rationally stated. His opponents, on the other hand, considered faith to be purely and fundamentally an act of the will.

This resulted from the fact that they considered the object of faith as having an absolutely supernatural character which could not be apprehended in the way of ordinary knowledge. It could be appropriated only through spiritual experience which gave it validity.

His reputation was already high when in his supreme audacity he ventured to enter the field of theology and applied his dialectics to its problems in a way which involved him in suspicion. St. Bernard was the most distinguished living man. Neither Pope nor King had half the influence which he exerted. He was the great preacher of the Second Crusade, and its tragic failure did not destroy his influence. But he was not a man of any great metaphysical or philosophical powers, and he rested upon authority without the slightest question or hesitation. There was a natural and fundamental opposition between him and Abelard, and the distrust which Abelard's speculations aroused in St. Bernard's mind led to the scholar's ultimate condemnation and disgrace. Much as we may sympathize with Abelard, his temper of mind and general attitude of pride and arrogance had probably as much to do with his condemnation as his heresy. He died in retirement: a sad, broken-hearted, and humble saint of God, if we can believe the friend who was with him to the end.

These men, interesting for their originality and vigorous characters, were merely the pioneers of the future. They furnished, however, an inspiration which never died out and their names are better known than those of some of the later ones who can claim with better right the name of Schoolmen. These, however, could not come until the intellectual conditions were prepared for a wide and systematic study carried on upon a definite intellectual method, and for this the universities were essential.

In the thirteenth century the eager-minded of all the races of Europe flocked, as if led by some impulse which they could not control, to the great centers of human thought, and especially to Paris. The conditions under which their studies were pursued are almost inconceivable to the modern mind. There were then few of the instruments of learning which are now considered essential. Books were rare and costly. In the early part of the eleventh century Lanfranc had collected at the Abbey of Bec a library which included no less than sixty volumes, which was considered a very remarkable collection, and the number had not increased materially by the thirteenth century. The accommodations for students were of the worst, even if that term could be used at all for what they had. Each student was literally fighting for his own hand. The account which Erasmus gives of his own experience three hundred years later makes the picture the more appalling. The crowd, the tumult, the noise, the angry strife and bitter dispute, the coarse and ignorant mass of students, point to a condition so frightful that it seems inconceivable that anything could be accomplished. But there were two things which are the real foundation and essential of every university and without which all intellectual work is but an empty sham. There were minds that must know, and there were men who were able to meet these minds with their own hard-won gains and a like passion for truth. There were teachers to inspire, and scholars who hungered for this inspiration. So in cold, dark and crowded hall, in cathedral cloister or in the open air, mind met mind, and the play and the clash of the keenest intellects of the age were at work in the schools making Europe ring with a strife as eager and more lasting, as well as more important, than the conflict of arms which was the common habit of life in those centuries. Of the enthusiasm for philosophical studies in the thirteenth century it has been said that there has never been an age in which there was greater zeal for the highest studies.

The number of students which is given is most probably greatly exaggerated. Ten, fifteen, twenty and even thirty thousand is given for different times and different places. Comparing it with modern numbers and considering also the relative proportion between the population then and now it seems quite impossible. It would give a higher percentage than any other time since Europe was civilized. The important and impressive thing is that the influence of the universities was so great that nothing could be said or done in any important way without getting their judgment and support. One who knew much about this period has said: "The schools flourished in such great numbers and with such crowds of students that they became cities." No one country seems to have had the monopoly. Ireland as well as Italy was represented. Germany, France, and England also figured largely. The same writer has said: "Michael Scot, Alexander of Hales, Edmund Rich, Robert of Lincoln, William Sherwood, John of St. Gilles, all studied at Paris and the English were the most eager as well as the most turbulent of all the students." Most of these men knew nothing of what we call progress or development. They were chiefly bent upon gaining access to the accumulated knowledge of the past which now seemed for the first time to be at their service. The growth of the mind, the development of their own intellectual powers, the expansion of the spiritual energies of the soul, the extension of the intellectual horizon were in fact all included in this, though with many, if not most, such an idea would have been most energetically rejected. Their aim, as they understood it, was to obtain the truth already given, by means of which they could possess certainty and conviction. The significance of this new intellectual movement is expressed in the statement of a writer of the Middle Ages who sums up in a phrase the forces which were regarded as the very foundation and life of the world of his day: Sacerdotium, Imperium, Studium—the Church, the Empire, and the Universities, and from this position the Universities as representative of the meaning and worth of knowledge, have never been displaced.

As we look back and notice the changes which were taking place, the great spiritual ferment, the unrest and intellectual agitation, the political and social movements which mark the times, we recognize clearly that the world was on the threshold of a new age. Heretofore religion had been largely confined, except in a mechanical and institutional way, to the clergy and the monks. The layman as such had no interest in, nor inspiration from, the regular order of things. Through its sacramental system the Church provided for his salvation not only in this life, but in the future. The mass of the people were utterly ignorant, but the growth of the cities and an increased social consciousness, led to a development of the democratic spirit which had in it the promise of a great unknown future. The rising spirit of democracy and individualism, with its emphasis on personality, was perhaps, in a religious way, more manifest in the north of Europe than in the south. A personal religious spirit began to develop among the people, independent of, and more or less antagonistic to, the Church. This movement, of which the Beguins and Beghards are the most striking expression, was, however, soon left behind or absorbed by the orders of mendicant friars founded by Dominic and Francis.

The Church had waited for the people to come to it. Francis and Dominic brought religion to the people. Instead of being a movement which appealed to the select few, to the souls worn with the passion for God, to the hearts heavy with the burden of life, to whom the monastic orders offered the best that they knew in this world, Francis appealed to the poor and the ignorant. He turned to the common man and woman who had to live the common life of the world. He made them feel for the first time in centuries that the world was God's world and that here and now one could lift his soul to God and find peace in His presence even though he were a peasant and a drudge. It was a new message, and the souls of men were thrilled as they heard the long-forgotten words and saw the strange, unearthly light in those dark, passionate eyes. It was the awakening religious individualism of the West. Yet even here the old leaven still worked and the ascetic instinct marked off the new Christians as lay members of the new order, not as children of God, living in the fullness and freedom of their sonship in a world which is entirely His.

As a result of this spiritual unrest and agitation the noblest and the best were drawn by the magic of the new life here unfolding. The new orders began with the deliberate purpose of dealing with the practical side of life and with that only. Yet the importance and power of the rising universities drew them to the benches of these scholars and the chairs of the teachers, and the Franciscans and Dominicans furnished the greatest names of those who represented the scholastic method and the scholastic spirit in their prime. The relation of the universities to the new mind of Europe is the most impressive and perhaps the most important fact to be recognized and studied. For it was in them that the human mind gained its greatest, if not its first, impulse to that intellectual freedom which has been the most characteristic note of modern times. The attitude of the ecclesiastical authorities toward them was constantly varying. There was an unconscious suspicion and distrust which often broke into violent opposition. For the elevation and supremacy of the reason, which was asserted by some, and conceded by almost all, is the primary and underlying fact of these centuries. Grabmann, a modern Roman Catholic theolo-

gian who has been one of the most ardent defenders of
the Schools, says: "The aim of the scholastic method is
to gain, if possible, an insight into the contents of faith
through the application of reason and philosophy to the
truths of Revelation, in order thus to bring the supernatural truths in their essence closer to the human spirit, to
make possible a systematic, organically developed body
of truth, and thus to be able to solve the objections which
on the ground of reason have been made against the
truths of Revelation. Thus the scholastic method gradually developed for itself a definite outer technique as well
as a definite form." In spite of all dogmatic definitions
and limitations the fact is that both in statement and
defense the worth of reason was constantly asserted and
it was always used. The verbal assent to authority, even
the willing recognition of it, can in no way conceal the
fact that reason was the underlying force, and its satisfaction the final aim, of all these efforts.

No finer minds or loftier spirits appeared in the thirteenth century than were those of Erigena, Anselm, and
Abelard, but the whole ordering of human thought had
passed through a great change. New problems were before the schools. New material was added to the growing
supply. The old problem of the Universals was brought
to what might be called a compromise by the keen dialectics of Abelard. The three definitions were formulated for
the Universals. The first was that the idea, or universal,
had an existence anterior to that of the particular or
individual, what was called the "ante rem." This was the
Platonic view. The second found the universal in the particular or the individual from which it was abstracted for
purposes of thought: this was the Aristotelian view and
was called "in re." The third, which was more or less
nominalistic in its thought, was that only from the particular or after the particular, could the inference be
drawn and the universal derived, which was described as

"post rem." These views were all realistic in thought as well as expression, but in their combination they made it possible for a choice and opened the way for new developments in thought and logic. The problem of the Universals, thus settled and accepted as a general assumption, dropped back out of the controversy and the mind moved on to new tasks which arose out of deeper study and a more systematic application of the Aristotelian logic and metaphysics.

The question naturally and inevitably arises, why did Aristotle take such a supreme place in the great work of the Schoolmen? Are there any hidden and obscure factors in his temper of mind which are still unknown? Was there, so to speak, a kind of psychological sympathy between the mind of Aristotle and the great minds of this age which led them to feel that here was the teacher they most needed? Were the conditions of knowledge such that his method appealed with greater force than that of any other? I have no means of answering all these questions, but the latter can unquestionably be answered in the affirmative. We know that at first the authorities looked with hesitation if not suspicion upon the study of Aristotle. We know also that it was finally forbidden, then qualified and ultimately accepted. One writer who has made this problem a subject of investigation finds two reasons at least why Aristotle became the great "Master of those that know" to the Middle Ages.

The first lay in the fact that their earliest acquaintance came indirectly and imperfectly through Arabic and Jewish authorities. However strong the dislike and however bitter the hostility against the Saracen it was impossible to prevent his thought and knowledge from finding access to the Christian world after the closer contact which was brought about by the Crusades and the later commercial relations between the two peoples. Some Christian students even went so far as to go to Spain to

study in the great universities there established, and thus
in some instances aroused deep suspicion and alarm. In
Southern Italy also, and especially at the court of Frederick II, the Saracen scholar was as welcome as the Christian and was often more learned and cultivated. The
Arabic schools had inherited with their other conquests
that of Aristotle and some of the most learned were eager
and devoted students of his writings. From the Christian, Mohammedan, and Jewish standpoints alike many
of these writers soon ran into heresy, or what was called
heresy. They constructed systems of their own which
contained elements of Aristotelianism, but there were also
many Neo-Platonic and pantheistic elements. Avicenna
and Averroës became names of ill-omen to the ears of
Christians, and their doctrines, under the name of Aristotle, spread far and wide. This roused a profound un-
easiness in the minds of the Christian authorities, and
the necessity for some measures of correction or repres-
sion became apparent. The first, and the more popular
one, was that of persecution and extermination. This was
tried with hideous success in the case of the Albigenses
and other sects who were more or less tinctured by the
new thought.

The other method, to adopt the more reasonable way,
was by a genuine and partly scientific study to attempt to get at the true mind of Aristotle through a
study of new translations, and additional treatises of the
philosopher. The result was a new interest in him and
a fuller command of the real sources. Albert the Great
(1193-1280) was the one perhaps who contributed most
to the new understanding of Aristotle, but his great
scholar, Aquinas (1227-1274) was the one who applied
it most exhaustively. But all was not Aristotle which went
by his name.

One must not think of the scholastic period as one in
which thought was carried on along definite lines of

cleavage between the debaters. The Schoolmen were not separated into schools or groups of well-defined opponents. The time came when this was to a large extent true, but in its earlier stages the movement was, taken as a whole, a great spiritual ferment with a great variety of cross currents and hidden forces. Not only was the earlier realism always present, but it was combined in all its different forms of expression with nominalistic tendencies, and the whole was shot through with an element of mysticism which asserted itself even when it was inconsistent with the logical and philosophical basis assumed.

This mysticism arose out of the Neo-Platonism which was the heritage of the great past. It appeared in the greatest variety of forms. Sometimes it was almost purely intellectual, like the original Plotinianism: sometimes it was based upon the yearning of the soul for the Infinite and the Eternal. Again there was a blending of both, and the attempt was made to construct a theological system by the accepted logical methods in which the root or source, however, was the mystical feeling. Most of these writers appealed to the Pseudo-Areopagite whom they regarded as fundamentally Christian but whose writings are now regarded as owing little or nothing to Christian sources. Had the men of that day known more of Christian history they would have seen that the real author of the mysticism of the Middle Ages was not the Areopagite but Augustine, and, through Augustine, Plotinus. It was not then an innovation, but the long and living tradition of the Christian Church. The language of the Christian mystic is changed but the thought is the same. When Hugo of St. Victor taught that man, enlightened by divine grace, was capable of raising himself in this life to the actual contemplation of God and thus have an actual foretaste of the Blessed Vision, he did not know that Plotinus had said the same thing. When Richard of

St. Victor taught that the higher powers of the soul, sense, imagination, memory and reason, cease being active in the state of ecstasy we find ourselves back in the last days of the classic world. In such a state all consciousness of the outer world vanishes, and even the inner world, the world of self-consciousness, disappears in the vision which floods the soul. This is the language of Neo-Platonism but it is also the language of the human soul. These men were Christians and mystics, committed to a spiritual attitude toward God by those deeper emotional qualities which the abstract conception of God can never satisfy and also, no doubt, partly in reaction against what seemed to them the excesses of the dialectic method.

The same element is to be found in even the greatest of the scholastics. Thomas Aquinas is the dialectician and philosopher par excellence. He denies the validity of Anselm's "a priori" argument for the existence of God and declares that the knowledge of God is not immediate but inferential. The whole weight of his intellect is bent upon asserting the force of the "a posteriori" argument, and the "a posteriori" alone. Yet strange as it may seem, the same mystic touch appears here again. In spite of all his attempts at coördinating his thoughts and truths into a logical and consistent system Aquinas is led to an even more complete assertion of some of the earlier mysticism which he found in Augustine. The "Visio Dei" which hovered before the eyes of all the saints and was the dream of all those who yearned for God haunted also the imagination and the spirit of him who is regarded as the greatest of the teachers of the Latin Church in the greatest age of its history.

The vision, St. Thomas thinks, is not possible to man under ordinary conditions. It can happen only "in raptu," which is the equivalent of the Neo-Platonic ecstasy. In this "Ecstasy" the human soul does not cease

to inform the body, but is snatched from the senses and
their organs through a supernatural enlightenment and
an inner working of God. This is done in order that the
soul may be purely active in Him, and in Him alone.

The complete and perfect fruition is, however, reserved for the future. There is no proof or justification
offered for this position by the logical method which St.
Thomas used in the demonstration and establishment of
his theological system. And yet this mysticism is found
almost everywhere running through the entire thought
of the Middle Ages and forming an integral part of the
Scholastic thinking. Indeed some have asserted that it is
an essential part of the Schoolmen's theology from whatever standpoint it is viewed. To be sure, in some instances, it may be a reaction from the dry dialectics of
the schools, and yet it is incorrect, as Willmann has
pointed out, to put the mystic and the scholastic in opposition. The genuine scholastics are at the same time mystics and the thorough mystics have by no means rejected
the science of the schools. Mysticism points to something
significant in the spiritual life of the times which is not
clearly expressed in the scholastic systems, though indeed it may be, and no doubt is, implied in them: that is
the larger and deeper sense of personality which has its
roots in the deeper spiritual experiences or aspirations.
For the mystic is essentially an individualist in the most
vivid and intense form.

The real problem concerning the mysticism of the
Middle Ages is not to trace it to its sources, either literary or traditional, but to explain why it took such a
deep hold upon the life of men, and why its influence
steadily strengthened as the centuries rolled by until ultimately it was the chief, if not the only, form of piety.
The solution is by no means an easy task. For great
spiritual movements or long-continued spiritual moods
have their roots deep in the constitution and the temper

of the human soul. The value of this present life was, in the mind of the men of the Middle Ages, a purely relative one: that is, they all, without exception held the view that it was preparatory for the life beyond. Time and eternity were in violent and hopeless contrast. Before the immensity and awfulness of the latter the days and years of man's life were but a span. This was not a new way of looking at life. It is a distinctly human view though it has been regarded as a peculiarly Christian view by all ages of Christian writers.

Yet at bottom it is essentially pessimistic and negatives or changes the character and meaning of Christ's redemption. If His redemption, as a practical experience, is to be relegated to the future and the whole meaning of His salvation is a kind of other-worldliness, then this view is true. But the Gospel itself points out that our present life may be charged with meaning and worth when Christ is made the center and the source of all its living energies and inspirations. Salvation is a present fact, an actual, living, immediate experience. In the light of it and by the power of it the everyday fellowship with Christ makes life a splendid thing. The imitation of Christ was supposed to be the inspiring motive of the best and the noblest. But this imitation too often was a purely external and physical one. The Poverty of Christ became the watchword and standard of those who were struggling to elevate the life of the soul. Nowhere is manifest that calm and serene sense of the fullness of life through the actual and immediate presence and power of Christ in the whole breadth and sweep of man's being.

The deepest and most fundamental emotions and convictions of any age always find their highest and finest utterance in verse, and so it was in this period of man's history. The mood of divine despair, the utter longing and hopes of the soul of the Middle Ages are mirrored in those great hymns which have lasted through the ages, and which for their power of expressing what was most deeply felt have never been surpassed in any period. St. Bernard of Cluny reveals in his great poem the wistful and undying longing of the soul, sick of life and dreaming of the far unknown future which hung like a vision before his aching eyes. Our English hymn, "Jerusalem the Golden," is but an echo of a mood which once filled every pious heart and found its expression in those wondrous words:

"Hora novissima, tempora pessima sunt. Vigilemus!"

Another note perhaps even deeper is struck in the solemn strains of that great hymn which rolls upon the ear with the thunder of that dread which filled the hearts of men:

"Dies iræ, die illa!
Solvet sæculum in favilla,
Teste David cum Sybila."

There is yet one more in which the whole passion and tenderness of the medieval soul poured itself out in adoration of the Virgin and which still moves our sympathies and stirs our affections, though it does not meet the deeper passion which has grown out of the longer and larger experiences of Christ.

"Stabat mater dolorosa
Juxta crucem, lachrymosa,
Dum pendebat filius.

In the spiritual life of this age we are face to face with a great complex made of traditions from the past, of inheritances from many an antique source. In this strange world we find the name and fame of Aristotle standing high above all others. It is difficult to find a satisfactory reason in the mere desire to correct mis-

apprehensions or false interpretations and uses. He was
chosen before all others and yet it is not easy to see why.
For even in the case of the most ardent Aristotelians
there is much which is not Aristotle although it went
under his name. His system and his method were accepted
and used by many who had often other thoughts than
his in their minds, and who mingled, with their Aristotelian formulas, ideas and interests which would have
been strange and foreign to the cool intelligence of the
great Greek.

The second reason which has been assigned for the
medieval study of Aristotle and his complete acceptance
is, that he was adopted on account of his method. His
system of thought seemed better suited for building up a
Christian science than that of Plato. For these men
started out with the fixed idea that all truth was known,
or could be known, and that a complete statement of the
universe of knowledge could be reached and also formulated. If this could be accomplished the greatest task
then before the world would have been achieved. No hint
is even suggested that such a dream might only be a
dream. Just a few words on the method of Aristotle may
help to understand why he captured the thought of these
times so completely that he was left without a rival.

Though Aristotle is known by the general reader
chiefly as the founder of the syllogistic logic, yet this in
turn was built upon his metaphysics and his categories,
or was theoretically united with them. The value of the
syllogism in detecting error in an argument has always
been recognized, but that it makes no discoveries and
does not advance human thought in any other way than
to clarify it is best known only to students. Aristotle
himself did a vast amount of research and investigation,
and upon the results so reached he built up his system of
thought. This has been generally called the deductive
system. That is, he starts from certain definitions or

postulates which he believes he has already established and erects his structure upon these. But Plato had been the teacher of Aristotle and the latter was profoundly influenced by the system of his great predecessor. It was the fundamental points in Plato which formed the ground of Aristotle's thinking and gave the ultimate form to his metaphysics, out of which all the rest grew by the application of the logic which he himself had invented. Plato's great contribution had been his theory of ideas. To him there was a world of reality in which existed an invisible series of ideas which were the pattern of all that is in this visible world. The two worlds stand related to each other as creating force and created product. Matter was molded by these ideas into the visible world with its shifting phenomena, but they stood eternal, unchanged, the ultimate ground of all that is. Yet a wide chasm separated these two worlds and Plato had found no bridge. Aristotle planted the ideas as the ground of the existence of each thing in the thing itself. The idea, or the cause of the particular thing was not outside of or apart from it, but was within it and was the organizing cause of its existence. Now if it were possible to reach a determination as to what this idea was, separate it from the individual, define its essence, then it would be possible to know reality and achieve knowledge.

Aristotle believed that the result of the mental process by which the mind drew out or abstracted from the individual that which gave it its specific character exactly corresponded to the facts. That is, that the concept represented the real essence of the objects included under it. Truth in a logical judgment, that is, the mental representation, corresponds to the essence of the object or objects described in the judgment. This means, of course, that the forms of speech correspond to the forms of being or reality. The concept therefore is the precise expression of the object which it denotes, and the essence in turn corresponds to the concept. In the process of defining we state or recognize the essence of the thing defined. To put it another way, the logical, subjective concept has a real objective correlate in the essence immanent in the objects of the concept.

If one asks what the essence in reality is we are told that it is the cause of each thing being what it is. Now this concept which expresses the essence is always a Universal. That is, it does not denote a particular thing or object, but a kind, that which is capable of being thought, but which does not exist apart from the thing in which it is manifest. The attitude of the modern mind is almost exactly the opposite of that of the medieval. To the modern mind the individual is the real, fixed, positive foundation for thought, and the universal is only the descriptive term, the basis of classification. To the Schoolman the individual or particular is the changing, passing and imperfect; the universal is the real and permanent. This arose from the fact that to the Schoolmen the identity of thought and being was fundamental, and that, therefore, the logical proof was an evidence of the fact, not only of an actual mental operation or concept in the mind itself, but of a reality external to thought, but discovered and stated in its terms. The argument was that the universal could not be known if it did not exist in reality, and the proof seemed to be offered in the conviction that it could not be predicated of real objects if it itself was not real. That is, that humanity or goodness could not be predicated of man or of the good if they did not have a real existence in themselves beyond the description which the mind had given for the purpose of classification.

The way then to get at truth was to think, and by logical determination to reach the essence or universal. Now that you have reached the universal by abstraction what guarantee has one of its truth or reality? This could be affirmed from the fundamental conviction that it could not be known or thought if it did not exist in reality. It is this purely logical and dialectic method of determining truth that puzzles the modern mind. The only facts or most of the facts come from purely mental operations, and there is no test devised through comparison with the evidence which facts themselves offer for deciding what the truth actually is. The Universal then was the ultimate aim of thought and when this was reached, it represented the fixed and unchanging as well as unchangeable truth. If the Universal was the very highest truth there was no need to interest one's self in the ordinary facts of life, but by a sheer mental effort to seek for the essence, the concept, and having reached this one could go no farther. A Roman Catholic writer has stated the aim of the Scholastics with a complete confidence not only in the methods but in the results. "The concept or the whole of these truths constitutes the ideal being of things; it precedes their actuality and persists after their destruction, because this whole or ideal, this world of concepts, is seen in the light of the immutable, the necessary and the perfect." This emphasis upon the Universal naturally led men to seek by abstraction the highest Universal. The highest conception must naturally be Pure Being, or, as it was ultimately described by further abstraction and definition, Pure Act, "Actus Purus." From this central and Supreme Universal all thought must proceed, for this is the most perfect and certain of all truths not only from a spiritual point of view, but also from the logical and metaphysical. If it is asked why this is so the answer is that the higher the abstraction the more reality it has, and that this is preëminently true of God the Absolute, for the Absolute is that which it is impossible to think of as not being. One is strongly inclined to agree with the French critic who describes the radical vice of this philosophy as "L'idolatrie de l'abstraction et l'intemperance de l'affirmation."

With this imperfect statement of the underlying principles of the Scholastic Philosophy we can see why Aristotle was chosen by the Schoolmen as their teacher. They knew little about the world around them and cared less, so far as any intellectual or scientific interest was concerned. They had begun to think and naturally sought for some method by which their thinking could be brought into a reasonably systematic form. Their own culture and the culture of the times did not furnish them with any intellectual methods and they were driven to seek them in the past. Aristotle seemed, for the purpose they had in view, to furnish the best method they knew. They started from certain assumptions. The truths which were assumed to be given they never challenged. The main thing for them to do was to determine what was the relation which existed between the truths of Revelation and the intellectual tradition of the past. The rising tide of intellectual energy also called forth a need for stating the boundary line between intellectual investigation, or the limits of reason and the theological and doctrinal definitions set forth authoritatively by the Church. The chief effort made was to show that if the mysteries of the faith cannot be determined by pure reason, they are at least not contrary to reason. More and more, however, the tendency was to limit the range and application of reason to these mysteries until the field of that which was to be accepted on authority was enlarged. The final result was an opposition between Faith and Reason which led to the position that things were true for faith which were not true for reason and vice versa, that there were truths of reason which were in no way consistent with faith.

The primary defect, however, of the scholastic method was one which was fatal to true science and blocked the way to a real progress in knowledge. The Schoolmen accepted the Universals, the conceptions and definitions they had reached by logical methods, as fixed formulas, final and authoritative, and not simply as results to which science had thus far attained. These became therefore permanent principles valid for all future scientific activity. The Schoolmen began with the Categories of Aristotle and studied everything under the influence of his logic. Now the Categories are not infallible, nor do they stand unaffected by the tests to which they have since been submitted. Yet upon these they built their syllogisms, or rather applied their syllogisms as the perfect method of proof. The syllogism was the simplest and apparently the most rigid form of logic, and consequently if the logic be true the conclusion must be inevitable. One great difficulty which they did not recognize was that the conclusion was already involved in the premise and the syllogism was only a different and more definite way of stating or expanding the inference already implied in the premises.

A further difficulty was one which also they never seemed to realize and that was that the premises were always assumed and never tested in a truly scientific way though the ingenuity of their logic seemed inexhaustible. If there is a flaw in the premises the farther the reasoning process advances the greater the error in the conclusion. It was next to impossible to correct this method by strict observation, for it was a metaphysical and logical age, and the study of nature and of facts was entirely ignored and intellectual definitions and distinctions held the field in all thinking. Even when there was a study of facts, as in the case of Albert the Great, the method was not fundamentally changed and he simply indicates the gradually aroused interest in things outside the mental processes which engrossed the main thought of this period. Among the many causes which produced this attitude of mind undoubtedly the ascetic temper of the age had a primary place. Something too may be due to

certain inherited philosophical traditions with reference
to matter itself. It was regarded as largely negative and
its pure potential character put it so much out of consideration that the mind worked only with and in its own
activities, disregarding the offer of knowledge which lay
all unexplored in the outside world.

In addition to this the method itself was largely hostile
to scientific knowledge or scientific research. Rejecting
the individual and the particular as the passing and the
changeable they sought only the abstract and permanent.
Holding this view of the particular it could never be an
object of science, nor, at least by implication, a source
of knowledge. One must plunge beyond the particular
to the Universal, to the inner essence, the permanent being, which makes it what it is. They all agreed in this,
that the proper object of science was not the particular
but the Universal. They declared that the highest and
most certain science is that which has Being for its object
since Being is the great Universal and therefore the
highest and greatest reality. They did not move along
the path of knowledge which was the result of actual
demonstration, but by the way of logical theory. In the
order of existence God comes first. He is the Highest
and Truest Being and therefore they began with Him.
In this they were running true to form, for the first
premise of the scholastic logic was: "Scientia est de Uni-
versalibus." These universals, which appear to us as
being only words or distinctions in the mind itself, were
accepted as a substitute for, and an infallibly accurate
statement of, the thing. St. Thomas repeats again and
again that the definition is the thing: "Definitio enim est
idem res."

Starting, as the Schoolmen did, from God, the highest
Being, and the necessary origin of all systematic thought,
assuming truth to be apprehended chiefly by the intellect
or in an intellectual form, the question arises as to man's

real and actual knowledge of God. Can the intellect
grasp the Being of God with the same certainty and
understanding that it does the fact of its own activity, or
the facts of human consciousness? Again, is it possible
to obtain an accurate and scientific knowledge of God's
nature as of the subjects of other sciences? Having
divided truth into natural and revealed truth and having
placed the character and nature of God preëminently
among the revealed truths, as was perfectly proper, and
having also asserted that these truths so revealed must
be accepted on authority, the further question then arises,
what relation does the intellect bear to these truths? If
the assumption is, as it seems to be, that the Supernatural
or Infinite cannot be apprehended by the powers of the
intellect, how can there be any real knowledge of revealed
truth? Even Faith which is called in to accept them
does not really know what it accepts. The terms chiefly
used as descriptive of God describe something outside the
capacity of the human mind to grasp or even to represent to itself. The danger lurking in this position revealed itself ultimately in the declaration or statement
of the Double Truth. That is, a thing or statement may
be true for theology which is not true for philosophy and
the reverse is also true that something may be true for
philosophy which is not true for theology.

The whole authority of truth itself was thus involved
and imperilled and any foundation upon which the soul
could rest was taken away and the whole problem of
truth was left in the air. In St. Thomas's day, however,
this danger was not clearly perceived, though he seemed,
in a way, to anticipate it by giving a real and valid
authority to the faith which is "acceptance," and by
asserting that the capacity to believe these supernatural
truths was infused into the intellect by God Himself. A
careful student of this period has said: "Faith in the
Schoolmen of the thirteenth century rests not upon the

evidence of its object like other knowledge, but upon the 'Virtus Credentis.' " It is in fact the obedient submission of the human intellect to God. But this result cannot be obtained through outer testimony like that of Scriptures or of miracles, but only through the illumination of the mind by the Eternal Light. Through this enlightenment the intellect gains the capacity and the impulse to see and apprehend God. This is the "Fides Gratuita," a different thing from the "Fides Informis." The subject of this "Fides Gratuita" is not the mystical vision of God but the "Articuli Fidei."

This infusion of Grace to which St. Thomas refers is a divine act and guarantees and authenticates the new knowledge given in Revelation. The process passes entirely out of the field of the regular method by which man ascertains the truth which forms the body of his knowledge and in so doing creates a secret uncertainty as to the method itself. How are we to know when God infuses this Grace except in the Sacraments? In the last analysis, the basis of the Scholastic method was primarily Hellenic. It really placed knowledge, intellectual knowledge, however obtained, as the ultimate means of salvation. As to the Greek, so to the Schoolmen, the intellect is the way of redemption. Lying back behind this intellectual method were certain assumptions which were never logically or consciously stated. These assumptions are involved in the very logic itself. First of these was the theory of Ideas which is at the root of much Greek thought after Plato, and which was taken over by the Schoolmen. Out of it arose also the great controversy over the problem of Matter and Form. This debate was an effort to settle the origin of the Universe as a whole, and to determine the nature of the individual. All varieties of objects are the manifestation of their Ideas. Speaking roughly the Idea stamps itself upon Matter or takes Matter out of its formless and potential condition and gives us the world as it is. The Idea is the source of all the divisions into Genera and Species and is also present in each individual. The object of science is to determine the nature and number of the Ideas and so to get at the inner character and constitution of the universe. Whether we approach the subject from the point of view of Plato or Aristotle, the conception of the Universe which lies behind the theory of Ideas is a purely fixed and static one.

The Schoolman's whole system was a philosophy rather than a theology, and it failed in both respects. Assuming the Aristotelian foundation as a basis for his theology he fell into the same fundamental error, viewed from the religious and Christian point of view, which lay at the heart of Aristotelianism. Aquinas starts with the Aristotelian axiom of a First Cause, a Primal Mover, Primum Mobile, and from this, the whole order of the universe follows by a process of logic. As a philosophical interpretation it must stand or fall by itself, for it is a philosophical and not an ethical or religious principle at all. A certain ethical value may be imputed to it or may be involved in it, but as a religious statement it has little or no value. It is true, man feels the natural desire to know the First Cause in its reality, which he already recognizes in its effects. This desire is a perfectly legitimate one, and in its satisfaction it may be assumed that there is a certain religious value. But from the very nature of the case this First Cause is in reality unknowable, under the present conditions of the human mind. The limits set to its powers preclude the possibility of such knowledge, and it is only by injecting a promise for the future that any spiritual satisfaction can be attained along this path.

Aquinas denied any value to the argument of Anselm and limited the mind to the inferences to be drawn from the logic of cause and effect. The promise for the future, on the other hand, meets only in part the desire which moves man, for what belongs to the future is related to this life only as an object of faith taken in the sense of hope. But hope has no necessary religious value, inasmuch as it has no necessary religious inspiration. It is introducing into the intellectual field of logical demonstration elements which belong to another side of life. Moreover in order to give a religious value to this system a body of Revealed Truth was introduced as a supplement to the natural truth. But in so doing these truths were often so separated from the field of reason that they were left to rest entirely upon authority. As a consequence the very Fatherhood of God was left outside the field of thought and reflection. So it was that the way was open for the theory of the "double truth" which worked so disastrously and marked the end of the scholastic effort.

The fundamental error in the whole scholastic method, considered as an attempt to construct a logical and scientific statement of the whole of truth lay in the fact that there is no clear moral and spiritual recognition of God as a Person or of man as a person. Of course, terms were used which seem to imply such a recognition, but when the inner relations of the thought are analyzed the truth of this statement is manifest. When we study man in his actual human life, in those earthly relations which make up the complex of his existence we find that the social bonds, the touch and movement of one life upon another, constitute the great forces or means by which life is elevated and inspired. We pass from the lower to the higher more swiftly and surely through the vision and force of human excellence than by the strength of any theoretical definitions of human life and conduct. History is but the expression of the working of this spiritual law which goes deeper than any logic of the schools and works with a mightier power than any other influence to which man may be exposed. The primary truth of Christianity is that God declares Himself in Christ as the Father. He is a Person, with all the characteristics of personality raised to their highest power. Man must be a Person else he cannot enter into any individual relations with this Father who is a Person. Here we move in the world of the spirit, of the highest reality, for nothing is so real as personality. Out of this central fact and this spiritual likeness springs the possibility of a communion, not accidental, occasional or peculiar, but one which is the very heart of human life in its Christian interpretation.

We cannot put any divine benevolence or charity in the place of this relation with the Father. It is not created by the bestowal of any external benefits, or the conferring of material advantages, or even of intellectual or spiritual blessings. It is the fellowship of the soul with God. The person must meet the Person if all the perfections which can flow from one life into the other are to be realized. If it be so in our ordinary human relations it is far more so in the relation between God and man. For the heart of the Gospel is that Man is His child, and, as Augustine said long ago: "Thou hast made me for Thyself and my heart is restless till it find rest in Thee." Among the men of the Middle Ages this was not realized either in life or thought as a present or possible experience here, save indeed among the mystics who broke away from the path of orthodox teaching and followed the instinctive and insatiable desires of their own hearts. Even to the mystics God was an inscrutable being, not primarily a Father, and they hoped and dreamed of an intercourse which might perhaps be attained after long and bitter self-renunciation and hard and stern denial. The tenderness of the divine love which asks only for love failed to be seen.

The controversy over the Universal inevitably led to psychological investigations, or at least to logical en-

quiry, as to the processes of thought and the origin of
ideas. Instead of being satisfied with the earlier Realism
the movement of thought advanced to Nominalism in
which it found a better definition of the facts of human
thought and the processes of intellectual activity. Yet
as we see in the great debate over Individuation, the
psychological advance was checked when the richest results were at hand. The question naturally arises whether
after all there was any question here at all. The problem
as stated seems like a logical or verbal refinement resting
upon false interpretations of facts or abstractions which
were only necessary for thought or logic but with no
ground in objective reality. The debaters assigned to
these abstractions an existence or a reality beyond the
thinking mind, and thus regarding them as elements of
the real world, they asked themselves by virtue of what
principle did the individual or the particular separate
itself from the Universal, and in what relation did Matter
and Form stand to each other in this process. Yet these
differences and distinctions upon which they laid so much
stress were after all only for logic and had no real existence outside and apart from the objects or realities in
which they existed. If Matter has but a potential existence, called into being by spirit, how can it be the source
of the Individual as St. Thomas asserts? Had these students advanced far enough to examine into the meaning
of self-consciousness, they would have discovered that it
implies the individual. "I exist because I am conscious
of myself." This consciousness is, moreover, a simple and
unitary one, not a process which is continued from the
primary consciousness to the inference, implication or
conclusion of individuality. We do not need all this
scaffolding to explain the origin of self-consciousness or
of the being of the individual unless one is involved in
definitions of matter, which, to say the least, are purely
metaphysical and logical. Yet in spite of these limita-

tions there was a real advance in psychological science, and many of the problems were felt if not stated or solved. The force of church authority exercised perhaps an unconscious restraint upon further advance, for it was only when the mind freely took upon itself the task of exploring its own deeper meaning that there was any marked progress.

Aside from the indirect contributions there were many direct ones. The Schoolmen practically created the whole terminology of logic, philosophy and theology, and what they did not create they transmitted. Many of their theories, speculations and interpretations were adopted bodily by the Protestants and have been their bane or blessing according to the individual beliefs of the student of history. Many have helped and perhaps more have hindered, the true advance of thought. Most of the practices which produced the religious revolution of the Sixteenth Century were built upon or supported by the teaching of the Schoolmen, if they were not directly taught by them.

But turning from general considerations let us take a little closer view of the one who not only expresses most completely the spirit of the Schools, but who also gave to that spirit its finest and fullest expression.

Thomas Aquinas, the Angelic Doctor, the Angel of the School, stands out as the greatest theological figure of the Middle Ages and the foremost teacher of the great Thirteenth Century. He was preëminently a systematizer and not a great creative mind like Augustine. He arranged and grouped the accumulations of the past, but he stated no new principles which became the basis for new and independent thought. St. Thomas was born in 1225 or 1227. He was of noble birth and imperial descent. The blood of Barbarossa flowed in his veins and he was cousin to the great Emperor, Frederick the Second, that great enigma of the Mid-

dle Ages. He was born in Aquino in the kingdom of
Sicily and was early sent to Monte Cassino, the famous
foundation of Saint Benedict, for his education. The
troubles of the times made his stay there shorter than
perhaps it would otherwise have been, and he thence went
to Naples to continue his studies. His intense devotion,
his earnest and pure spirit were soon felt by those who
had an eye for a man. The new Mendicant Orders, the
Franciscans and the Dominicans, were already in the full
movement of their marvelous history. St. Thomas was
born only a year before St. Francis' death and yet when
he was still but a boy these two Orders were leading the
world.

They were drawing from all classes, and from all parts
of Europe, the young, the enthusiastic and the gifted.
The Dominicans had from the beginning marked out the
intellectual field as their own, although the rivalry between the two orders soon led the Franciscans into the
same path. The Dominicans, in spite of the bitter opposition of his family which went even so far as to use violence, eventually triumphed, and won to their order the
young man upon whom such great hopes were placed.
He was apparently only a boy when the great decision
was made, yet there is not a sign or hint that at any
time during that arduous and intense life he ever wavered
in his choice. As a Dominican he was sent to the North
to study under the greatest of the Order and one of the
greatest minds of the Middle Ages, Albert the Great.
The generous sympathy of the older man was not touched
by the least jealousy, and he did all in his power to
develop and enlarge the mind of his pupil. He early
prophesied that his voice would soon be heard, and heard
as no other voice of his age. The story of the years as
they pass is monotonous from the outside. There are
few, if any, striking events. His mind was buried in the
problems which were before the minds of the men of that

age. Albert the Great was the most learned man of his times, and his learning was not confined to the ordinary material of the Schools. His mind had ranged far and wide, and he had gathered together all that was then accessible to the seeker, in the path of knowledge. His was perhaps the most universal mind of the Middle Ages, and all that he had, and all that he saw, was poured into the soul of the most receptive pupil of his time.

Looking merely at the output of St. Thomas, as it is given in his published works, and recognizing the fact that he died in 1274, not fifty years old, it is hard to understand how he accomplished the mere physical labor involved. In addition to that, these brief years were filled with other tasks, for the Papacy, for his Order, and especially by his lectures to his students. Yet, in a way, all his work was of a very high order. He dealt with all the questions which were troubling the minds of men, and he also dealt with them in a spirit which always strove to give due weight to the arguments of his opponents. He often stated their positions better than they had been stated before. He answered them also in the same calm and deliberate tone, though in a clear and somewhat colorless style, which left no doubt about his meaning. He dealt with the least important parts of his argument with the same care and fullness that he devoted to the most important, and one is inclined to feel that he wasted a good deal of time and energy.

But it was the Middle Ages, and men's minds then were not so clear as now regarding the relative value and importance of things, or as to the real basis upon which affirmations have a right to be made. The subject of "the Angels," for instance, occupies an amount of space and an emphasis of thought which few would devote to the matter in our day. His greatest work, however, was left incomplete. One wonders if it ever could have been finished by his method and with the detailed attention he gave to it, in the course of a far longer life. But in the "Summa Theologica" the fundamental and essential aspects of the Scholastic Philosophy are at least suggested when they are not presented. The "Summa" became at once the handbook of the Schools and was quoted as an authority inferior to none by almost every writer and teacher of his own generation. Rivals of course arose and his system was submitted to some severe if not effective criticism, but it remained, and remains to this day, the authoritative exposition of the theology of the Latin Church. Recently there have been efforts made, by no less authority than the Pope himself, to have it used as a textbook in all the Roman schools, and to fix it as the standard of all theological judgments.

To examine in detail this attempt at a complete theology would be impossible. The criticisms of it run into volumes. The points in it which have been shown to be unsatisfactory and not in accordance with the larger knowledge since gained have been already indicated. Into the particular aspect of his work which relates to the subject in hand it will be necessary to go with more detail.

The question as to the meaning and value of Faith as presented by St. Thomas carries us into the very heart of medieval theology and to the conception of the Gospel which prevailed in that period. This conception was still the Latin. That is, it took the legal view that faith is primarily the acceptance of religious truth on the authority of either the Church or revelation. It was, fundamentally and psychologically, intellectual in its essence and meaning. It is true that Augustine was still regarded as the great authority and as the gifted creator of western theology, and St. Thomas was supposed simply to have given to it the medieval expression. Yet with respect to faith neither Augustine nor St. Thomas departed from the accepted standard of interpretation of this

fundamental subject. It had passed over to them from
the earlier period, during which the psychological character of faith as an inward state or relation of the soul
with God was changed to an intellectual acceptance of
theological formulas. So long, however, as the religious
assurance was purely objective, that is, resting upon
authority, there could be no sense of personal certainty,
nothing to meet and satisfy the growing individual consciousness of responsibility and personality which was
raising new spiritual demands.

In their fondness for definitions and distinctions the
Schoolmen attempted to express the meaning of faith in
new terms, or with refinements of expression, which had
no historical or even psychological grounds. We look in
vain in the New Testament for anything corresponding
to such terms as, Fides Implicita, Fides Explicita, Fides
Informis and Fides Formata which are of such universal
use in the writings of the Schoolmen. More than that,
excepting an occasional reference to St. Paul, which generally has nothing to do with his own statements about
faith, one might even conclude that he had written nothing and even thought nothing in particular upon this
subject. The whole section which St. Thomas devotes to
faith in his "Summa" does not seem to indicate the
slightest acquaintance with the passionately personal and
vivid consciousness with which St. Paul expresses himself on this matter. The subjective or psychological expression or definition of faith as described by St. Paul
nowhere appears. The whole conception of Aquinas was
conditioned by the legalistic and objective statement of
the New Law, the "Nova Lex," and consequently it had
primarily an intellectual character. This intellectual
character determines or conditions the process by which
Fides or Faith becomes the personal or subjective possession of the believer. Faith has its root in intellectual
knowledge. On this the belief rests, whether the knowl-

edge is the result of logical demonstration or that of acceptance on authority. It was in the same group of spiritual experiences with knowledge, as it appealed to the same side of the nature, that is, the intellect.

It was, in fact, however, on a lower plane and consequently of less value than what was defined as knowledge. In differentiating between knowledge and faith, which they classed under the same intellectual category, the Schoolmen attributed to knowledge a specific character of certainty. As a psychological experience, however, faith did not and could not possess this positive character of certainty which belongs to knowledge. Faith had, in a way, a certain resemblance to opinion, with which also it is contrasted, inasmuch as there is wanting to it that clear intellectual grasp or vision upon which knowledge is founded. Yet in order to save the authority of faith, and quite in contradiction with the theory, it is placed above knowledge. It is said to be of a higher order than knowledge because it rests upon the authority of the Veritas Prima. This Veritas Prima is the absolute ground or reason for accepting as true that which faith holds. What believes these truths is the human intellect. The intellect is moved to accept the truths not simply by their inherent truthfulness, but by the will which decides the mind to believe. At its roots, then, belief is an act of the will. A rather mechanical and artificial character is thus given to the whole process.

St. Thomas in his statements about Faith merely sets forth in perhaps more logical and scientific language the generally accepted position of the chief writers of the Middle Ages. Hugo of St. Victor asserted that faith was the certainty of the soul about things which were not present to it as contents of its own consciousness or as subjects of its own observation. Consequently it stands between opinion and knowledge. The former, opinion, is a lower and knowledge is a higher state than faith.

Hugo also insists upon the complexity of this state of faith, regarded from its psychological character. It is an act of the intellect because what is involved in it is a matter of knowledge. This follows from the fact that what is accepted contains what is believed. Hugo introduces here a distinction which St. Thomas does not seem to have adopted. He states that faith, in its essence, is an act of will, because that which as knowledge is offered to the mind for acceptance is held by the will to be true. This knowledge, however, is not what could be called scientific, but rather hearsay.

All this seems very abstract and lifeless when placed side by side with the New Testament, so simple, so direct, so personal and intimate. It was in fact an effort to put into scientific or theoretical form the immediate experience of the human soul with God. It failed because it did not realize the inwardness and spirituality of the Gospel of Christ. It made the intercourse of men with God dependent upon certain intellectual affirmations or apprehensions, or rather upon some interpretations of what the relations really were. As an actual basis for this experience of God what was called Grace was introduced and so emphasized that it was ultimately the whole expression of God. Grace in turn became operative only or chiefly through the Sacraments, and the whole of the Christian life was reduced to mechanical and material terms, and there was left no inward experience on which and by which the soul could live.

No sooner, however, had the complete exposition of the medieval theology found its statement through St. Thomas than a process of dissolution began. This was the result of the attack by one of the most vigorous and subtle minds that this whole period ever knew. The rival school of the Franciscans put forth as their champion, Duns Scotus, who immediately began the attack. No one in the long course of medieval thought was so in love with verbal refinements and verbal distinctions. Apparently there were no facts but words, and what could be done with them. Every ingenuity of logical distinction, every speculation which thought could suggest, became at once the basis for further inferences, until the mind was plunged into a blinding cloud of purely mental and verbal distinctions. Those monstrous terms, "Hæcceitas," and "Quidditas," with many others took the place of clear thinking. There was no appeal to experience or reality: for him the only realities were these subtleties whose twistings and turnings were the despair of his contemporaries. Out of it all arose in greater clearness and prominence the old "Double Truth," of knowledge and faith, of philosophy and religion. The latent skepticism of the scholastic system came now into full light. The human mind had gone as far as it could in this direction and finally turned in revolt from this world of empty words to the real facts of life. After its noble beginning and its long and triumphant course the end of Scholasticism was tragic enough. It fell into abject decay; it lost all relation with the living forces within which lay the future. The contempt of the world was poured upon the last of the Schoolmen and their methods in the scornful epithet, "Dunce"!

CHAPTER VII

MARTIN LUTHER AND THE REVOLUTION
OF THE SIXTEENTH CENTURY

"A change was coming upon the world, the meaning and direction of which even still is hidden from us, a change from era to era. The paths trodden by the footsteps of ages were broken up; old things were passing away, and the faith and the life of ten centuries were dissolving like a dream. Chivalry was dying; and all the forms, desires, beliefs, convictions of the old world were passing away, never to return. A new continent had risen up beyond the western sea. The floor of heaven, inlaid with stars, had sunk back into an infinite abyss of immeasurable space: and the firm earth itself, unfixed from its foundations, was seen to be but a small atom in the awful vastness of the universe. In the fabric of habit which they had so laboriously built for themselves mankind were to remain no longer.

"And now it is all gone—like an unsubstantial pageant faded; and between us and the old English there lies a gulf of mystery which the prose of the historian will never adequately bridge. They cannot come to us, and our imagination can but feebly penetrate to them. Only among the aisles of the cathedral, only as we gaze upon their silent figures sleeping on their tombs, some faint conceptions float before us of what these men were when they were alive; and perhaps in the sound of church bells, that peculiar creation of mediæval age, which falls upon the ear like the echo of a vanished world."

These remarkable words of Froude were true not only for England but for the whole of Europe. For the first time, what we call the modern world came into full view through the storms and darkness of the passing age. The times and the circumstances which indicate the beginnings of this new movement in history are not easy to determine, but far back in the past there are many signs of coming change. Thomas Aquinas, the culmination and fullest expression of the medieval spirit, completed his task, which was to endure forever, and went to his rest in 1274. Nine years before he died another Italian who was to bring to his land and to the world a far, far greater glory was playing in the streets of Florence never dreaming of his great fame and his great tragedy. He "in whom ten silent centuries found a voice," with the unerring instinct of his mighty genius, chose his own vulgar speech and despising all the traditions of the past, rejecting the stately Latin verse of even him whom he had chosen as his guide he spoke to the future in a language which has never died and which incarnated in it all the loftiness of his own soul, the noblest spirit of the past and the heroic dreams of the future. The difference between Aquinas and Dante shows the coming of a new spirit into the world.

Other events less important and much less far-reaching had already taken place. The dying St. Francis had seen the dream of his aspiring spirit destroyed by the iron hand of the Church and had gone broken-hearted to his grave. But his inspiration, though strangely misunderstood and distorted, still survived and created a spirit of revolt which tore the reorganized order with strife and bitterness, out of which sprang heresies and schisms. Old heresies of the past which had lived hidden in the dark corners of the world and in the dim hearts of men again began to play a part they had not played in centuries.

Under the great popes of the early thirteenth century the Church stood above all kingdoms, above even the empire itself. In the fourteenth century it had sunk to a mere tool of France and the great Babylonian Captivity had begun. The immense vitality of the institution is, however, revealed by the fact that after the long struggle was over it was able to return to Rome and renew, if with much diminished power, its former place not only in Rome but in Europe. Though its loss had been so immense, yet when the struggle began with the free political instincts of Europe and the new spirit of national life as represented by the Councils, it was able to defeat all the attempts at reform whether at Pisa, Constance or Basle and crowned, or seemed to crown, its victory by the burning of Huss and the death of Jerome of Prague.

Much has been said of the glories of the thirteenth century, but little or nothing of the silent misery, the hideous grossness, the widespread and overwhelming poverty. The enormous energy, the undying and inexhaustible vigor which rose above these terrible conditions reveal the immense power of that new desire which was springing up in the hearts of men. Still the stream was flowing toward the light and from many sources besides the invincible energy of the human soul new forces were coming to the slowly awakening mind of the western world.

That the Middle Ages really came to an end in the thirteenth century is evident because in that same period we see the coming into play of those very forces which were in their great evolution to be the dominant features of that later period which we call the Renaissance and Humanism. Two civilizations were struggling for existence in the fourteenth century, the old medieval ascetic ideal and the new and human ideal inspired by the aroused intelligence of the eager spirits who sought in the antique world of light and of knowledge the power to live in the wider world which was opening before their eyes.

The lingering echoes of a glorious past had ever haunted the mind of Europe and through it the great figure of Vergil had wandered, clothed with a strange halo and a mystic power. Beyond him lay another world whose outlines were only dimly imagined: the world of Greek art and Greek letters: the world of a mind free from the tyranny of ignorance and the authority of power; a world so splendid in its freedom and so magnificent in its accomplishments that men yearned to know only that they might wonder and admire. Slowly the past came back, the writings so long buried and forgotten became the great desire of many a seeking soul. Poor and lonely students pored over the dim pages not only of the great Latin writers, but of those whose names even they had never before heard. Besides Aristotle, whom they had first learned to know through the Saracens, and who had wrought so greatly that the world had a new history of thought built upon him, came another, the magic of whose thought and the charm of whose style made the shade of Aristotle fade away before the lofty spirit of Plato. The Revival of Learning, as it is called, is only the revival of the past, and it is a story of the most romantic interest. It throws over the squalor and barbarism of the centuries during which it grew a glory which has hidden from most eyes the hideous life which lay below. But it was not in the form of philosophy that the Greek first seized upon the minds of the men of the Renaissance, but rather as letters: that is, the expression of thought, emotion and life in literature.

No figure is so representative of the coming age, none so immediately significant of the approaching change, as Petrarch (1304-1374). The torch which Dante had lighted was passed to him but it shone with a different light and a less intense and somber beauty. The inspiration which led him was less personal and individual, it was drawn more from classic springs and was more in harmony with the rising spirit of his age. He saw the present less through his own eyes than through the eyes of the past. He turned resolutely and deliberately from the ideas and ideals of the ecclesiastical world of which he was a member to the freer and, as he believed, the nobler spirit of the past.

The Babylonian Captivity was practically coextensive with the life of Petrarch and he was at Avignon in the closest and most intimate contact with its inner life. His description of that life is such that no modern historian has dared to turn it from its Latin original into any of the languages of modern Europe. The picture is a ghastly one and though it may be that the court of the Pope was worse than the life of the lower clergy, yet it could not have existed as it was without the most debasing influence upon the whole life of the hierarchy. It was this perhaps, more than anything else, which did so much to arouse the indignation of the rulers and the people, causing them to insist so passionately upon the need for reform. How useless that demand was is shown by the next century, the Century of the Councils, as it has sometimes been called. Neither Pisa, Constance nor Basle were able to remedy the condition, and the account of the situation at Constance is one of the most disgusting possible. Meanwhile the Church, having fallen behind the intellectual interest and the moral aspirations of Europe, became a drag and a menace to the new life which was coming into the world. The political and social development out of which our modern world was to emerge had already begun. Before St. Thomas was born Magna Charta had been signed and the foundations for the political and religious freedom of England were laid. The Hundred Years War and the historical results dependent upon it were yet to be fought and found. But France was becoming the France of later generations, and the growth of the cities which is the characteristic social feature of the passing Middle Ages had already begun, and the feuds and rivalries, the intense social activities of a stirring life were creating a new type of human experience. The Holy Roman Empire was not yet a mere phrase of historical rhetoric, and Guelph and Ghibelline were terms to rouse the most passionate interest and already divided peoples, cities and kingdoms into two camps. But the great names of the future were to be no longer chiefly schoolmen, ecclesiastics and soldiers; others representing

new interests and forms of experience were to throw a
new splendor over the common life of man.

Giotto had pointed the way for the wonderful development of art in the days that were to come, but Petrarch
is still the name which stands for most, and has given the
stamp to the moving scenes of those shifting years. His
aim, in its widest definition, might be called that which
is associated with letters both ancient and modern, that
is, culture. It was the freedom of the soul, untrammeled
by precedent and unrestrained by arbitrary authority,
which he sought. As always, it was in poetry that this
spirit found its fullest satisfaction and its highest expression, and the poetry of Petrarch belonged to the type
which is fed by the classic spirit. His literary activity
was of the most varied character and his triumphant
career showed that a new field was opening in which such
a genius as his could play a higher part than had been
played for centuries. His passionate patriotism was mod-
eled after what he believed were the ancient traditions of
Rome, and the Latin spirit, blended with the new Italian
consciousness, made him the most representative man of
his age. Wide as his culture was and hospitable as his
spirit was, to all ideas, he never knew Greek, and the
deeper basis of the ancient culture was hidden from his
eyes. Yet in spite of these limitations he has been called
by many careful students, "The First Modern Man of
Letters."

It was his determination to walk in his own path, to
follow his own inspiration, and to live his own life, which
marks a new note in history. In a way he represents in
no imperfect manner the manifestation of that passionate
individualism which is one of the central forces of the
Renaissance, and has become one of the most striking
differences between the modern and medieval world. For
though there were men of the most notable and impressive
character in those earlier centuries, they did not have the

conscious purpose of developing their own lives and characters and making their own souls the object and aim of
their endeavors. To be themselves, and live again in the
full freedom of the boundless energies of which they were
becoming conscious, was the deliberate purpose of the
most powerful and energetic spirits of the coming world.
Men found other and greater interests than hitherto, and
theology occupied in their minds another place than that
which it held in the Middle Ages.

The world beyond, which had absorbed the attention,
fascinated the eye, and filled the imagination to the ex-
clusion of all else, finally found its fullest and most
splendid expression in Dante, and then suddenly and
swiftly passed away and gave place to a new and intense
preoccupation with this present life. The two great
authorities which had dominated the Middle Ages: the
classical heritage with its intellectual energy and splendor, and the church doctrine which was said to be above
and beyond reason, and rested for its power upon divine
revelation, now stood in directly opposite relations. In
the earlier period the classical element was subordinated
to the theological and ecclesiastical. Now the classical
was placed supreme and a long struggle began which is
not yet ended, but during which the theological never
regained its earlier supremacy.

Over against the authority which the Schoolmen represented, rose another force destined, in its effects, to dis-
solve all the structures and the very authority which the
medieval life had obeyed with fear and awe, that is, the
spirit of free inquiry. The individual now came to take
a place in the conscious life which the mass had never
possessed. A new standard of values was set up in the
claims which were not only asserted but realized for the
individual soul as such and everywhere. In the long past
the "a priori" of authority, both ecclesiastical and intellectual, had been the foundation of all thought and action,

and the ascetic interpretation of life was accepted in the same spirit. Now began a new method of thought, springing out of the very schools themselves, with Friar Bacon as its first representative, as Francis Bacon was its highest. This method was "the experimental" one. The testing of facts, the examination of reality, not only in nature, but in thought, and the gradual construction of a new world built upon foundations hitherto either unknown or despised, were the final results. The very earth which had been ignored became the teacher for the new spirits who sought the secrets not only of time but of eternity. Now for the first time since the ancient world had passed away, with all its struggles and all its glory, the rights of reason were proclaimed with joy and exultation, and over against the blind and ignorant faith demanded of all, was declared the inalienable right and duty of man to think and search.

Italy had lighted the fire of the new learning and Italy was looked upon as the Sacred Soil by every one who yearned for more light and more knowledge. The glamour of her great achievement led men from far and wide into the same path. Down to the land of sunshine and wide skies, down to the home of ancient learning and liberty the men of the North flocked as five centuries and more they had gone to the Holy Land. In spite of all that is repellent and brutal, in spite of its arrogant skepticism and physical grossness, the passion for knowledge, the weary labors to achieve, the unlimited renunciation for its sake, make this period of one of the noblest pages in the history of the human mind.

The singular individuality of the most striking of these men, as for example that of Pico della Mirandola, has too often been assumed to be the product of the studies pursued. This peculiar individuality is regarded as a rebirth of the antique spirit, but this is true only so far as the thoughts and forms of expression are con-

cerned. In reality this new type was a rebirth of the
original humanity. These men felt as men of no generation had felt for centuries, the joy simply of life itself
and the delight of the free exercise of all their human
faculties. The background against which they stood was
the ascetic metaphysics of the Middle Ages with its
earnest and fearful outlook on the other world. To such
a view of life man's present existence and this present
world were only preliminary and painful. Against this
the men of the Renaissance reacted with passionate vigor,
and they found in the classical culture that which would
strengthen the new spirit though it did not create it. It
did, however, help to give a pagan tone to life and
stamped the whole movement with an air of revolt.

At this same time another event of the greatest importance added impetus to the spread of knowledge and the
independence of the scholar. The invention of printing
like the invention of the steam engine three centuries
later was revolutionary. As the latter changed the whole
social structure so printing revolutionized the whole field
of education. It was the invention of the people and not
of the princes, and whatever it might do and did do for the
princes and scholars, it did more for the people. When
the new knowledge came it flooded Europe with new light.
Words showed they had hands and feet, as Luther said,
and they went everywhere. They wrought in the souls
of men as nothing else, not even acts of councils or decrees of Popes. Ideas are as invisible as air and yet carry
with them life or death as was soon to be seen. Before
the days of printing books were scarce and costly, and
in many cases only manuscripts of the most imperfect
character and in the worst condition were available.
With the new invention followed the whole branch of
textual criticism which was not much less important than
the possession of the text itself. In addition books became cheap, or relatively so, and the new process led

almost immediately to such splendid results that the best examples of the great printers of this age stand alone. Important, however, as this may be, the chief value of printing lay in the fact that one who could read became his own teacher, and he who had a library had all the essential elements of a university.

In the field of theology itself a great change was taking place or had taken place. Duns Scotus, in his reaction against St. Thomas had dissolved and destroyed the stately and elaborate structure which represented the culmination of the Aristotelian scholasticism. This ultimately led either to a contempt for all intellectual constructions or to a plain declaration of the inability of man either to understand or accept, in any living way, the dogmas which were set forth on the authority of the Church. The dogmas were accepted as true, but no one could possibly know whether they were true or not, and the irrational character of all belief was declared or implied in the ironic logic of the Nominalists. If all the rational conceptions upon which dogma rested, or seemed to rest, were destroyed, the intellect could only submit without understanding or comprehending the dogma. To the great body of the faithful the Gospel became only a mass of affirmations which one must believe without reflection and without love. This was what was meant or implied by the term, "Fides Implicita." The skepticism of Occam thus led only to a blind obedience.

Theology as a science or a rational process of human thought was ruined and all study became merely an idle discussion of empty abstractions, which had no profit for the intellect and no value for the inner life. Such a condition of the higher field of thought would, and did, inevitably lead to reactions upon the life of the people of the most unfavorable kind. To these the Gospel of Jesus Christ was in reality either unknown and entirely neglected, or it became for them merely a mass of religious observances, practices and works, which were recognized by the Church as meritorious. If this was the condition to which organized and official religion had come, yet there were within it and still more without it, evidences of a different spirit.

Individualism, the sense of the value of the personal and individual life of the common man, had appeared in the religious realm as at once the impulse and the consequence of the Franciscan movement, and was slowly spreading through all these centuries. This in spite of the defeat and untimely decay of the real Franciscan aim. In the generations immediately following many of the new phases of religious thought took on the character of heresy, or at least were tainted by it, in the eyes of the Church. In many cases this was undoubtedly true, but Wycliffe and his follower, John Huss, were far nearer in spirit to the mind and motive of Christ than their enemies and destroyers. Not in England only or Bohemia, but far and wide through the Rhine country and in quiet groups a new lay spirit of piety was silently working. The longing for better lives, the wistful yearning for fellowship and communion with the Master, the pathetic efforts to shape their lives as He would wish, the lonely struggles in a world so hard and so gross, the brutality and the cruelty which frightened and shocked these tender spirits, all this has been told again and again. Yet all these souls were still under the power and swayed by ideals which were passing away. The darkness was still too thick for them to do more than catch a faint glimpse of that great world of light for which their souls longed.

The humble efforts of earnest and pious souls to lift their generation a little higher toward the light must always be of singular interest and significance. The Brethren of the Common Life have left their mark both on the history of piety and the history of learning. One of their members founded a school at Deventer in the fourteenth century and, strange to say, these humble souls were among the first to welcome and introduce into the North the new learning, which came as a breath of life, from that far-off land of the South. Two names stand out among their scholars, utterly unlike in every way, except perhaps in their testimony to their teachers. They were not contemporaries, but the wide gulf which separates them shows how completely the horizon had changed in one generation. Thomas à Kempis died soon after Erasmus was born, and to many he is far better known than the great humanist, but for his own day and generation Erasmus is the outstanding figure. About the personal life of Thomas we know little, but about Erasmus and the European world of his day, we know much and we know it at first hand.

Desiderius Erasmus was born at Rotterdam, October 27, 1466. Both he and his older brother were love-children, born out of wedlock, and lost both parents while still very young. The father had attempted to provide for their future, but the guardians to whom the property was entrusted promptly proceeded to rob the children. Then in order to protect themselves they took measures to dispose of them as so many helpless children were disposed of, by putting them in a monastery. Erasmus was a fair-haired, blue-eyed, delicate child who had even when very young struck his teachers with his unusual ability. These very gifts of his were used against him and he was told how great the opportunities would be for carrying on the studies which he loved. So, like Luther, he entered the order of the Augustinians, in a monastery at Stein, near Gouda. He was a monk at nineteen and later he was ordained priest. A closer contact with the monastic life dissipated all his hopes and dreams of its glory. In those years he learned a deep and undying hatred of monks and of the whole monastic system. He hated their stupidity; he hated their dullness and coarseness; he hated their ignorance and brutality with a hatred which never abated to the day of his death. And he hated Fish!! He said his head was Catholic, but his stomach was Protestant and the horrors of those years he never forgot and he never forgave.

Soon, however, he was able to break away from the confinement and associations of the cloister and was chosen as secretary to the Bishop of Cambrai. The desire of his heart was to be gratified. It is singular, but striking, that he never seems to have had any interest in the studies which were pursued in the schools. The "New Learning," the classical world, now being rediscovered was the very heart of all his ambition from the first day until the last. He went to Paris, and after some years' study there his wanderings and his writings began. He went from France to England, from England to Germany, from Germany to France and Italy and the endless round kept on. He was driven by some instinct, some insatiable thirst, which never let him abide and never let him be silent wherever he went. And it was always the same; wherever he was, the sparkling wit, the winning spirit, the eager longing for light won him the friendship of the best and the bravest in that new world which was still in its dawn. Popes, cardinals, bishops, emperors, kings, princes, scholars, students in every land welcomed this new spirit, so full of knowledge and inspiration, so ardent for the best things of the mind. His writings went through many editions, and his attacks upon the dullness of the leaders of the old schools, and the methods so long in use, won him a fame which brought letters and praise from all sides.

When Erasmus began, Luther was but a boy, and remained for long years unknown, and even when known drew from the great Humanist no particular sympathy. Erasmus was a man of letters. His interest was in learning; his aim was knowledge. His sympathies were generous, but he wished to live a quiet life, and thought that the great matters which really concerned the welfare of the world should be settled by men of learning and not brought into open debate before an ignorant and incompetent crowd. Besides, many of the questions which were moving the spiritual life of the world made no appeal to him. His nature was neither deep nor passionate. To many earnest men he seemed but a trifler, and the wild tumult of soul through which Luther passed was something of which he knew nothing, could understand nothing and perhaps cared nothing. Their aims were different, and a natural antagonism, not only of method but of purpose, lay between them. The calm and somewhat scornful spirit of the man of letters hated indeed with fastidious dislike the grossness of life; but the moral loathing and the awful horror for the spiritual degradation of soul which moved Luther seemed to him but wild exaggeration and needless emotion. He did sympathize with many of the things for which the reformers were struggling, but his method was that of slow and steady education, and a gradual removal of the most objectionable things in the existing order. He did not understand the real issue.

That issue was,—which was the greater evil,—to endure the corruptions or to rebel? Erasmus did neither; hence the pathos of his career. The years carried him into unknown waters and stormy seas where he could not pilot his vessel. His later days were harassed and vexed with endless complaints. As the struggle deepened reproaches and demands from both sides made his life miserable and he might well cry out: "A plague on both your houses!" He died suspected by the mass of Catholics and disliked by the mass of Protestants. Only the few on both sides who still preserved a sense of the real value of letters thought sadly and spoke kindly of the great scholar who had done so much and yet seemed to have done so little. His contributions were, as we all know, very great, but new and more powerful figures were coming on the scene who in the very fury of the storm rose to heights the little scholar could not reach. At the very crisis of the century, when the forces stood face to face for a life-and-death struggle, the one whom both Holbein and Dürer delighted to paint passed to the rest he had so long sought and never found. Much that he did is now forgotten except by those who care for the things of the mind, but the edition of the Greek Testament which he published in 1516 gave the impulse to and became the foundation of modern Biblical scholarship. It shook forever the authority of the Vulgate and opened the door to a new movement in a field which had not been worked in centuries.

Another name far less known, but of great importance in the preparatory work of the new reform was another German, a contemporary, but an older contemporary of Erasmus. John Reuchlin, whom, with Erasmus, Hutten called "The eyes of Germany," was born at Pforzheim in the Black Forest in 1455. He was therefore eleven years older than Erasmus. After studying in different places in Germany he finally went to Paris and it was there that his career as a scholar really first began. He traveled much and studied much. He visited Italy like all the young and eager spirits of his age, and finally settled at Basle and began to teach. He was a born teacher and with his commanding presence and eager interest in the new learning he gained a wide influence. His fame spread until he was regarded as the first humanist of Germany. When he added Hebrew, which was almost, if not entirely unknown, to his list of accomplishments, he was easily the first man of learning in his native land. His position and authority were so firmly established that he became a final court of appeal to all who had any position in the world of letters.

In the year 1509 an event took place which was to give him a new position before the world. One John Pfeffer-korn, a converted Jew, "ein getauft juden," believed that it was for the best interests not only of his former co-religionists, but also for the cause of the Church, that all Hebrew books should be burned. This preposterous plan was received with great approval by many ecclesiastics, and by all the ignorant and bigoted in the Church. But theological zeal did not have quite the free hand it once had had, and the authorities, before whom this scheme was placed, laid the whole matter before Reuchlin. He of course gave judgment against it and his opponents were furious. The Dominicans, who at this time held the desirable office of inquisitors for all Germany and were preëminently the heresy-hunters of the day, prepared for war. The theologians of Cologne and all who sympa-thized with them united against this one man. In their eyes Reuchlin was thrice damned. First for knowing anything at all; secondly for knowing two more lan-guages than any of them knew, and thirdly for knowing the accursed language of the Jews who were the enemies of Christ and his Church. This was neither the first nor the last time in history when men have aimed at a litera-ture the bitter hostility they felt for the people who cre-ated it.

The whole affair was infinitely stupid, but the cry went out, and the whole pack of theologians, ecclesiastics, monks and rabble were banded together against the first scholar of Germany. It was a clear warning to the hu-manists, if any was needed, of what was before them if they continued in the direction they were now moving. To the scattered and independent groups of young and ardent students this attack was like the blast of a bugle. The attack on Reuchlin indeed failed, but what had hitherto been but an uneasy and restless movement gained clearness and force. Men knew that something more was coming. This was but the first skirmish before the battle. The reply which came from the Humanists was one of the fiercest blows yet struck, the scornful and contemptuous volume containing the "Epistolæ Obscurorum Virorum." This was overwhelming, and the ridicule it excited and displayed deepened the bitterness and hate of the solid body of conservatives.

The French Humanists were, almost without exception, favorable to reform. They were offended not only by the ignorance, but by the grossness of the common life of the mass of the clergy. The old controversies and the wretched debates about scholastic subtleties irritated them as they breathed the freer and purer air of the new inspiration. This unanimity remained unbroken until the struggle had become one of arms and not of minds. Even in the latter case we find that all the reformers had passed through the school of Humanism. Also this passion for letters was, in many cases, united to a deep and tender piety. As has been said of them: "They celebrated the double triumph of piety and science, of the classics and the Gospel. They were at the same time disciples of Christ and of the classic tradition. The word 'Christus' was printed in capitals and was for them the secret of life."

What they earnestly and faithfully sought was a real and true knowledge of the Scriptures. They wished to remove all the medieval growths and accretions. They wanted to bring about a peaceful reform without withdrawing from the Catholic Church. The prevailing attitude of these men was sweetness and toleration. As the course of events unfolded itself their position became more and more difficult. The reform took on a character which seems to be in harmony with the French spirit, with its love of logic and clear definition. A new dogmatism thus arose, opposed to the old, and created an impossible situation for persons of a generous and tolerant dispo-

sition. These had no vocation for martyrdom, and many
of them could echo the phrase of Rabelais, "They were
reformers only as far as the stake."

Among the best-known of this class of scholars and
thinkers were LeFèvre d'Étaples, Berquin, Briçonnet,
Sadolet, Moroto, Rabelais, Margaret of Navarre. Of
these d'Étaples is the best example to illustrate the religious situation in France at this time. Jaques LeFèvre
d'Étaples, or as he was known in the world of letters,
Jacobus Faber Stapulensis, was born in Picardy about
1450 and died in 1533, three years before Erasmus. He
early went to Paris to pursue his studies and afterwards
to Italy. The awakening spirit of the new learning moved
him deeply and yet the ordinary attitude of many of the
humanists did not appeal to him. It was the matter and
not the manner that he chiefly sought. A pious and
earnest soul, he was strongly drawn to the study of Scripture and prepared new versions of most of the books of
the New Testament, the object of which was to lead men
to a better and truer understanding of them. In his
exegesis he sought to discover the actual meaning of the
writings as it was understood and intended by the writers
themselves. Consequently he went below and beyond the
traditional meaning as expressed either in the patristic
or scholastic interpretations. A young and ardent band
of pupils gathered around him, but when they were asked
to go to Meaux with Bishop Briçonnet to purify and revive the Church the outcome was inevitable. The rising
opposition of the ultra-conservatives was arrayed against
them. In the very year that Luther threw down the gage
of battle to the Church LeFèvre also challenged the established views. This ultimately led to the condemnation of
all such opinions by the Sorbonne. In vain d'Étaples
tried to occupy a middle ground and prove his faith by
accepting the customary practices and ceremonies of the
Church. Yet his heart was with the reformers, and his

disciples carried to their logical conclusions the principles which governed his own thinking. When he died both sides claimed him, but his convictions and principles became in reality the foundation, upon which the later French reformers built. The issue was already drawn. The common impulse which lay at the heart both of the French and the German was the same in spite of the fact that the French was an independent growth, having its roots in the national mind and spirit and was not a mere reflection or adaptation of the German. Hence the stigma of heresy which was already placed upon the more vigorous and more radical German movement was not transferred to the French school of innovators. Yet there was a profound difference between them and this difference became more evident as the movement developed.

One likes to linger over these great beginnings and these new spirits. In a way they seem more intelligible than the greatest and can be measured by standards which are, and have been, in use for centuries. It is when one comes to a figure of one who stands apart from and above even the great men of his day that one feels how ineffective are the methods and inadequate the standards hitherto in use.

Martin Luther towers above his generation and his world as perhaps no other figure in history. He is unlike any other man either before or since. His strength is so great, his gifts so many, his figure so massive and huge, that his very faults and defects rise to a measure beyond those of other men. No one has been more bitterly hated and none more passionately loved. The hatred is so great that it has lived three hundred years, and men write of him to-day with the bitter anger of a contemporary. He still stands for millions as the one enemy in all the long history of the Church for whom there is no forgiveness. No charge so vile, no slander so base, that it has not been repeated and believed. Great as was the number he roused against him in his life, the number since his death has been vaster and more formidable.

And he has been loved as it has been given to few men to be loved. Loved not in an intellectual and sympathetic manner, not in any calm and detached fashion, but with an ardor and passionate devotion, with an intimate and personal affection which few have ever called out in the same way. His faults and his virtues, his strength and his weakness are not merely historical facts, but living experiences to men removed from him by three centuries of time and by an almost infinite distance in ways of life and thought, education and culture.

The forces which had been at work for three hundred years met in him. "His spirit was the battle ground of two ages." The struggle which had been begun by the Humanists was, in a way, blind and ineffective. The reform which Erasmus and the religious humanists aimed at was an impossibility. They started with the assumption of an Infallible Church, and this conception was based upon the traditions and decrees of the past, including in these the scholastic theology as the full and final expression of ultimate truth. To attempt to reform such an institution was not only undesirable, but impossible. Between the two points of view as represented by the Church and the Humanists there was a fundamental opposition of ideas.

Luther says of himself that he was a peasant and the son of a peasant, and his character shows the marks of this close and intimate relation with the fundamental facts of life, just as in the case of Burns, Carlyle and Lincoln. His whole life was hard and stern. He met the fierce face of things in childhood, and all his years were years of toil and strife. The most striking thing about him is his enormous energy. In the days of his fiercest struggles he worked with a fury which was more like that of a force of nature than of mere human energy. In the violence of his toil he forgot either to eat or sleep, and he kept up this titanic effort month after month and year after year. In those sixty-four years of life he changed the whole course of European history. He lived in a great age, and yet in a very marked way he rises above all other men, not simply by his gifts, or by that which he accomplished, but by the sheer weight and mass of his being.

It is hard to find words to tell just what he was and how he impressed men, but in the words of Gulliver, there is an approach, when he described the Brobdindnagian: "He appeared as tall as an ordinary spire steeple, and took about ten yards at every stride." He moved as no other one did with a freedom and sweep which included the whole range of human emotion. He was the greatest humorist of his day even though that age held Rabelais. He exhibited an infinite variety of moods, the swift passage from tenderness to sternness, from playfulness to the deepest and most somber passion, from a coarse jest to the awful sense of the infinite mystery of life. His humor was neither the broad, genial and sunny laughter of Shakespeare, the sparkling wit and malice of Voltaire, nor the bitter and mordant scorn of Swift. It was more like the fury and volcanic explosions of Carlyle which often ended in a hearty laugh. How tender and how deep he was two familiar examples will make at once clear. The first is his letter to his son.

"Grace and peace in Christ, my dear little son. I am pleased to see that thou learnest thy lessons well, and prayest diligently. Do thus, my little son, and persevere; when I come home I will bring thee a fine 'fairing.' I know of a pretty garden where merry children run about that wear little golden coats, and gather nice apples and pears, and cherries, and plums under the trees, and sing and dance, and ride on pretty horses with gold bridles and silver saddles. I asked the man of the place, whose the garden was, and whose the children were. He said, 'These are the children who pray and learn, and are good.' Then I answered, 'Dear sir, I also have a son who is called Hans Luther.

May he not also come into this garden, and eat these nice pears and apples, and ride a little horse and play with these children?' The man said, 'If he says his prayers, and learns and is good, he too may come into the garden; and Lippus and John may come, and when they all come back, they shall have pipes and drums and lutes and all sorts of stringed instruments, and they shall dance and shoot with little crossbows.' Then he showed me a smooth lawn in the garden laid out for dancing, where hung pipes of pure gold, and drums and beautiful silver crossbows. But it was still early, and the children had not dined. So I could not wait for the dance, and said to the man, 'Dear sir, I will go straight home and write all this to my dear little son Hans, that he may pray diligently and learn well and be good, and so come into this garden; but he has an aunt, Lena, whom he must bring with him.' And the man answered, 'So it shall be: go home and write as you say.' Therefore, dear little son Hans, learn and pray with a good heart, and tell Lippus and John to do the same, and then you will all come to the beautiful garden together. Almighty God guard you. Give my love to aunt Lena, and give her a kiss for me. In the year 1530—
"Your Loving Father,
"MARTIN LUTHER."

The other letter is to the Chancellor Bruck:

"I have lately, on looking out of the window, seen two wonders: the first, the glorious vault of heaven, with the stars, supported by no pillar and yet firmly fixed; the second, great thick clouds hanging over us, and yet no ground upon which they rested, or vessel in which they were contained; and then, after they had greeted us with a gloomy countenance and passed away, came the luminous rainbow, which like a frail thin roof nevertheless bore the great weight of water."

His sagacity was instinctive, even in matters which were apparently outside the circle of his actions or his interests. Again and again he opposed the judgments of the political leaders and guides of his party, and in almost every instance he was right and they were wrong. His convictions in all these cases were based upon his religious faith and not his political experience. The cardinal instance which is urged against this conclusion is his attitude in the Peasant War. Here he opposed the peasants violently, fiercely, and at times, it seems, really brutally and cruelly. His words have been repeated again and again, and it is said he forever alienated the poor, oppressed classes to whom his Gospel had first come as a new and glorious revelation of a nobler life. That his attitude here seems wrong cannot be denied. Neither can the fact that the conduct of the peasants was such as to provoke fear and horror be denied. That Luther was in complete sympathy with their aims can be clearly proven, but the means they used were abhorrent to his whole nature. It was inconsistent with the thought of the Gospel that such means should be used, and we know it was only reluctantly, half-heartedly, and later in life, that he even accepted the position that subjects could take arms in defense of their faith against the lawful rulers of the land. He had no faith in the arms of the flesh, and that he compromised at all, is only stronger evidence that his inner conviction was against such a theory.

With each new need of his country and his age he seemed to develop a new faculty or power. His passion for music, which never left him from the days of his childhood to the sad years when he was drawing to his end, made him feel the worth and power of song in the service of God. So, in the simplicity of his soul, he set out to meet this need, with no dream of doing anything more than to give metrical and rhythmical form to his spirit of worship. Among his hymns some have remained in use ever since, and the greatest of all, "Ein Feste Burg," became what Heine called it, "The Marseillaise of the Reformation," and to-day it still has power to stir the soul like a trumpet. His fame as a preacher spread through all the land. There had been none like him before, and, in his power, none like him since. It was not only the simplicity, directness, truth and weight of his language, but the intense passion of the man which beat like a bell in every word he spoke.

If anything were needed to prove how little learning has to do with the life of the soul itself, that is, with the very heart and meaning of existence, Luther would and did reveal it with tremendous power. It is here that his difference from and superiority to the humanists comes most clearly in view. The humanists opposed the old order as vehemently as Luther but from a very different standpoint. Asceticism which is always one of the signs and symptoms of a degenerate and decaying social ideal or culture, was scornfully and bitterly attacked by the humanists. Against this pessimistic asceticism they set a vigorous and optimistic individualism whose root was largely æsthetic and intellectual. This æsthetic cosmopolitanism had, however, no appreciation of the common man or the coming democratic movement. Its religious character too was largely moral and critical with no creative or constructive power behind it or within it. The deep longing and passion for salvation, a salvation which should be immediate and personal, did not appeal to them. They either did not feel it or they did not fully understand it. Consequently they could not and did not avoid becoming a band of select, aristocratic intellectualists who made no appeal to the deep heart of life, nor to the common race struggling with the sorrows and temptations of a bitter existence. Man was more than mind and to the humanity of the soul humanism had, in the last analysis, nothing to offer.

Luther's standpoint was entirely different. At bottom it was neither theoretical nor scientific; hence much of the difficulty which later expositors have found when they have sought to build up a Lutheran system of theology. Everything was with him practical and religious, and the impulse which guided him was the longing for a truth,

primarily for life and not for thought only. He wished
for some common, living source of energy and being, for
himself and for others, but the energy of a life-giving
power is there. This came to him not as a matter of sudden inspiration or the happy discovery of a moment. It
sprang out of the very travail and agony of his soul. He
wanted to be with God. He nearly died in the struggle to
realize or attain to this union. He puzzled all his teachers
and filled many of his comrades with anger and scorn.
He felt himself alone and apart from the life of the world
of his own day. Yet no man lives outside of or uninfluenced by the actual life around him. Especially is this
the case with men of great and original endowment, the
great thinkers, the great poets, the great reformers.
They gather into their own bosom all the currents of
thought, emotion, longing and hope of the hidden life of
their world. This was peculiarly true in the case of
Luther and was the explanation and reason of his power.
One of his own countrymen has put it very truly: "What
Luther said, all men knew long before; but Luther said
it." "Was Luther sagt, das wusste man langst; aber
sagte es Luther!"

In spite of the hardships of his youth the eager soul
found health and help in the poor circumstances of his
life. It seems but a barren soil for such a great growth,
but as has been well said: "What the lion eats, turns to
lion." The path was hard, rough, and bare through those
early years but it led him in due time to Erfurt. This
university was the one of all others in Germany where
the new spirit was working most strongly. The youth
there had caught the light that was spreading over all
Europe. The studies were those still customary in all the
great schools founded chiefly on Scholastic methods, but
some of the teachers infused a new sense of freedom and
energy into the work of the schools. What few indications we have show that the young boy of eighteen was

keenly alive to his opportunities. Luther had entered
with the intention of studying law. While he was passing
through the regular course of studies other thoughts were
troubling his mind and his spirit was stirred by strange
and perplexing questions. He had been brought up
strictly and piously, for his father though a hard, stern
man was an honest and God-fearing one.

Before those college years were passed the whole career
he had planned was swept away by a new stream which
bore him into a strange and wonderful future. The
reasons for his becoming a monk have been stated again
and again. But outward events often pass human lives
without making any impression, and the thunderstorm
which made him vow to leave the world was only the occasion, not the cause, of this great change in his life. Sufficient that he entered the Augustinian monastery in Erfurt
in 1505 when he was but twenty-two years old. He was
a most rigid and obedient monk. He rose rapidly in the
esteem of his convent and in 1511 he was sent on a mission to Rome. The Renaissance was at its height. At this
very time Michael Angelo was painting the Sistine Chapel,
for we know that it was finished before 1512. Yet all the
glory of the present and the tragedy of the past in that
marvelous city, swept by his unseeing eyes and left no
trace either in his mind or his memory. Other thoughts
were haunting him and other dreams were working con-
fusedly in the soul of that poor, unknown, beggar monk.

Almost immediately after his return from Rome he was
sent to the newly established University of Wittenberg
where the rest of his life was spent. His brilliant talents
and his energy of character soon made him the leading
figure there. New work opened up before him, though at
each step he shrank from the new responsibilities. He
was made teacher of theology and also preacher in the
City Church. The unknown strength and unexpected
powers of the man were revealed by these new opportuni-

ties. Men felt that a new force was at work the outcome of which no one could see.

The date October 31, 1517, is regarded as the birthday of the Protestant Reformation but it did not in the least mean anything of that kind to him. It was simply his personal protest made in the customary manner against something which he felt was working frightful injury. The subject of Indulgences has been threshed over for generations; yet when one considers, not the refinements, qualifications, explanations, and subtleties of the theologians and ecclesiastics, but the mind of the people to whom these offers were made, it becomes another and very simple matter. They thought and believed that they had the opportunity to purchase for money, not only the remission of penalties for past sins, but the permission or freedom to commit future ones. There does not seem to be the slightest doubt that this was the common opinion. Against this the whole nature of Luther revolted. It was the most anxious and eager desire of his own soul to find peace, to obtain forgiveness of sins and victory over that inclination or disposition out of which all sins, not only of the mind but the heart, ultimately spring. To such a man this whole transaction seemed a dreadful sacrilege, not only against God, but against the human soul. He therefore flung himself against it with all the energy and passion of his nature. He did not look forward in the least. He supposed and expected that the whole wretched business would be at once stopped by the authorities so soon as they realized what was being done.

His words thrilled Germany as none it had heard in years. He himself was driven by his own indignation to speak, but he left it to other and wiser hands to settle the problem. Immediately, however, a bitter controversy sprang up, which sooner or later involved not only the scholars and theologians, but the whole mass of the people. He was only thirty-four years old at the time, and was thinking chiefly of his own busy life in the quiet little town where he had been sent. But down beneath the endless labors, his soul was struggling with problems which he found few could understand and fewer still could sympathize with. He plunged into the study of the Scriptures, and by his lectures delivered with no patristic or scholastic explanations, he roused an interest in the Bible that had not been felt in centuries. With each new struggle he was driven to a further study and to a much clearer realization of what was really moving him and which was slowly revealing the real meaning of his life.

The great year, the "Annus Mirabilis," the year 1520 had come. Luther was at the height of his power. He was now thirty-seven years old, and the long travail had brought him clearness and courage. The three great documents of this period, "The Address to the German Nobles," "The Babylonian Captivity," and "The Freedom of the Christian Man," are the most perfect expression of the inner meaning and purpose of his own life and of the movement itself. Never since has a clearer, broader, more triumphant statement of the essential meaning of Protestantism been made than what is set forth in these three tracts. Nowhere else either does one find so perfectly stated what is in the heart and soul of a man. At once he rose before the world to the stature he has ever since occupied in the eyes of all people of discernment. He carried Germany in the hollow of his hand, and no one before or since has expressed the inmost desires and spirit of the national soul as did this humble, simple monk of Wittenberg. Whether one likes him or dislikes him, this fact stands assured, that he made the Gospel something to men that it had not been since the beginning, the reconciling and vitalizing force of all the nobler and higher activities of human society and of the human soul. The whole of the world and the entire breadth and variety of human life, in all its manifold forms of expression, were gathered together in the largeness and strength of Christ's living inspiration.

At last the great day came when he was called before the rulers of the earth. The Emperor in person, the Pope through his representatives, the princes and nobles of all Germany were gathered together there at Worms, and the man who had troubled Israel was called upon to recant and repent. Many writers are fond of describing this scene as one wherein a poor, unknown monk threw down a bold and defiant challenge to the whole world of established authority. If this be the case Luther did not feel so or say anything to justify such a view. He was not in the least bold. He was a brave man, but he admits that he was very much frightened, so much frightened in fact that he became confused by those great figures and those stern and hostile eyes. He asked for time—delay. When he did at last answer, it was in no arrogant manner, and when he was dismissed and came to his friends, he cried out, "I am through, I am through." He had no thought of himself except a fear lest he should fail to speak the truth. What God had made clear to him, that he must stand by. He was only a young monk, conscious of his ignorance, conscious also of his rashness. He was bold about one thing only, that was the truth as God had made him see it. What happened to him was of no importance. Strangely unlike the popular champion he is so often represented to be.

It is said that he stood for "Freedom of Conscience." Undoubtedly he did but not as is so often understood. If it is meant that he stood for the right of each man to do and to think what seemed best in his own eyes and to his own conscience, it can only be said that nothing would have seemed more bewildering to him than this. He stood for the truth which he felt God had revealed to him. It was for this truth and this alone that he made his stand. The truth had seized him and he was simply a servant of

it. He was not claiming any right of freedom for himself, but what he did claim was that when once the truth
had come to a soul that soul must submit itself to that
truth and obey God and follow Him. There does not
seem to be the least self-consciousness in the man, and he
made no claims whatever for his own judgment or opinion
as such. "Show me that this is not God's truth. Prove
out of His word that I am wrong. Give me the truth and
I will obey it for it is the voice of God." Such humility
may seem to some more like ignorance or arrogance, but
it can hardly be said to be the declaration of independence in the sense so frequently imputed to his words.
There is much that goes to show he did feel the value and
importance of full liberty of conscience and yet it is not
his primary thought, for the fact is he did not consistently
hold it through life. Most men of his generation felt
much as he did. Later on when Calvin burned Servetus
there was a general chorus of assent if not of approval.
None who believed in the freedom of conscience, as we
now understand it, could possibly have either approved
or sympathized with that hideous tragedy.

When the Old and the New stood face to face in a life
and death struggle each party was driven by the logic of
events to state its position. The Catholic party stood for
an infallible Pope and an infallible Church. They believed sincerely and honestly in this infallibility as they
do now. In the temper of men's minds, and with their
limited experience of any other conception of life, their
opponents were driven to set up another orthodoxy and
another infallibility. To the Pope and the Church the
reformers opposed an infallible Bible. Thus two infalli-
bilities stood face to face and each man must choose his
side. Freedom of conscience sprang out of Protestantism
but it was not the conscious aim or purpose of any of the
reformers to make this a universal or leading principle.
The historical results of its application have been attrib-

uted as direct motives, to men whose whole purpose was far different.

By 1525 the situation had so developed that the two great forces were at length clearly defined. On the one hand a real and earnest effort was made to purify and restore the spiritual life by a return to medieval principles and to reëstablish the medieval Church. With this effort went a revival of the old ideal of piety, as expressed in the Middle Ages, but freed from the corruptions and abuses which had attended it. A new interpretation of the forms and activities of the monastic spirit came as an outgrowth of this effort, but it was not fully manifest until the time of the Counter-Reformation somewhat later. On the other hand, and in vital opposition to this movement, was the introduction of a new principle, "The Freedom of Conscience," which in its expansion and application endeavored to free life from the dead hand of medieval authority and plant itself as a factor in the personal, religious experiences of the individual. One renewed the bondage of the Middle Ages and the other aimed to set the individual free to develop his own religious character.

However widespread this clash of opposing principles, however differently it expressed itself because of characteristics peculiar to the persons and nations involved, the great German was the living source and the constant inspiration of the new world which was coming to its birth in such unheard-of pains. His acts and his words were the subject of constant attack and constant wonder. His marriage with a former nun, which took place in 1525, made it clear to all that there was no possibility of either a reconciliation or a compromise. The Church party was scandalized and horrified, and the Protestants were, many of them, dismayed and depressed, not because of the marriage as such, for many monks and priests had already married, but because it was Luther. Yet out of this untoward act, as it was regarded, flowed some of the most beautiful and tender expressions he ever uttered, and what it meant for the future of Protestantism and the world was long in being understood. The last years of his life were still as full of labor and debate as ever. One cannot follow in detail all the events of those swift and changing years, but the meaning of what he was and what he did remains to be examined. It is not possible to consider all the attacks and criticisms which were directed against him, but a short statement of the most important and the most frequently repeated will throw some light upon the spirit of his enemies, as it then was and in many respects continued to be. The position of an heretic is one we need not consider. Any one, who at any time varies from the established customs, convictions or creeds of a given party or age is regarded as a heretic by all those who hold to the past.

To the Catholic of the sixteenth century and to the Catholic of the nineteenth century Luther was and is a heretic. This is a foregone conclusion, an established assumption which is not in debate. To the Protestant such a claim and such an indictment do not weigh very heavily. A heretic, however, is by assumption capable of all major and minor sins. Therefore Luther was, and still is, charged with immorality. If it is immorality for a monk to marry a nun, Luther was immoral; but to assume this is really to beg the whole question. In order, however, to explain this marriage or adultery it is necessary to assume a gross and immoral mind, and the act is only one expression of his guilty soul. So it was charged against him at the time that this was only the culmination of a long and wretched course of immorality, hints of which are scattered throughout his whole history. Grisar, the last of the great Roman critics, admits that there is no evidence in act at least, and that his reputation stood very high until his revolt from the Church. It is intimated, however, that any one who was capable of this would also be capable of almost anything else. Here also it is not a question of evidence, or of morals, but of point of view.

Another charge, repeated again and again, ever since his day, and with great bitterness, is the violence and grossness of his controversy. There is not the least question about the violence or about the fact that it is regrettable. Yet there is something about the complaint which strikes one as at least singular coming from its source. For what was the language used against him? He was charged with all the misdeeds a heretic was capable of committing. He was said to be possessed by a demon. He was the enemy of God and the Church. He was a blasphemer and an infidel. It is curious that every party in power always feels that any language it may use toward its enemies is not only permissible, but justifiable. It is perfectly true that Luther struck harder and straighter, and shook as no one had ever done before, the authority of the Church and the credit of its leaders. He surpassed all others in the weight of his blows. The inability of his enemies to reply effectively was not due to lack of inclination, but to lack of power. But they learned, if not in that generation, soon later. Mark Pattison, who well knew the story of the period, has said: "In 1605 Carolus Scribianus, the Rector of the Jesuit College at Antwerp, produced the 'Amphitheatrum Honoris.' . . . It is difficult to give the English reader any idea of this production. It must suffice to say that it is one of the most shamelessly beastly books which have ever disgraced the printing press. Even the titles of its chapters could not be reproduced in these pages." It was received with universal applause and approval by the whole Catholic party. Nothing Luther ever said can be compared with this.

The coarseness which is alleged against him undoubtedly holds. Yet all the facts need to be stated. Everything Luther has said has been quoted again and again, and most who read these passages know nothing about the habits and manners of the age. Beside Luther the majority know only Rabelais and he is spoken of with horror. Yet Rabelais had as his intimate and confidential friends some of the most distinguished men of his age in the world of learning and of letters. Those who know Margaret of Navarre know her as the friend of higher learning, as a poet and a mystic, the protector and friend of the noblest spirits of her day, but they too often forget that she was also the author of "The Heptameron," which very few at the present day would regard as particularly edifying reading. The worst that can be said of Luther in this respect is that he was a man of his age. The best perhaps, that he was far higher than most, though not up to the standard of present-day controversial literature.

A far more effective and far more acute attack has been made upon Luther's attitude toward his own mission and his own work. It has been rather scornfully and derisively said that he thought and said he was inspired. No doubt the charge is quite true. One may even go farther and say that few have fully appreciated the profound depth of the feeling he had that he was not moving or acting in his own interest or for his own purpose. He felt that his life had been guided in strange and mysterious ways through the years that had passed. He had the deepest conviction that he would be guided through the events and years which were to come. He did not think of himself, he did not speak of himself. He submitted himself wholly, mind and heart, to One who, he believed, would guide him aright. This is the common and universal attitude of all those of whatever age and race the human soul has honored and revered. Moses and Socrates as well as Luther and Galileo felt they were bound to bear witness and offer their lives for the truth which they had been sent to proclaim. They were jeered at as vain, presumptuous, and egotistical. They would have been not only this but something far worse had they dared to stand up before the world and declare that it was their own wisdom and their own wit which made them come before a world so confused and uncertain and profess to know what path was open for the feet of men. If a man does not believe that his highest duty is the will of God, if he does not feel sure that He who made him will not despise the works of His own hands; if he is not sure that if he beg humbly and pray fervently God will guide him and direct him so that no power of man can prevail against him, then he will fail utterly and completely to lead the restless, troubled spirits of men to their Father's house.

Another charge, of far less importance, but still very effective to-day, is the one which seems to have a certain justification in the language which is used to describe the movement. It is that the whole movement was simply and only destructive, negative, and therefore ineffective. This latter phrase is not, however, used, for it is manifestly not ineffective; otherwise the excitement which followed it would have been quite without explanation. But the very term negative implies ineffective. Great movements never spring from negations. If there is no vital and constructive principle or spirit behind a movement it will inevitably and invariably collapse.

Luther's whole history is a history of development. Each period of his life was a change and growth, and that consistency which is regarded as the highest test of character by so many, could not in the least be claimed for him. He was always moving forward, always expanding and reaching out, always widening his horizon and realizing more fully the sweep and greatness of life. It was this immense energy, this incessant unfolding of new powers and forces which gives his life such a freshness and vigor. He was a new man each day, and each day he faced life with a fullness and force of undiminished energy. All that came to him was transmuted into new power, and his ability of assimilation is the amazing thing about him. Whatever he took to himself came forth as part of a new vitality in which the character of the old food is hardly to be recognized.

Each new stage brought a new stream into the current of his life. After an early training in the scholastic method, as exemplified in the Scotists, the soul of medieval mysticism came to him through the sermons of Tauler and the German theology, whose depth of piety he understood and felt. Though an Augustinian monk he did not know Augustine well before 1509, when he had been transferred to Wittenberg and had begun to teach. It was through him that he came under the influence of that Neo-Platonic strain which is everywhere manifest in the earlier writer. Yet in spite of all the influences brought to bear upon him and mixed in the complex of his own consciousness, the originality and individuality of his own religious experience stand out clear and supreme.

The sense of sin as guilt, as something which separates and alienates the soul from God, making it in itself an object worthy of punishment, that is, the sense of the bondage of the soul by sin, are not characteristic notes of either Tauler or the other mystics, and yet they are of the very essence of Luther's religious consciousness. The mystics sought union with God and strove with all their might to attain it, but they did not set forth the divine forgiveness as the very foundation of this union. Moreover, his conception of the Christian life was directly opposed to that of the mystics or mysticism, in its previous historical manifestations. It always taught a renunciation of the world and flight from the same. It placed the moral values of life and the active cultivation of the

Christian character in life itself as means to an end, the ecstatic vision of God.

So also of Luther's relations with Augustine. In him Luther found a depth of religious feeling which he found nowhere else in antiquity outside the Bible; but his debt to Augustine is far less real than he himself believed it to be. He found in Augustine a declaration and exposition of original sin which appealed to him most profoundly. With Augustine, however, sin was largely, if not wholly, a physical matter, a fleshly desire, owing to its historic origin; with Luther it was a moral and psychological fact, a matter of primary personal experience, having its source in the spirit or will and not in the physical instincts. According to Augustine grace was the divine factor by which a progressive regeneration took place, which, however, would be accomplished in the future only, in the final union of the soul with God. The consciousness of sin and the failure of life are not met by this postponement to the future. It was the present consciousness of sin which Luther realized with such depth and passion and which this explanation or prevision did not in any way meet.

The influence of Augustine and the later Schoolmen was mingled in his statements regarding both the bondage of the will and election. The later Nominalists held that God could confer or withhold "Grace" according to His sovereign will, irrespective of the character of the individual. This of course practically destroyed any moral basis for election. Luther was unwilling to accept such a conclusion, and adopted the logic, if not the form, of Augustine. This in turn left the whole matter still in darkness, a mystery concealed in the Will of God. For practical purposes the matter remains and must forever remain unknown, since it belongs to the inscrutable Will of God.

It is one of the most marked facts in religious history that the greatest and profoundest souls, those most deeply conscious of the saving and redeeming love of God in Christ have been the most humble and complete in the acknowledgment of the working of God's will in their salvation. They have rejected with a feeling of impiety any claim for participation in this supreme work. "Not unto us," has been the adoring and grateful cry, and in the depths of their pious souls they have attributed all to God. The very sense of their own weakness and sinfulness makes it impossible to believe that any act or thought, any motion or mind, which led to the new life, could have any other source than the loving Will of God. Stated in logical form and according to the laws of philosophical thought one lands in a cold, relentless determinism. Yet fidelity to religious experience has led many, if not most, to accept this conclusion rather than in any way invalidate or modify the awful tenderness of God's all-conquering love. It is a paradox, but it is the paradox of the devout soul, and not the iron rigidity of logic which it so much resembles. Between the language of the fatalist and the language of the saint the difference in statement seems again and again invisible, but between the soul of the fatalist and the soul of the saint the difference is immeasurable. The dispositions or characters from which these theories, so similar in form, issue are as utterly dissimilar as the theories are alike.

Luther's religious position was in violent and destructive opposition to the current and established system. One common method characterized the great teachers of the past, whether they were agreed in detail or divided into schools. The dominance of logical and philosophical ideas determined the method, and the result was a system or scheme which was to represent all the knowledge of the past and determine the place and power of all future knowledge. The aim of the Schoolmen was a complete

Christian philosophy. There were, and therefore could
be, no independent philosophical investigations for these
must inevitably and invariably trespass upon the field of
theology. The whole course of scholastic speculation reveals the fact that the very conception of philosophy then
in control demanded an absolute dependence of all thinking upon the authority of the Church. All the terms of
theological thought were either borrowed from philosophy or colored by it. The motive was intellectual and the
method was that of the schools. Salvation was through
knowledge and the Sacraments, and the system was based
upon the foundations supposed to be established in the
debate upon the Universals. The Schoolmen began with
the greatest and highest Universal, the pure abstract conception of Being. They found in Aristotle a definition
of the "Primum Mobile" as pure energy, from which all
life is derived and upon which it rests. To modify this
original Aristotelian term by the introduction of Christian ideas was not difficult, but it made the Gospel after
all a system of philosophy. The term Christian was added
to philosophy, but it did not save it. From the abstract
to the concrete, from the universal to the particular was
the widely accepted method.

Against this whole scheme Luther revolted with all the
energy of his passionate spirit. Mere intellectual belief
in, or acceptance of, a metaphysical God made no appeal
to him. He rejected the whole system of abstractions
and definitions and, instead of beginning with a logical
concept, he began with the living Person and living splendor of Jesus Christ. This was to him the great historical
reality. He needed no proofs of His character and no
evidence of His power. Therefore the only God in whom
he could trust, the only being in whom he could rest in
pure and childlike faith was the Father of Our Lord
Jesus Christ. He did not begin with God and come to
Man. He began here upon earth, in the life and character

of Jesus Christ, in all its human tenderness, in all its divine mystery, and through Him he turned his eyes to the Father who had revealed Himself in Christ. For theology he substituted religion and for logic Christian experience. He appealed from the doctors with their theories to the plain story of the Gospel with its universal appeal to the deepest human instincts. He did not start with any "a priori" or speculative idea of God. He did not rest upon any scholastic definition or philosophical formulas, no matter how well supported by authority, but upon the revelation of God in Christ.

In Christ and in Christ alone is the Father known as such. In Him and in Him alone do we see the heart of God. It is from this Center that we rise to God. From this living revelation alone do we know what is His essential character and what His attitude toward men. This was his deepest conviction and his fundamental faith. Its foundation was thus wholly Christian, practical and personal, not abstract or logical like that of the Schoolmen. Such a revelation of God inspires in the heart of His child a sense of living and loving dependence upon God. It is His mercy and forgiveness which move the soul to repentance and thanksgiving. But it is in Jesus Christ that this revelation takes place; He it is who forgives our sins, who died and rose for our salvation, and through whom God gives to each soul that turns to Him righteousness and blessedness.

At first and for long even, Luther did not realize or appreciate what his own experience really meant for history or for his relations to the thinking and practices of the past. He was always strongly conservative. He still clung to the old doctrinal statements, though they had a new meaning for him, or at least did not seem to be necessarily in conflict with what he now felt was the deepest truth of his life. There was also a certain naïveté about him, so marked in fact, that we do not find him either rejecting or attacking ideas and practices which were in violent contradiction with his new evangelical convictions and feelings. Many of these, however, had been already severely criticized by others, who did not in the least share his thoughts or aims. He still believed, or thought that he believed that the Church could not err. The infallibility of General Councils was accepted and asserted by him. He still spoke of salvation in terms of medieval thought, as something yet in the future. Though he used the term Faith again and again it still often had the old meaning of "hope," as found in the Epistle to the Hebrews rather than in the Pauline sense. It was only gradually, as his spiritual life developed, that he became conscious, through his union with Christ, that salvation was a present, living experience, and not something to be postponed to the future. This final step in his development took place long before he realized its significance, or found either form, thought or language, suitable for its full expression.

The significance of this change, from doctrine to experience, from dogma to history, from speculation to fact, came more clearly to light in Luther's conviction of the place which Christ took, not only in the thought, but in the actual life of each individual. Faith could not any longer be the "holding as true" certain statements, however certain, but an immediate and personal relation with Jesus Christ. The means by which the life of his Lord should become his was taught in the word of God, in the life of Christ and in the experience of those whom He had inspired, and through whom each one was to learn the way.

This way was the way of faith. Saint Bernard had announced the doctrine of Justification by Faith, though without in the least grasping any of the religious consequences of it. It is one of the curiosities of controversy that those, who at one moment accused Luther of unheard-of novelties, in the very next breath declared he had said nothing more than had already been said by one of the greatest saints of the Middle Ages. The mere affirmation of historical or even metaphysical truth in no degree corresponded with what Luther declared to be the meaning of Scripture. Of course the defenders of the old view had no alternative except to declare that the Church was the only authorized and divine interpreter of Scripture. But the New Learning had already gone too far and had taught men too much for this argument to prevail with those upon whom the bonds of Church authority had begun to sit rather loosely.

To his adversaries his attacks on "Good Works," and his substitution for them of Justification by Faith, seemed too often merely the exchange of an actual and definite line of conduct and an outward expression of obedience for a purely mental attitude which was accepted in place of works. This easily made mistake of course rose out of the fact that those who opposed him had still in mind the old conception of faith. In the beginnning too when Luther first recognized the spiritual and religious significance of faith he failed to see that from his standpoint the old historic institutions were in many respects in direct and violent contradiction with it. When Augustine, to whom he felt he owed so much, had set forth his doctrine of Grace, Election, and Predestination, he asserted them with the utmost emphasis and earnestness, yet he failed utterly to realize that they were inconsistent with the theory of the authority of the Church and "the power of the keys." This inconsistency neither Augustine nor his successors ever succeeded in harmonizing. Yet Augustine accepted the authority of the Church and declared it to be one of the grounds for his acceptance of the Gospel.

Like him Luther also failed at first to recognize in any way either the logical or the religious inconsistency of his

position though in a later period he felt compelled, or
was driven by the inward movement of his own life, to
break with the historic Church which stood upon quite
another plane of religious thought and feeling. The influence of old ideas and habits of thought was a source
of difficulty not only for Luther but also for his friends.
He drew his convictions of the meaning of faith neither
from history nor from theology. The two factors which
determined his entire position were the Holy Scriptures
and his own religious experience. The inward unrest, the
spiritual dissatisfaction which tormented him, drove him
more and more to a study of the Scriptures and especially
of Saint Paul, in whose religious life he found so much
which reflected his own. That he always understood Saint
Paul or always stated the complete thought of the great
Apostle can hardly be maintained since the inner history
of the Apostle as well as of Luther had much in it which
is now, and probably always will be, unknown. But what
he did draw from these two sources he has so fully and
completely stated that there is no real difficulty at this
time in knowing what he meant.

In the earlier years, when he was still deeply moved
by the new light which had come to him from the German
school of mystics the indwelling of Christ was strongly
emphasized. The sense of this inner life brought peace
to his anxious mind and troubled heart, but for the tremendous part he was to play in the active and regenerat-
ing movement of the world, this more or less quietistic
feeling was no sufficient preparation. Then it grew upon
him that the indwelling of Christ and what it had accomplished in him and for him were the necessary, preliminary conditions for a realization of the fullness of his
Christian life.

When Prierias asserted in his controversy with Luther
that there was no assurance and no absolute certainty of
the forgiveness of sins in the sense in which he declared

it, there was no question of the profound importance of
the struggle now on. It was in the discussions on faith
that Luther's standpoint came out most clearly. The
scholastic distinctions on this point filled him with the
deepest anger. He says, in speaking of "Fides Informis"
and "Fides Formata": "We also put a difference between
a counterfeit faith and a true faith. The counterfeit
faith is that which heareth of God, of Christ, and of all
the mysteries of his Incarnation and our redemption: yea,
and can talk godly thereof, and yet there remaineth nothing else in the heart but a naked opinion and a sound of
the Gospel. For it neither reneweth nor changeth the
heart: it maketh not a new man but leaveth him in the
vanity of his former opinions and conversations, and this
is a very pernicious faith. The moral philosopher is not
much better than a hypocrite having such a faith. Wherefore if they would make a distinction between faith
formed (and take it as the Scripture taketh it) and a
false or counterfeit faith, their distinction should nothing
offend me. But they speak of faith formed and made
perfect with charity, and make a double faith, that is to
say, formed and unformed. This pestilent and devilish
gloss I utterly detest. Although, say they, we have faith
infused called 'Fides Infusa,' which is the gift of the
Holy Ghost, and also faith gotten by our own industry,
called 'Fides Aquisita'; yet both of them lack their form
and perfection, which is charity, and are formed with
charity. This is to prefer charity before faith, and to
attribute righteousness not to faith but to charity.
Wherefore, when they do not attribute righteousness to
faith but only in respect to charity, they attribute to
faith nothing at all. Moreover these perverters of the
Gospel of Christ do teach that even that faith which they
call faith infused, and not received by hearing, nor gotten
by any working, but created in man by the Holy Ghost,
may stand with deadly sin, and that the worst men may

have this faith: therefore say they, if it be alone, it is idle and unprofitable. Thus they take from faith her office and give it unto charity; so that faith is nothing, except charity, which they call the form and perfection thereof, be joined withal. This is a devilish and blasphemous kind of doctrine, which utterly defaceth and overthroweth the doctrine of faith, and carrieth man clean from Christ the Mediator and from faith, which is the hand and only means whereby we apprehend him. For if Charity be the form and perfection of faith, as they dream, then am I by and by constrained to say that charity is the principal part of the Christian religion, and so I lose Christ, his blood and all his benefits, and now I rest altogether in a moral doing, even as the Pope and the heathen philosopher and the Turk doth." "Faith is nothing else but the truth of the heart, that is to say, a true and right opinion of the heart as touching God."

Here the line is clearly indicated which distinguishes faith, as he meant it, from faith in the Latin conception. It is the answer of the heart, not a mere "cum assensione cogitare." Faith is neither law nor works but "an assured confidence which apprehendeth Christ. A certain steadfast beholding which looketh upon nothing else but Christ, the Conqueror of Sin and death and the Giver of righteousness, salvation and eternal life." "The greatest wonder ever upon earth is that the Son of God died the shameful death upon the Cross."

"And here it is necessary that you know the true definition of Christ. The Schoolmen, being utterly ignorant thereof, have made Christ a judge and tormentor devising this fond fancy concerning the merit of congruence and worthiness. But Christ according to his true definition is no law-giver, but a forgiver of sins and a Savior." "Christ therefore thus joined and united unto me and abiding in me, liveth this life in me which I now live: yea Christ himself is this life which I now live. Where-

fore Christ and I in this behalf are both one. Now Christ
living in me abolisheth the law, condemneth sin, and de-
stroyeth death; for it cannot be but at his presence all
these must needs vanish away." . . . "So Christ living
and abiding in me taketh away and swalloweth up all evils
which vex and afflict me. This union or conjunction then
is the cause that I am delivered from the terror of the
law and sin, am separate from myself, and translated into
Christ and his kingdom, which is a kingdom of grace,
righteousness, peace, joy, life, salvation and eternal glory.
Whilst I thus abide and dwell in him what evil is there
that can hurt me? In the mean season the old man abideth
without and is subject to the law: but as concerneth justification, Christ and I must be entirely conjoined and
united together, so that He may live in me and I in Him.
And this is a wonderful manner of speech. Now because
Christ liveth in me, therefore look what grace, righteousness, life, peace, and salvation is in me, it is his, and yet
notwithstanding the same is mine also, by that inseparable
union and conjunction which is through faith: by the
which Christ and I are made one body in spirit. Foras-
much then as Christ liveth in me, it followeth that as I
must needs be with him partaker of grace, righteousness,
life and eternal salvation: so the law, sin and death can
have no place in me." "Faith must be purely taught:
namely, that thou art so entirely and nearly joined unto
Christ, that he and thou art made as it were one person:
so that thou mayest boldly say, I am now one with Christ,
that is to say, Christ's righteousness, victory and life are
mine. And again, Christ may say, I am that sinner: that
is, his sins and his death are mine because he is united
and joined unto me and I unto him. For by faith we are
so joined together that we are become one flesh and one
bone, we are members of the body of Christ, flesh of his
flesh and bone of his bones: so that this faith doth couple
Christ and me more nearly together than the husband is

coupled to his wife." "So do we say, that it is Christ which furnisheth and adorneth faith, or rather that He is the very form and perfection of faith. Wherefore Christ apprehended by faith, and dwelling in the heart, is the true Christian righteousness." "True Christian righteousness is that righteousness whereby Christ liveth in me, and not that which is in our own person." "For Christ, on whom our eyes are fixed, in whom we live, who also liveth in us, is Lord and Conqueror of the law, sin, and death, and all evils: in whom most certain and sure consolation is set forth in us, and victory given."

The quotations could be repeated indefinitely, but it is hardly necessary. No such language had been heard since St. Paul's voice had gone silent. A new world of the spirit and for the spirit unrolled itself before the inward vision of mankind. A world of power and of passion, of freedom and of greatness, like the vision of the sons of God which filled the soul of the Apostle. It is all there; all that spiritual splendor; all that high elevation; all that great nobility of soul which St. Paul believed was the life of the sons of God in Christ Jesus. It is perfectly obvious, in view of such language, that the act of faith on the part of the individual, that is the personal belief, cannot be regarded as a work which merits or earns in and by itself justification. It does not in any way mean that an interior and spiritual act is substituted for an external act, or what in the language then in use could be regarded as a "good work." It is not the subjective faith of the individual which makes righteous before God, but the appropriation and identification of the soul with Christ, to whom we are united, and who becomes the living energy of our lives. Faith is thus not an idle quality or intellectual apprehension, but a living force and power working in the life and for the life, in real fact, Christ himself. The old questions of the relation between faith and the intellect or the will have no longer any relevancy. It is not a matter of the will or intellect alone, but the whole personality is involved. It is the possession of the life by another spirit, which in its action and influence creates new centers of power and life, and plants the seeds of a richer and larger personality.

In the imperfection of the scholastic definition of faith the want had been supplied by love. Faith in itself was insufficient, so love was imparted to the soul by which the possibilities of the fullness of life might be realized. But this fullness was not and could not be a present possession, so that faith necessarily became more hope and anticipation than anything else. But the presence of Christ in the soul and to the soul, not only implied but furnished an abundance of spiritual energy and life which would transfigure the whole existence. Christ is, as Luther said, the jewel which is held in the ring, but not made by the ring. This union with Christ is real and spiritual, not external or mechanical.

As the union is a matter of the soul it is also hidden and secret. If it does not exist no authority can confer it or create it. The whole meaning of personality thus takes on a new significance. Nothing can be a substitute for the personal communion and fellowship of the individual with his Savior. For it was as his Savior that Luther looked on Christ. It was not only as an indwelling spirit, leading and guiding the uncertain feet, but as one who had a real and energetic relation with the soul itself, One who took away not only the control of sin, but the burden of guilt. It was not only the Christ in us, but the Christ for us, a truth far larger and richer in meaning than any which had hitherto been apprehended, of the intimate relations which are possible for the soul of man.

When Luther speaks of the believer applying all the powers and spiritual greatness of Christ to the soul, he is only trying to put into words the new sense of this relation to Christ. All that is Christ's belongs to me not because I have earned it or deserved it; not even because I have discovered it and appropriated it, but because Christ has revealed it to me, and in his entrance into my soul has made it all mine. He wants me to have Him and offers Himself to me and it is only through His presence and His gift that it is possible for Him to become mine. Each man who has experienced this intercourse and communion can and does say, "He is my Savior." No individual and no institution can create or guarantee this interior and personal communion and union. At its roots it is the most individual and mysterious experience of which the human soul is capable. Time and space and life and death are swallowed up and abolished. The blessedness is not a future possibility, but a present personal and infinite experience. Therefore each individual must experience it for himself. He must believe and he must stand fast in his own faith. One cannot be conscious of this blessedness through the faith of another or of all others. A complete revolution was thus brought about in the religious life of man. Even the most authoritative and autocratic affirmations of earlier teaching had never claimed as much as this. All that had been said before was that submission and obedience would guarantee the future, but for the present the best that could be hoped for would be that one could so live as not to fail to gain the final reward and heavenly rest.

The Schoolmen, drawing their own inferences from Aristotle and post-Apostolic Christianity, had approached ethics from the point of view of the act rather than the agent. Virtuous acts became the ground and cause of virtue. The inevitable inference, of course, would be that if one performed these acts one would be acting virtuously before one was virtuous. The psychological absurdity of this assumption does not seem to have been realized. Life could then, on its moral side, be reduced to a catalogue of definite acts, and the establishment of habits based upon this list of actions would constitute a virtuous life. Almost all the ethical teaching was engaged in defining duties and virtues. These in turn were supported by ecclesiastical authority as the necessary way by which salvation could be attained. Acts became sins which were no sins and acts became meritorious which were not self-evidently such.

Luther swept away all the theory and practice of virtue as developed by the Schoolmen. His language was perfectly simple and perfectly clear. It was the language of Scripture, the very words of Our Lord Himself, which he never dreamed of modifying or questioning. He believed them to be the final authority for all and accepted as such by all Christians. "An evil tree bears not good fruit nor a good tree evil fruit." "Now it is plain that the fruit bears not the tree, nor does the tree spring from the fruit, but on the other hand the tree bears the fruit and the fruit springs from the tree. Since now the tree must be before the fruit, and the fruit does not make the tree either good or evil, but the tree makes the fruit. So also must the man in person be pious or wicked before he can do good or evil works, and his works make him neither good nor evil, but he makes the work good or evil. . . . Works do not make a man believing nor do they make him pious, but faith as it makes a man pious so does it also produce good works. . . . We reject good works therefore not on their own account but on account of the evil additions and the false perverted interpretation of them." In applying his principle to daily life he says: "It makes no difference to the soul whether the body wears holy clothes or not, as the priests or the monks: not if it is the church and the holy city, not if it is surrounded by holy things, not if it prays bodily, goes on pilgrimages and does all good works which can be and are done by the body. There must be something else which brings and gives to the soul piety and freedom. . . . The Christian useth the world and all creatures so that there is no difference between him and the infidel. . . . Yet notwithstanding there is a great difference. For I live in the flesh I grant, but I live not of myself: but in that I now live, I live in the faith of the Son of God."

This would seem to destroy all outward differences and make good works not only useless and unnecessary, but possibly misleading and injurious. So many of his opponents thought, angered and astounded by his sweeping language. Yet the balance was never really destroyed nor the reality of life denied. He takes up this very objection when he says: "If faith is everything and alone regarded as sufficient to make pious, why then are good works commended? Thus we would be good and do nothing. . . . Mein lieber Mensch, not so: it would indeed be so if thou wert only an inward man (innerlich), and had become entirely spiritual and inward (innerlich) which will not happen until the last day. . . ." He wishes to lay the emphasis where it really belongs. He wants to get at the root from which the outer life actually springs. He seeks to discriminate between cause and effect, and find the vital and organic relation between character and conduct. The order in which these stand determines the reality and essence of the life, or else reverses it and robs it of all sincerity and clearness. "All things which are attributed to works do properly belong unto faith." For works must not be looked upon morally, that is, as having a definite and independent value of themselves, without any reference whatever to the purpose or motive which inspires them: "but faithfully and with a spiritual eye. Faith is the divinity of works, and so spread through the works of the faithful, as the divinity throughout the humanity of Christ." "The whole life of a Christian man is this, namely, that inwardly it consisteth in faith towards God and outwardly in charity and good works towards my neighbour. So that a man is a perfect Christian inwardly through faith before God who hath no need of our works: and outwardly before men whom our faith profiteth nothing, but our charity and our works."

In his vision of a new society filled with the spirit of Christ and bound together in a common loyalty and delight in the goodness of God, he says: "When Adam and Eve were in Paradise they laboured not to become pious and righteous through works for they were already without sin, but God put them in the Garden to plant and tend it and they worked to please Him. This also is the nature of the works of a believing man, because through faith he has again been placed in Paradise and newly created, and he works only to please Him." Such language is not simply pious rhetoric borrowed from the far-away vision of the past, but an inward and living conviction. He felt that man was not only redeemed, but life itself was redeemed, and all the old fear and dread of the common and worldly facts of life were banished forever. Here and now, in the land and in the city, in the homes and friendships which God had given to each one there was the foundation for a new and noble life. Deep in his heart was the truth which Augustine had so daringly proclaimed ten centuries before: "Love God and do as you please." The love of God had sanctified all life and the spirit of Christ whom Luther felt he could trust. Thus living to the full extent of his energies he passed beyond the hard limitations within which life had hitherto been held in bondage. All authority, save that of God alone as revealed in Jesus Christ, was open to challenge.

Luther has been set forth as the great figure whose aim was the establishment of "Freedom of Conscience." If, as many suppose and assert, freedom of conscience means that one may think as he pleases, Luther did not care for that at all. "Christian Freedom is in faith which produces it, not that we may walk vainly or do evil but that we require no works in order to obtain piety and blessedness." Unfortunately the older he grew the more he was impressed by the lawlessness which arose out of the abuse of those very principles for which he stood.

Jesus Christ has been since the beginning the Christian ideal. Yet in the interpretation of this ideal there have been the greatest differences and the most immense variety. As this interpretation has changed from age to age so has the practical expression of it varied. The movement in the life of Europe which we call the Reformation marks a great advance if not the greatest advance in the development of the spiritual life of man of any which had been made since the Apostolic Age. For at bottom it was a contrast and a conflict between two spiritual ideals, one of which had held sway for centuries and had molded or influenced the life of every race and every age where it was present.

In the first centuries of Christian history, when the Gospel was regarded as a hostile and dangerous power to be ruthlessly destroyed, the common mind of the Brotherhood fixed itself in admiration upon the one type which rose above the commonplace and everyday life of the ordinary believer. This was the Martyr. He became the hero and the ideal, for he represented, as his Master had done, the supreme sacrifice. It is true, the spirit of the martyr was often quite different from that of his Master, but such inner distinctions are not always apparent, or ever emphasized, in the flood of glory and reverence which crowns his head. The influence of the martyrs and confessors was far greater than that of any other group of men in the early Church. The regular officer, however efficient and saintly, sank below the fame of those who suffered for Christ. Through them the mightiest passion of the soul, the desire for an ideal, seemed to find a concrete and living expression. They,

above all others, were the ones who most truly expressed
the valor and spirit of their Lord.

When the time came that martyrdom was neither general nor frequent; when the Church took its place at the
head of the great forces which were leading and governing the Empire; when those who suffered were, in the
majority of cases, heretics or schismatics in the popular
mind, the situation became altogether different. The old
passion still lived, as it lives still in the human heart, but
it took a new turn, and one which, in the length of time
during which it prevailed and the amount of influence it
exerted, stands alone in the history of the Church. Instead of the renunciation of life, which was the expression
and fruit of the martyr spirit, the renunciation of the
world and its pleasures, became the great ideal. Monasticism became the highest conception of the perfect Christian life. It became, therefore, the greatest force in the
life of the finest and noblest spirits in the Church for
more than a thousand years. The ecclesiastical and the
political expression of the organized Church stood far
below the life of the world-renouncing monk himself.
Monasticism looked with distrust and sometimes with horror upon the secular character of the Church around it,
and resented every effort to force any of its members out
of the seclusion of their life into the hard glare and
worldly habits of the institutional Church. It was jealous
of its seclusion and became a Church within or above the
Church which stood before the world as the representative
authority of Christianity. It so completely absorbed into
itself the highest Christian ideal then known that a reform of religion always meant a reform of monasticism.
They were so closely and organically connected that it
was impossible to separate, even in thought, the Gospel
and this specific manifestation of piety which had
gathered into it all the higher spiritual instincts and
impulses of centuries. All reforms were attempts to en-

force more completely the separation of life from the world.

Thus the great mass of the people were not only put on a lower plane; they were really and practically excluded from even the possibility of realizing the Christian ideal, since this was possible only by repudiating most of the facts of life and most of the ties which made up man's duties and delights. Of course such a situation had many serious consequences. A double standard of morality sprang up with the most disastrous results for all. The secular Christian was not expected to rise above the very lowest standard which the accommodation of the Church permitted. No real spiritual attainment being possible a mechanical theory of the Church and the Sacraments provided a substitute for personal character. The laity were put in the background and the Church became the instrument for a mechanical salvation. The early faith that the spirit of God found its dwelling place in the heart of the believer was reserved, by implication at least, for those alone who separated from the world. The idea that the Father had taught each child to address Him in his soul yielded to the idea that those outside the sacred brotherhood must depend upon the holiness of the Church. There could be for the mass no experience of salvation, no vivid sense of the presence and love of God within him. That was a dream, at most a hope; and all through the centuries, from the death of Augustine to the end of the Middle Ages, there was a profound spiritual despair whose depth we now cannot measure. Not here and now, but there, beyond this world, was the one hope of the soul. To work out this salvation, to assure man of redemption was the end and purpose of the monastic ideal. The lonely struggle was haunted again and again by uncertainty. The mechanical and external relations of the Church to the soul left a great want unsatisfied. In the supreme manifestation which the monastic spirit

found, that of the Franciscans, the same inevitable results
followed. Francis sought to bring the world and God
into closer relations and fill the souls of men with the
same delight which lifted his sunlit spirit up to God. But
even in this noble and energetic attempt the old leaven
still worked. The ideal was too strong, and the laity
whom he sought to reclaim for the highest privileges of
sonship were only monks after all, in another and modified form. World-renunciation was still at the heart of
it, and it was the poor who were the rightful heirs of
salvation. The deep anxiety and fear of the soul never
slumbered, though a tender and gracious spirit flowed out
upon a parched and thirsty world. God might save one,
but one must serve Him day and night in fear and wonder and leave the world to rot in its natural weakness.
The very root of the monastic ideal, the vows which lay
at the heart of it, Obedience, Chastity, Poverty, lay outside and beyond the common religious life of the world
and were impossible for the mass of people with their
common duties and their daily tasks.

So the universality of the Gospel ended in an aristocracy which stood apart from and above the average life
of man. This ideal revealed itself ultimately as an enemy
to personal salvation and to the highest spiritual experiences, except for the few. It was a magnificent attempt,
if you please, to make personal and individual salvation
the great end and aim of life, but if the Gospel of Jesus
Christ as set forth by Himself and His Apostles was true,
this was not the way. Ecclesiastical obedience, physical
asceticism, and the rejection of the common family life
of mankind, were the roots of this ideal, and it failed.
An ideal which is not possible and practicable for all men,
everywhere and always, is, and must ultimately be, a
failure. The Roman spirit, by transforming the Gospel
into the "New Law," strengthened the hold which the
monastic ideal had obtained and reduced the whole

spiritual life to a rigid system of external rules and practices in which consisted the essence of the religious life. The freedom of the spirit was reduced or in bondage to observances and legality, and salvation, in its last terms was a bargain which found its final expression in the theory and the practice of indulgences. Nothing more mechanical and unspiritual has ever been conceived as the essence of religion than the form to which it was reduced at the end of the Middle Ages, and the best men recognized this fact.

In the new ideal which was presented to the world in Protestantism the sense of individual responsibility and personal character stand in the first place. This new sense of personality should not be confounded with that which is so striking a feature in the Renaissance. The Renaissance represented a strong and deep sense of the individual as the possessor of powers and qualities in his own person which demanded the right of self-expression. To the men of the old school, and those under the influence of the old ideal, a spirit of the Humanists seemed like mere mad willfullness. In the case of the Protestants also, to the men of the old order there seemed to be no difference between them and the Humanists. Protestantism was only a more aggravated case of rebellion. Many of the men of the Renaissance, like Erasmus and also many of the Italians and French, in spite of their self-assertion still professed attachment and obedience to the Roman See. The position of the Protestants seemed to be on the other hand inspired by the instinct to revolt carried to its most logical and violent conclusions. The spirit of the Humanists was one of intellectual independence and the assertion of the rights of the individual reason. The ground of the Protestant revolt was an inner obedience, a sense of obligation to an impulse or inspiration which they could not disobey. In the beginning the Protestants did not wish to break from the

Church with a bold declaration of independence, but there was within them a consciousness which called for obedience. This obedience brought them into conflict with the old historic authority which had hitherto claimed and maintained control over human thought and action.

Protestantism was in no sense a mere intellectual struggle, nor was it essentially a demand for personal freedom, however right such a position might be. It was, on the other hand, a passionate sense of a new relation, of the overwhelming authority of the inner life which the personal presence of God's love and forgiveness through Christ had wrought in men's souls. This consciousness was necessarily intensely individualistic, and it brought with it an increased sense of personality. More than that it testified to a new and larger personality. It was not simply the consciousness of a real and separate individual endowed with certain personal and original qualities, but that of a new person, a man who had in addition to all these the consciousness that he was a child of God. Christ had claimed him for His own and called him into fellowship and communion with God. The immediateness of this relation did not by any means destroy all the values of the existing institutions, but it entirely altered their relation to men. The Church no longer stood between man and God as an indispensable and infallible mediator. It still occupied a necessary but a far more subordinate place. The individual was thus at once raised to a position where he must face for himself and enjoy for himself the newly realized relation under its most intense and personal character. To those who felt as Erasmus did it still seemed possible to acknowledge the church authority and yet preserve their personal liberty. The compromise was made or attempted, but even those who accepted it recognized that in real force and weight of character Erasmus stood far below the great Protestant leader.

Character gained a new meaning and a new sincerity. It imposed new obligations, demanded new sacrifices and foreshadowed a new type of manhood, the development of which no one could possibly anticipate. It implied change, it meant growth of some kind since the old immobility had been destroyed, and the old restraints had been broken through. The new life in Christ and with Christ left the future open and the static conception of life passed away forever as a controlling force. The new life of Europe gained in depth, reality, and a strange sense of its own possibilities and mysteries. A new and nobler loyalty to duty and spiritual responsibility: a larger and more fearless outlook upon life and a deeper and more awful sense of God's presence became the dominant characteristics of the new piety. In the spiritual history of the individual his interior experiences were profoundly changed. Prayer, which is the highest privilege and expression of the soul became the common attitude, not of the saint in the cloister or of the priest at the altar, but of the humble and the ignorant. One of the great facts of the last three centuries has been the household religion of Protestantism and Protestant Europe. The head of the family presented to God the petitions and the adoration of his household, a social unit which was henceforth to be a fact of far greater significance than it ever had been before in the religious consciousness of men.

The family was to be no more a compromise representing the lower instincts and the coarser tendencies of human nature, but one of the highest, holiest and most sacred institutions which the soul possesses, standing as the very model for the Church itself which in its highest and most impassioned description is called the Family of God. The father of a family, nobly fulfilling his great responsibilities and sharing the best in his soul with the children who looked up to him came to stand on a far higher plane of spiritual worth than any hermit, monk, ecclesiastic or pope, as such. From this central conviction of the present worth of the family as the most fundamental and sacred organism of society new values radiated through all the immense variety of social life. All the various relations created by an highly organized society are but opportunities for the expression of that inner spirit of sonship to God and brotherhood to man which is the very heart of the Gospel. No restrictions, no limitations, no prescriptions, could here be either demanded or allowed. Out of the full soul the stream of sympathy and patience, of service and of fellowship would flow forever, so long as Christ is living within and pouring out the tides of tenderness and strength which poor human life needs.

This was the Protestant ideal. This was the dream of those who wanted a fuller and larger life. To say there is nothing positive, creative or new in these fundamental principles or claims of the Reformation is simply to display an ignorance of history so profound, and an inability to realize the relation of cause and effect so complete, that discussion is unprofitable and useless.

It is perfectly true that the immediate and even remote results of this great movement were for generation after generation agitation, unrest, revolution, and war. It is true that there has been no rest for the foot of man or peace for his soul. It is true that change and not stability has been preëminently the character of all the centuries since the sixteenth. It is true that the high hopes and the great dreams of that century were not fully realized nor have been yet. It is true that failure has followed failure but each failure has been met by a quenchless courage, and a passionate hopefulness. The Reformation, however, was so far from being a failure that it is absolutely certain that at the heart of these last four centuries, as the inspiring energy of all that has been finest and best, have been the forces set free by the Reformation, and above all the men who did so much to make that century the cradle of the new era towers the figure of Martin Luther.

CHAPTER VIII

THE COUNTER-REFORMATION AND AFTER

THE change which the great movement of the sixteenth
century produced in the world did not consist merely in
an addition to human knowledge, great as that was, the
discovery of America, the invention of printing and gun-
powder, the establishment of the Copernican system and
the vast growth in knowledge of the past, resulting from
the Renaissance; all these were of primary importance,
but they had behind them something even more significant. Mankind, at least in western Europe, had reached
a new stage in its development and what came after was,
as distinguished from the past, not merely some new intellectual achievement, but a new culture, using that term
in the largest sense of the word. It was not simply that
men knew more, but that they saw life with different eyes
and had different aims and interests. Nothing that then
stood remained as it was or continued uninfluenced by the
new atmosphere which men were breathing.

The boast of the old Church was that it never changed,
but the Roman Church that represented the old faith at
the end of the sixteenth century was in some very important respects a Church which in its outlook and spirit
was one so different that it, too, might be called reformed.
Harnack has said: "The decrees of the Council of Trent
are the shadow of the Reformation." Actually the action
and re-action were mutual. It is impossible to understand
the changes which took place then in the life of the
Church unless one recognizes this primary fact. It is in
vain that men and institutions declare that they will not

288

be affected by any of the changes taking place around them, the growth in knowledge, the rise of new intellectual interests, the power of new moral forces, the sway and sweep of new deals. The old institutions and organization remained unchanged perhaps, but they are filled with a new spirit.

The new temper of the Church appeared in several manifestations, as first in the revival of monasticism. The old orders had grown so useless and so burdensome, that they were hated by all, both learned and ignorant, and even the best of their members were perfectly conscious of their failure. The Church was unwilling to abandon an institution which had done so much in the past and with which some of the greatest names in its history were associated. So while the old orders were not discontinued, new ones were founded which were utterly different except in name, and which affected in time the spirit of many of the older orders. The new orders were established for the welfare of society and not of their members. From one point of view they were philanthropic and social organizations designed to meet the needs of a world that was suffering pains and seeing sorrows to which the eyes of the past had been too often either closed or indifferent. This devotion to the service of man was rewarded then as always, by the most enthusiastic admiration and devotion. To the earnest and devout souls among the members of the old church this new development gave an opportunity which was most eagerly welcomed, and the names of the founders of these new orders and the members who devoted themselves to them are among the most unselfish and high-minded of that age. The practical and definite objects to which they devoted themselves changed in many ways the actual life of the Church and brought within its influence those who had been neglected and those who had been repelled by the secular and worldly life of the leaders of the preceding generations.

It was a moral revival of the most significant character and was of untold benefit to just those elements of society which in the changing order of things were bound to bear the burdens and suffer the consequences of the changes unless there were manifest a spirit of sympathy larger and more generous than had prevailed for many centuries. Probably none of the attempts to reëstablish the Church in the hearts of its members did more than this revival of monasticism with its fresh spirit of unselfish and Christian devotion. While loyalty to the Church was always assumed, the aim was personal and individual. The welfare of men from the point of view of the pains and sufferings of life was the chief purpose of these whole-hearted and unselfish idealists.

A second manifestation of the new spirit of sixteenth-century Catholicism was quite unlike the first. It was called the Index, or, to give it its full and correct designation, the "Index Librorum Prohibitorum." The Church in its anxiety to preserve its members from unfavorable or injurious influences had always, from the days of Cyprian at least, felt called upon to warn its members against books which might injure them either morally or spiritually. The consequence was that the field over which this limitation on their intellectual freedom was drawn was so extensive that it was practically determined by the sole judgment of the individual bishop or by the Church in its assemblies. The right to decide on this matter, especially by the Pope, was almost never disputed and it was exercised in every case of heresy or controversy with an iron hand. At the time of the Reformation the amount of controversial literature was almost beyond belief. The discovery of printing, too, had changed the situation. For the first time in the life of man the sources of knowledge were made generally available. The greater danger made the Church feel a greater need for protection.

The Index suddenly found itself one of the most important and most powerful agencies in the hands of the Church. Lists were made of all literature which met with papal disapproval and regulations were established which should enforce with heavy punishments the failure to observe the prohibitions. As time passed new lists were issued to meet the new flood of heresy or danger. What this meant to the intellectual life of the countries or groups where these decisions were in force may easily be imagined and the effects are manifest more clearly to-day than they were even in the sixteenth century. Knowledge, for and in itself, the exercise of the reason, the investigations of the deep problems of life, all these fertile sources of the growth and freedom of the soul were condemned and banished from the life of those who recognized the authority of the Church to fix the limits of the operations of the human mind.

The institution of sixteenth-century Catholicism which has most impressed itself upon the popular mind is the Society of Jesus. The popular mind has not been far wrong in its estimate of the significance of this new order. It has had a great influence upon the inner life of the Church judging by the immense controversial literature upon the subject and the wide differences of opinion even among the writers of that communion. Its influence upon Protestantism has been almost none, although it has been endowed by popular imagination with the most subtle and sinister power, transcending almost the capacity of the human mind to measure. It is supposed to be the ever watchful enemy of Protestantism which is working secretly and silently for its destruction and in its unsleeping hostility never fails to avail itself of all events by which it can work injury to its unconscious foe. No evidences, however, are given for all these assertions, and the very nature of the order makes it impossible that it should accomplish what it is supposed to

achieve with such ease and such fatal accuracy. Few
great organizations, with such a widespread reputation
have accomplished so little that was really of any value,
as this great company, so singular in its organization,
so devoted to its aims and so untiring in its efforts. To-
day it has probably less influence than at any other time
in its history.

Its story has been told recently by one of its own members and here there is space only to deal with its beginnings and the causes and persons instrumental in its
establishment.

Ignatius Loyola was born in a little town in Spain in
the year 1493. He was thus about ten years younger
than Luther against whose work his whole activity and
energy were directed. He was a soldier, and after being
badly wounded he found himself deprived of all the hopes
he had once entertained of a great military career. The
age of chivalry was not yet passed in Spain and the spirit
of the wandering knight was still alive in him. By one of
those strange revolutions which take place more often in
passionate natures than in calm ones, his thoughts during
his long recovery were turned to religion. As the knight
of old devoted his life and his arms to the cause of his
lady, so now it came to pass that this stern Spanish soldier determined to devote his life and labors to the cause
of the Church. The saints and the Virgin favored his
purpose, for it was an age of visions and nowhere were
they more manifest than among the ardent spirits whose
memories were filled with the glory of the great past and
who dreamed dreams of another age in which the Church
should again be at the head of society as it had been in
the centuries that were past.

Filled with this great dream the wanderings and struggles of Ignatius began. With an iron resolution he gave
himself to the preparation for his great task. No dis-
couragements daunted him and no difficulties or labors

were too great for him. He realized that to be in any way qualified for the undertaking he had proposed to himself he must be equipped with the necessary learning, as he understood it. So at an age when most men were busy with the mature task of life he entered himself as a student in the University of Paris. The probabilities are that John Calvin was a student there at the same time. They never met, but it is something to be noted that the two men who represent most fully the militant spirit of the two great forces of the day should be working side by side, to prepare for the great struggle which in the next generation was to fill Europe with strife and carnage.

The details of his story have been told so many times that it is not necessary to repeat them here. He met with much opposition even among the wisest men of his own communion, but at last his earnestness triumphed and the Company of Jesus was organized in the year 1537, a year after the death of Erasmus. This was the strange and sinister answer to his cry for moderation and charity. The Order professed itself to be the Pope's special servant. His power and authority were the one end of its existence. He alone had any control over its operations and in return the Jesuits were always the most ardent and faithful defenders of the papal claims. Amid the increasing confusion of the world, they stood as a pretorian guard surrounding the throne and devoted heart and soul to its defense. As the claims of the papacy and its abuse of power had been one of the chief causes of the revolution, so now in a passionate reaction and a blind contempt for the opinion of the most thoughtful members of the Roman Church the Society of Jesus labored to strengthen the very agency which had been the source of so much scandal and indignation. Its growth and organization were determined by the military instinct of its founder; and though the number was never large, the unrelenting energy and the definite purpose which guided it gave it an immediate and immense success.

Loyola knew what he wanted and knew how to get it, and so in its particular field, which was chosen with extraordinary sagacity, it achieved results which on the surface seemed almost marvelous. The government of the Order was absolutism carried to the very limit of human obedience, and soul and body were surrendered in cheerful submission to the will of the spirit which guided all its activities. Against the growing sense of personal character and personal rights it flung itself in an absolute denial and a relentless hostility. No individual instincts, claims, or duties were recognized: rather the Society demanded the most complete and unqualified subjection of the whole being to itself and the cause for which it was fighting. Such a conception and use of human life in any age must carry with it the possibilities of a kind of success, but also of ultimate failure. At this age with the rising tide of new life and a new world of ideas, aspirations, and spiritual adventure, it was the most reactionary attitude conceivable. The Society's achievements were temporary, but it did help regain a part of the lost territory, and drove the Protestants to a more aggressive and unyielding attitude than what might otherwise have been the case. It checked, but it did not and could not destroy, the new life which was spreading.

The main efforts of the Jesuit were directed to controversy, education and ethics. The first was bitter, unscrupulous and obscene in many cases; the second was skillful, brilliant and superficial; and the last plunged into such wretched casuistry that in its degrading conclusions it destroyed the very foundations of morality and shocked the conscience of a not too sensitive world which poured out its scorn and contempt in the bitter and destructive denunciations of Pascal's "Lettres Provinciales."

Side by side with the agencies already indicated was

still another which had a long and terrible history. This was The Inquisition. No institution out of the past has called forth such bitter denunciations or aroused such feelings of horror and hatred as the Inquisition. Again and again it had been called upon to act, and again and again it had filled men with dread and the land with blood. Against all those who were called heretics or were even suspected of being such, it acted with relentless and remorseless cruelty. In the religious and political wars which filled the next hundred years its activity was incessant and widespread. Against the Protestants in every land where its offices could function it manifested its terrific power. Even against the poor savages in the lands of the West which came under the sway of Spain it acted with unhesitating and ferocious energy. England never forgot the terrible experiences through which it passed during the reign of Mary, and every sailor who fell into the Spanish prisons sooner or later was handed over to the Holy Office. The Netherlands were a field where its possibilities were revealed in all their terrors, and even the most prominent persons in state and church in the Catholic countries lived in dread of its stern and cruel domination.

The action of these various agencies was not, however, independent and accidental. The whole story of the Counter-Reformation is that of a thoroughly organized and united movement continued to the very close of the sixteenth century when the weakening of Spain and the death of Philip II brought an end to the long and bitter struggle. The struggle was not a purely religious one, as it seemed, for though it was in many instances prompted and guided by the hand of the Papacy, there were political forces which worked not only in harmony with the religious agencies, but one might even say, took the lead practically in all that was decisive of the final results.

During the Middle Ages the Papacy and the Empire were assumed to stand in the closest and most intimate relations, with the Papacy, generally speaking, standing at the head of the great European movements. The age of the councils had revealed not only the weakness, but the strength also of the Papacy. Nominally and ecclesiastically it won the long struggle, but the moral authority it had once possessed was clearly destroyed. The leadership passed to the Empire especially when it fell into the hands of Charles V. In 1527 the imperial troops sacked Rome and inflicted outrages and horrors far greater than any which either barbarian or Saracen had ever committed. This shows how low the prestige of the Papacy had fallen, for even the outward and formal respect which was preserved in all official relations was here contemptuously thrown aside. It also showed the Papacy where the real authority lay. Yet, while it seemed as if in all these events the Empire was still asserting itself, subsequent events showed it was not the Empire but Spain which used the office in the hands of Charles, and on his death the leadership was at once taken up by his son so that henceforth Spain was the true representative of the Empire. With this change the struggle was given an entirely different tone. The Spanish temper, hardened by many centuries of battle with the Moslem power, was bitterly and unswervingly orthodox; an orthodoxy so rigid and uncompromising that it aroused fear even among the faithful. The Church took upon itself the Spanish stamp which it never lost. The names of the chief actors in the great struggle everywhere are all Spanish, and the spirit is the same.

As a consequence all the forces worked in combination, and one of the chief instruments was the military power of Spain. The Spanish infantry was the most powerful and perfect military instrument then in existence, and in the hand of the dull bigot and the iron-hearted Alva filled the world with the terror of its deeds. These, then, were the chief instruments used by the Counter-Reformation: The Index, The Inquisition, The Society of Jesus, The Spanish Infantry. They were, however, more fatal for the life of the Catholic countries than for the Protestant, and for Italy in particular they may be called "The Four Horsemen of the Apocalypse," for destruction and decay followed everywhere in their path.

The most important event in the history of the Counter-Reformation, if not the most striking, was the new attitude, theological and ecclesiastical, which was represented by the Council of Trent. The great struggle of the fifteenth century between the mind of the Church, as expressed in the councils, and the Papacy, had left the latter with very bitter recollections and a profound dread of any such assemblies. It is true, the Papacy had won the battle, but it was at such an expense that, as was once said "another such victory would ruin it"; and there was not the least assurance that it would be a victory, if a like struggle should again take place. The growth of popular sentiment and the increasing power of the political institutions of the world caused an uneasy fear on the part of the ecclesiastical authorities that their influence was not what it once had been. When the demand was made to deliver Luther to the hands of the Church the request was quietly though contemptuously refused. When Luther asked for a General Council, backed as this request was by the common mind of Germany, if not of all Europe, the refusal was concealed under a number of conditions and qualifications which, however, did not deceive any one. The new Emperor Charles in his effort to settle the problem of his own dominions attempted to have a General Council called which would settle all the disputes, both ecclesiastical and theological, which had divided and disgusted all serious people.

The Imperial Diets showed in their declarations the

indignation against the papal abuses and the moral degradations which had followed from them. The popes were put on trial before the common conscience of Christendom and the language used, not only by the rebellious forces, but by those who were entirely in sympathy with the old Church, were in many, if not most, respects, the same. The common feeling was that a General Council, with the aid of the statesmen and rulers then directing the European governments, would be able to achieve results which would reunite the divided elements and remove from the Church those abuses which were the source of such undoubted evil. A reform of the Church in its head and all its members, which was the cry, did not look very promising to the Papacy whose chief representative at this time was one whom none respected and few feared. So ecclesiastical manipulation and the influence of many secret and separate ambitions and wishes brought about the interminable and inevitable delays which the Papacy desired. The political situation in Europe, the rivalries of the great chiefs, Charles V, Francis I, and Henry VIII, prevented any such concord and agreement as would compel the pope to yield. With consummate skill and much secret diplomacy he played one against the other and was thus enabled year after year to postpone the calling of the much-dreaded council. The demand which Luther had made, backed by the almost unanimous voice of the German people, for a General Council, was not answered until a whole generation had passed, when the great reformer himself was in his grave and the whole situation in Europe was entirely changed. The most powerful and the most earnest of the rulers devoted to the interests of the Church, Charles, was at least to see the desire he had so long struggled for satisfied. Yet his great aim, to bring Europe back to its allegiance to the Holy See, was now impossible, if, in fact, it had ever been possible.

For the fifteenth century had seen an immense development in national consciousness. The conflicts between the Papacy and the Empire no longer absorbed the attention or the energies of the new world. The struggle was one between nations, and the papacy was merely another element which could assist, though it could not control, the decision. The development of this national spirit made a universal church, in the old medieval sense, an impossibility; but this did not seem to have been recognized, though it was acted upon instinctively by all the forces then controlling Europe. With such vigorous and growing political units as the great countries which were now beginning to divide the map of Europe it was impossible that the Papacy or the Church should determine how these national forces and instincts should move. The state rose above the church in reality for the first time in history and became the decisive factor for the future development of European history.

A General Council, therefore, would inevitably be influenced by the new political situation. The dream of a universal church in the old political form in which it had functioned in the age of Hildebrand or Innocent III was still the dream of those who looked backward and took no note of the changes that were coming over even the most conservative thought of the world. It was this dream which had so long haunted the mind of Charles and which had affected all his conduct as well as his thought. This same idea and this same hope had their echoes in the minds of many other rulers, with, however, a difference. The new political jealousies, the fear of the tremendous power of the Empire united with the fierce energy and wealth of Spain made the new nations dread the control of Spain and the destruction of those political institutions which were springing up, more than they desired the unity of the Church. Even Charles would not suppress heresy unless and until he saw that it also involved a strengthening of his political position. Under these con-

ditions, including in them as we must, the declared independence of England which stood always as a possible
leader for all the insurgent and heretical forces of the
Continent, it is easy for us now to see that the restoration
of the old situation was, from the very nature of the case,
impossible.

The great figures had all passed away: Erasmus was
dead, Luther was dead, Zwingli was dead, Francis I was
also gone. The tremendous figure of Henry VIII, with
his ruthless energy and iron will, had passed from the
stage, and Charles himself, who had sought so long and
so honestly for a way out of these interminable struggles
and bitter and disastrous enmities was soon to retire, discouraged and broken-hearted, the ablest and most high-
minded ruler that his generation had known.

The Pope issued the call for the Council in March,
1545, but on account of the dissensions in Germany it did
not really meet until December of that year. Ranke said
no history of the Council had as yet been written and
none has been written since. The documents necessary to
give a complete and satisfactory narrative not only of
the order of events, but of their causes, are not yet available. Portions of the proceedings have been studied and
much light furnished, but the full account is yet to come.
At heart it was a struggle, as the other councils had been,
between the political powers and the Papacy, the powers
at one time working together against the Papacy and at
other times with it and against each other. Charles, as
the great representative in the political field, of the religious aims and wishes of the most loyal portion of the
Church, desired above all things that there should first
be a reform of the organization, a removal of all ground
for complaint, a correction of all the abuses which were
a stench in the nostrils of all decent people. This involved a complete overhauling of the papal system and
radical reform of the papal court. No pope could face

such a situation with anything but fear. More than that, Charles insisted that these practical matters should be made the first object of the Council, thus paving the way for a reconciliation with the Protestants who could legitimately refuse to consider any suggestions for reunion so long as the causes which had produced the original rupture were not removed. Fixing his eye upon this supreme matter the Emperor insisted that all doctrinal subjects should be left for later consideration. The Papacy desired to free itself from any such restrictions, and the Council placed doctrinal matters first. Finding, however, that this would produce a disruption of the Council, a compromise was made. Different subjects were assigned to different committees or bodies for discussion and examination.

The proceedings covering the different subjects were to move simultaneously to be later submitted to the Council in forms suitable for further discussion and final decision. Of course it was easy to see that in this way the matter could be so arranged that the interest of the members should first be engaged upon the theological problems. The minds of the ecclesiastics were more inclined naturally to this method of procedure, especially since the Protestants were not represented by any of their scholars or leaders. Taking up the theological matters first enabled the papal party so to act that it could insist that the Protestants, if and when they appeared at the Council, could be admitted only by accepting as valid the actions already taken. But the Protestants had refused to recognize the Council because it was called by the Pope, and their acceptance would imply, if not involve, a recognition of his authority. But, as a matter of fact, the possibility of any reconciliation was long since passed and the aim of the great leaders was hopeless from the beginning. The struggle ended as it had ended again and again in the triumph of the pope, only now more complete than it ever had been in the past. He came out of the struggle as the supreme master of the Church, the Bishop of the whole Roman Communion. It never was anything but a local council, and after a long and troubled history was dissolved in December, 1563, with two hundred and thirty-four cardinals, bishops, generals of orders, abbots and procurators present, the majority of whom were Italians. The doctrines as formulated by the Council were accepted by the Catholic powers alone, but the disciplinary decisions, and those acts which affected the political situation were never accepted by either France or Spain, and were approved even by the Empire only with reservations.

The significance of the doctrinal decisions of Trent lies in the fact that the medieval theology was now declared to be the dogma of the Church, whereas, before, it had not possessed this character, but represented merely the dominant view and theological conceptions of the age.

The reformed Catholic Church was thus purposed to exclude all sects and parties, which means that all these elements were to be suppressed or driven out to find a place in the broader and more expansive life of Protestantism. The later struggles within the Church reveal that the purpose was never completely executed. But the fates of Jansenism, and now of Modernism attest the success the new spirit in the Church achieved.

There were other important results of the council aside from those already mentioned. Theological seminaries were established in every diocese for the education of the priesthood, which was thus separated more and more from the life and atmosphere of the world. Frequent confessions were enjoined and confessionals were placed in the churches as fixed parts of the church building. Cardinal Borromeo had an active part in bringing about this innovation, that is, the fixed confessionals, but the Jesuits

were among the strongest influences in the reëstablishment and reorganization of the confessional.

With reference to faith it must be fully recognized
that there were many serious-minded members of the old
Church who were more or less in sympathy with what
may be called the more vital and personal view of Faith
as represented by Luther. This element was what was
left of the better part of the earlier Humanism, which
would have accepted without much hesitation or qualifi-
cation the language on this subject which the more broad-
minded and thoughtful Protestants used. But when this
subject was brought up for discussion in the Council, as
it soon was, the rigid and unbending orthodoxy of the
uncompromising members of the Council, vigorously re-
enforced by the Jesuits who had sprung at once to a
leading place in the new life of the church, rejected all
efforts at reconciliation. The restated doctrine followed
the path of the old intellectualism which rested upon the
authority of the Church and was affirmed by the accepting mind of the believer. In this statement nothing was
changed which is essential since the time of St. Thomas,
and the elaborations of the doctrine in the treatises of
the modern Roman theologians do not in any essential
depart from his foundation.

Hence there was and could be no reconciliation or
agreement on what was regarded by Protestants and
Catholics as a fundamental matter. The authority of the
Christian consciousness can never come to its full development if it is to be made dependent upon the authority of the Church. This is the fundamental opposition
and one which is also irreconcilable. It is no nearer a
solution in this twentieth century than it was in the sixteenth and it will never be solved in the future.

Turning from the old Church and looking at the history of the Protestant movement, we find that Luther

himself was at the end heartsick and discouraged. To him it looked as if all his hopes were doomed to disappointment and his dreams of a nobler spiritual life for the soul of man were fast fading away in the presence of the controversies and hate, the fierce animosities and open war which threatened soon to bury Europe in ruin and blood. Forces were at work which neither he nor any other man could measure, and the results of which lay far off in the future. Erasmus died in 1536 and Luther in 1546. To men then living the statement that the Reformation had been a failure would seem to be one which it would be difficult to deny. When men are suddenly lifted out of a state of bondage, whether intellectual or physical, the new freedom is an intoxication and a danger. Their experience has in no way educated them for the new conditions, and the penalty paid is the result of ignorance, and means, until experience has been obtained, many excesses and abuses, violent and brutal indulgence.

Wisdom and self-restraint, discipline and responsibility are of slow growth in the new and hitherto uncultivated soil of the spiritual bond-servants of the past. To give freedom to the soul without knowledge to use it is to bring chaos for a time, though out of the smoke and confusion men find their way to a finer and nobler type of living. Out of the huge ferment of this age has come all that is or has been best in these modern centuries, but the forces then operating were so confused that it is difficult to appraise them. All that men hoped for then, and sought with tireless effort we now see could not possibly be achieved, wonderful and splendid as was the daring which fired their hearts. The drag of the past necessarily delayed the full display of all the power which lay at the heart of this new experience of men's souls.

We see this when we look calmly and closely into the religious history of that period. One of the noticeable things, at least in its effects upon the course of thought,

is that all the men who counted for most were educated
in the old scholastic system. All that the mind revolted
from had its origin in this method. Luther never ceased
denouncing the heathen Aristotle, and the bitterest gibes
of all the men of the new freedom were flung at the subtleties and barren definitions of the great scholastic
authorities. When they were dealing with the great spiritual experiences which had wrought a new soul in them
they spoke with freedom and with force. But when this
religious experience tried to express itself in terms which
might be understood by others, they were flung back upon
the only method they knew, and used the old terms in very
much the same way, though perhaps without its verbal
excesses and emptiness.

The theology which Protestantism produced to meet
the attacks of the old church and to strengthen its position among its members was in all essentials the same as
that of their opponents. That is, they proceeded along
the same lines, used the same weapons and adopted the
same presuppositions. Methods of thinking are the last
things which change in the action of the human mind. It
was because the Protestant theologians still used the old
logic that they unwittingly were caught in some of the
very conclusions above which their religious inspirations
were lifting them. For they not only used the same logical method of deduction, but began with the same assumptions. Given the premises, the conclusions are inevitable.
Nothing new is added, no higher or larger truths are
revealed. The deduction is simply an expansion of the
truths already expressed in the premises and the only
apparent advance is by way of refinement, clearer definitions, and more subtle distinctions. Protestant interest
in such speculations and abstractions led to more and
more discussion and greater and greater definition until
there grew up a body of theology which in its essence
and method differed in almost no respect, except its aim,

from the vast body of Scholastic theology which had so wearied the robust and eager minds of the new age. One realizes how far removed Protestant theology was from the living mind of the world and from the vivid and passionate religious life of a century before when Calovius published his "System Locorum" in twelve volumes in 1655.

How Luther would have regarded this crystallization of his followers' thinking it is difficult to say. He had looked with a certain uneasy suspicion upon the dialectic skill of Melanchthon, his "dear Philip," and always felt irritated and sore over the different disputes which seemed to him to be mere verbal platitudes without life or inspiration. The decay of Protestant theology is one of the noticeable facts of the seventeenth century. After the death of Calvin there is no great name for more than two centuries and, indeed, we may say there was no great creative mind devoted to the field of religious thought until we come to Schleiermacher at the beginning of the nineteenth century. Scholasticism which had been rejected by the early reformers could not gain its old influence by merely changing its name.

The great names since the sixteenth century are the names of scientists, scholars, philosophers and discoverers, and not until the nineteenth century do we find any names which interest or influence the active and most energetic religious spirits of the time. There were great religious spirits but no great theologians, and again was reënforced the old lesson which is so hard to read or appreciate, that religion and theology are not in an organic relation, at least not in the order in which they are generally understood. It has been too often the assumption that religion was the product of theology, not the reverse. And yet this would be difficult to prove, for many acute theologians have been characterized by anything rather than a religious spirit. Piety disappeared and the old wretched controversies and distinctions filled the air again. Disputes arose about the language of Protoplasts and the logic of angels: whether a single drop of the blood of Christ was sufficient for the human race; whether the blood shed in Gethsemane remained united with the Godhead, and whether Christ at the Last Judgment would or would not show the scars of his wounds.

It was also a time of bitter party controversies and antagonisms, during which it was debated whether the Lutherans ought to regard the Calvinists as Christians; and it was openly asserted that one must avoid the Calvinists more than the Romanists. But why delay over these contemptible trivialities and ghastly irrelevancies?

In the growth of new methods of thought the thinking takes place and the method is adapted without any realization of the change or any deliberate and conscious application of the new method. It was so in these very ages when the world was slowly turning away from its past history and starting out on new voyages of discovery. Life, the world, the story of the past, all the living present and all the world's achievements had a new and powerful attraction for the new minds which were seeking fields for investigation. Verbal refinements and logical distinctions furnish no new light and no deep knowledge; but the life of man, the structure of society, and the organization of the Cosmos were all subjects to which men were turning with an eager and intense interest. Science was born, though it did not know the meaning of that which was taking place. Men were thinking in a new way and what they felt this new life required above all was facts. Now words were not facts, except as they stand for realities, and in this new world realities were flooding in upon them from every corner of the universe.

The theologians of Catholicism and Protestantism alike did little to help men in their new explorations for understanding. Copernicus marks the beginning of that revo-

lution which has changed forever the thought of the world
and man's place in it. Yet wherever the church could
control the action of the human mind, and keep men from
sharing in the newly discovered universe, it did so, and
even the Protestants were not as open-minded as their
own principles involved. When Luther was told about
the theory of Copernicus he said contemptuously, "He is
a fool." He said this, not because he knew anything about
the subject or had any theological prejudice, but because
he was supremely indifferent, and it was this indifference,
when it was not worse, that ultimately ended in an opposition akin to that of the old church, though robbed of
the power to inflict punishment for error.

The future belonged to science and philosophy, and the
advances made in theology in the last four centuries are
due more to the efforts and discoveries of the scientific
spirit and to the methods developed by the new philosophy
than to the independent action of theologians, either
Protestant or Roman. The man who opened the great
period of modern thought, which has by no means completed its work, was René Descartes.

Luther stands a hundred years after Huss. René Descartes in his intellectual development comes just a hundred years after Luther, for he says it was in 1619 or
1620 that he made his great discovery and laid the foundation for his "new Method." He was born in 1596, just
fifty years after the death of Luther and at a time when
the serious-minded men of his world were utterly weary
of the futile disputes about religion and were turning
away to interests which they thought far more important,
or at least more pleasant and interesting. He was of distinguished birth and easy circumstances though of a very
delicate constitution. The story of his life is a strange
one. He was educated at La Flèche, the great Jesuit
school, founded by Henry IV, and always professed a
warm affection for, and a deep gratitude to, his old

teachers. He had a passion for life and spent much time traveling, seeking every opportunity to widen his knowledge of men and society; and yet his system of philosophy is one of the most coldly abstract and purely intellectual expressions of human thought possible to conceive. In spite, also of his constant intercourse with men he was a recluse and after months of activity spent in the company of courtiers, soldiers, or scholars he hid himself so completely that only one or two of his most intimate friends had the slightest knowledge of his residence.

He left France to escape controversies and the incessant interruptions of his friends and went to Holland where the last twenty years of his life were passed. He changed his residence so often that it is now impossible to determine how and where some of his years were passed. He hated anything like fame and also feared it to a degree. He had none of the martyr spirit and preferred silence to any kind of reputation which his attainments might give him.

His system, as it is given to us by the writings which have survived, leaves many questions unanswered and these questions are not made any easier by his own manner of writing. He was educated by the Jesuits, as has been said, and therefore, one would assume, has been familiar with the scholastic philosophy. It has been said by one who made this one point a special study, that indications of his familiarity with the scholastic philosophy are evident throughout his writings, not only from his use of its terms, but also of its ideas. What real influence, however, the scholastic philosophy had over him, and what real part, if any, it played in the development of his thought is a different and more difficult question. He disliked controversy and he dreaded the condemnation of the Church or of the theologians which amounted to the same thing at this time. When he heard of the way in which the Holy Office had treated Galileo,

he at once withheld the publication which he had planned.
He also deliberately used phrases which had a familiar
sound and were apparently in harmony with the traditional views. In addition, he most earnestly declared that
his system was in perfect harmony with the established
theology, which it obviously was not, and in every way
he tried to conceal or soften the radical and revolutionary
character of the new method.

New wine is often put into old bottles and new thought
into old forms and in both instances the vessels are
broken. In spite of the attempt, if not at reconciliation
at least to assume such, Descartes' opponents were quick
to realize that a mode of thought was here adopted which
involved a radical break with the past and also a practical
rejection of its assumptions. It was also a challenge to
the whole intellectual basis of the ancient theology and
to the philosophy upon which it rested.

Descartes said he had grown utterly dissatisfied with
any of the knowledge, or what was offered to him as
knowledge, in the existing system of thought. There was
nothing in their assumptions which seemed to him in any
way to offer a solid foundation for intellectual progress.
They were accepted on the authority either of the church
or of the past, without having been submitted to any tests
whatever. How was he to get any valid basis upon which
he could rest with any absolute certainty of its reality
or truth? This was, of course, to put in question every
statement and to call for an examination of every assumption. Instead of accepting the old aphorism of Anselm,
"Credo ut intelligam," he put the exact opposite as the
primary attitude of the mind, "Dubito"—to doubt, not
in a skeptical or agnostic sense, but as a means of reaching some primary truth. What, after every analysis, is
the final and fundamental truth upon which one can rest
with absolute conviction of its reality and authority?
Following each question and assertion, examining each

proposition and fact he reached the conclusion that the ultimate and fundamental truth which was beyond any doubt or question was the certainty of his own existence. Or, to put it in a more personal way, the fact that thought existed no matter what was thought by the mind, implied the existence of a personal self-conscious being which did the thinking and this thinking necessitates something that thinks,—the certainty of a thinker. In his own phrase which has become the historic foundation for all modern philosophy, he stated it thus: "Cogito ergo sum." He started from the individual and the authority of his own personal consciousness and not the authority of the church or the past. Whatever truth there might be in the body of knowledge which was claimed as such it must ultimately find its verification in the fundamental facts of which the consciousness is the basis and the authority. He stood upon his own inner conviction and assurance of the ultimate and original truth of his own consciousness as a fact irrespective of the contents of that consciousness. One of the primary results, of course, was an unconscious, yet increased, sense of personality, giving to it a new value and a new significance. The organic relation of this philosophy with the deeper religious life of the age was thus unconsciously revealed.

Strictly speaking the Reformation was the religious reaction against the medieval interpretation of the spiritual relations of men. For the essence of Luther's position was rooted in the personal need for salvation as a conscious experience of the soul. Descartes, and Bacon too, represented the intellectual revolt against the scholastic philosophy and the personal need for truth as something which was a living possession. Thus the great philosophical movement inaugurated by Descartes sprang out of the same impulse, that is, the personal one, in which the religious reformation had its roots. They strengthened and reënforced each other in spite of the fact that Protestant orthodoxy was at times bitterly and vehemently opposed to the new philosophy. Protestantism was saved from its own scholasticism by the introduction of new thought and new spiritual experiences of freedom and of truth.

The Reformation had broken the authority of the Church over the operations of the human mind, and now philosophy for the first time since antiquity could work freely, unhampered by theological interference or control. In this new atmosphere it took up the task as it was left by the later Greek philosophy, with the addition of the later psychological investigations of the Schoolmen. There were also some contributions from the Arabian speculations, particularly the idea of self-consciousness. As in the history of Greek thought a revolution was wrought by Socrates when he turned the current of speculation from the cosmological efforts of the earlier physical schools to the study of man, so the foundation of all that is of value and significance in modern philosophy and speculation was laid in the Cartesian philosophy. More than that, one of the primary and most important elements of the new philosophy was its passionate assertion of the rights of reason, an assertion which had not been made with the same vigor since the end of the classic age. Against this too, the theological authorities, both Protestant and Catholic, made a bitter attack, and generation after generation the controversy has continued with decreasing interest and lessening power.

The ultimate test of truth is not authority, no matter how well authenticated, but its ability to prove itself true to the soul of man. A long course of investigation followed upon the original lines laid down by Descartes and it was not until Kant opened a new door that any fresh contribution was made toward solving the problem of human knowledge.

The great structure of scholastic theology was completed and crowned by the skill and genius of the greatest of the Schoolmen, St. Thomas Aquinas. No sooner, however, had his work been finished than it was attacked by one of the most subtle minds of the Middle Ages, or perhaps of any age, Duns Scotus. He, in turn, was followed by his greatest pupil, William of Occam, who by his nominalistic logic destroyed the very foundations of the scholastic theology. In so doing Occam prepared the way for a new system of reasoning. It is not probable that he had any anticipation of what would rise on the foundation he was preparing or that he recognized in what his practical method would culminate by his rejection of some of the fundamental conceptions of Scholasticism. In making the particular, the individual, the object of examination and investigation, the deductive method with its inferences from general propositions or universals was stripped of its authority. When this was done the way was open for the new attempts of thought which characterized the new age and made possible the scientific method of the post-Reformation thought of western Europe. If Occam's work was destructive or negative, the constructive work of the new era was that of a fellow countryman.

It is a significant fact that both Occam and Bacon were Englishmen, sharing alike the common feeling of dislike and distrust of the ruling Scholasticism. To Francis Bacon belongs the immortal honor of first stating the steps or method by which knowledge was to be reached. It was the revival or reëstablishment of science, and by this he meant the study not of what men thought or had thought about life and the universe, but what were the actual facts which could be discovered by patient and careful investigation. Unlike Descartes he was not so much interested in the mind and its laws, but in Nature and her laws, and the truth so long hidden there from the human mind. The new method, the modern method, as it has been developed and elaborated by generations of students, has been, first, to collect all the facts possible, as they are actually presented either in the life of the organism, institution, or society which is being investigated. Out of this mass of facts the mind must collect those which can legitimately and inevitably be bound together in their natural order. In other words, write a history of the organism, for history describes the real life, the complete and organized body of facts or truths concerning the particular subject of investigation.

The application of this method must necessarily be imperfect and subject to constant revision as new facts and new secrets come to light. This to many minds is a weakness and shows the inferiority of the new to the older and more abstract method. It has, however, this enormous advantage, that it cultivated in the mind a realizing sense of the inevitable limitations of human knowledge, a healthy and humble resistance to the dogmatic spirit and the complete rejection of any idea of infallibility in any field of human knowledge. Bacon was the first one to see all which was implied in these revolutionary steps. It is true that all the leaders of science and of thought were practicing the new method, but it was simply the immediate and instinctive response of eager spirits who saw a new path by which they could reach the goal that none hitherto had attained. They did not stop to define or determine what was the character or significance of their method; they simply used it and left for others to determine the intellectual significance and value of the new logic. Bacon gave it a name; he called it the "Inductive method," and the work in which he set forth the method he deliberately and intentionally contrasted with the Organon of Aristotle as the "Novum Organum." He meant to show that a new era in human thought had come and a new age in the history of man's spiritual progress.

Unlike Descartes, however, he found the beginning and the end of man's field of operation in nature. His study was objective where that of Descartes had been subjective, and thus he became the founder of modern Empiricism, as Descartes was the founder of modern Idealism.

The date, 1620, when this work was published, is one of the most significant in the history of the seventeenth century. It was also the date on which the great attempt at a new order of human society was to take its first step, and the fellow countrymen of Bacon launched their ships to build a new world for men to live in. So Bacon was to tell what that world really was and really meant for them. This date would be still more suggestive if, as seemed at one time probable, it was also the time when Descartes made his great discovery which he speaks of as almost a divine revelation; but the mass of modern critics seem inclined to believe that the reference is to 1619 rather than to 1620. At all events these two years mark the beginning of world changes of such immense importance that it is hardly possible to exaggerate them.

It has been customary for historians and especially for historians of religion, to lay the emphasis upon the theological revolution of the sixteenth century. But along with this, and perhaps no less important, not only in itself, but in its influence upon the development of religious thought since, was the philosophical movement which took place in the same period. It is in the new attitude of the human mind toward the problems of philosophy and science, the freedom and power with which this new development advanced that the supreme significance of the change lies. The whole change was one of spirit and method which slowly but gradually affected the whole realm of human knowledge and altered the entire outlook of man upon the world and the life in which he found himself.

To attempt to discuss or even review the events of

modern history and their significance would simply be to
dissipate all effort and reach no results. What is common would be lost sight of in the incessant shift and
change which have marked these eager and intense generations. If, however, we look at them as revealing the
operation of a new way of thinking, the result of new
motives and methods, we get a sense of the unity of this
history below all the changes and revolutions in life and
thought which have made them the most wonderful in
the experience of the world. Western Europe in the sixteenth century, by a gigantic and convulsive effort threw
itself out of the old orbit in which it had moved for a
thousand years and swung out into a new cycle. At the
same time the physical universe lost its old path and
moved into a space unknown and infinite and so vast that
the mind stands in awe of the hidden depths which are
still unmeasured and unknown. So the new spiritual
world of man is still moving on from revelation to revelation and from revolution to revolution and no man can
measure its orbit. It has been an age of endless discoveries and that which has touched the soul with the deepest
sense of mystery is not only or chiefly the new knowledge
but the possibilities which are revealed in the new instrument for discovery and the impossibility of determining
how its limits, if any, can be determined. There is an
eager and unappeasable passion for truth, a wide and
eager conviction that more light is breaking, more and
more a passionate conviction that farther and farther as
we go, farther still the great horizon will recede into
unknown depths beyond.

In every field of human life that which distinguishes
the past from the present, so far at least as the changing
world of knowledge and thought are concerned, is the
application of the new method to the existing facts of life
as they may be known and as they are revealed by more
careful, patient and methodical investigation. Nowhere

have the results been more startling or more disturbing than in the field of religion or, more specifically, in the area of life covered by Christian theology and history.

The application of the new method was gradual and, in many cases, unconscious. It was the instinctive suggestion which rose from habitual use, to extend the same habit of thought to the fields which seemed to present so many anomalies and contradictions. The history of the past, the world of ancient history was studied anew and with new tools of thought and new and startling results immediately revolutionized men's conceptions of the past.

It is not possible to give in detail all that has issued from the application of the scientific method to the field of religion; that belongs to the specialist whose duty is to trace the movement and give the results of the new application of science in a field hitherto held immune from what seemed so secular and irreverent a spirit. But gradually and with much difficulty the work has been done and now we stand where we can see some of the results. It is only necessary to consider a few of the facts to establish without any question the certainty and the reality of the changes which the inductive method as used in the history of religion has wrought in the world of thought as well as of life.

The Bible was accepted at the time of the Reformation by both Catholic and Protestant as the infallible rule of faith. It was the foundation upon which all rested and to which all was referred. The chief difference, and almost the only difference, was that the Romanist said the only authoritative interpretation was given by the Church. While the Protestant accepted the infallibility of Scripture, he claimed the right of interpretation for each individual Christian. This theoretical claim, however, was soon and effectively limited by the theological determinations or systems which were soon as thick as leaves in Vallombrosa. The infallibility of the Bible rested upon a

theory of verbal inspiration and a mechanical construction which left the mind utterly without any valid explanation of the contradictions or varieties of difference
which were everywhere manifest and which taxed the ingenuity of all its interpreters. There was one signal exception to this general consensus and that was Luther.
His attitude was one of independence, and though he
asserted his freedom in his criticism or understanding of
the Bible, it did not rest on matters of fact as revealed
by a study of the documents, but upon a purely subjective religious basis. The infallibility of verbal inspiration
could not sustain itself as knowledge advanced.

The various departments of study which have contributed to the change in the way the Bible is regarded
are too numerous to mention; textual criticism came first;
philology in its widest extent; historical investigations
of the ancient religions not only of Greece and Rome, but
especially of the great religions of western Asia; the
establishment and development of what may be called the
science of Comparative Religion and the historical background of the different books of the Bible, both of the
Old and the New Testament, in fact, the whole body of
that which to-day is called Modern Biblical Criticism.
The results attained have been established upon the solid
foundations of knowledge and the laws of reasonable evidence. In the grand outlines and the main conclusions
all scholars are agreed. The leading minds of all countries where these studies are pursued in a scientific spirit
stand upon one common ground and this unanimity of
agreement has been one of the strong factors in calling
for a closer recognition of the real spiritual unity of
Christian thought as something deeper and more universal than the special and peculiar theories or doctrines
which are the notes of the individual Christian bodies.
It was said long ago by one of the greatest scholars of
the seventeenth century that the differences between the

churches was largely due to ignorance of Greek grammar. It is true that this statement of Scaliger is quite too sweeping, but in the main idea that real knowledge, not tradition or prejudice, must and does bring the minds of men into closer agreement than anything else, is beyond question. The Bible of the best scholarship of to-day is a living book in a way that it never has been before.

One of the chief philosophical ideas which has been of immense value and assistance in achieving these conclusions has been that of the theory of development as applied to the course and growth of human thought and experience. We see in the Bible a record of the living soul of man at different periods of its history and under an immense variety of circumstances. We see that spirit struggling always upwards, seeking ever more light and finding it; growing into a clearer and firmer faith in a God of truth, of purity, of righteousness and of love. As the long story unfolds itself from the early dawn of history down to the days in which we live, the overwhelming conviction grows of One who has led the race in all its vicissitudes, temptations, struggles and failures to a profounder appreciation of His wise and patient guidance and to more serious and solemn faith in His infinite goodness. The human mind has been for years growing more and more impatient with theories and traditions, with the unnatural, unreasonable and inconsistent speculations of the past, and asks for facts. The Bible of to-day gives these facts, facts of human experience, facts of the spiritual life of man which can be tested and whose reality is proved by their present existence and their vital power. There is no record of man's religious experience so vivid and so real, so impressive and so awful, as that which the Bible unfolds to the eyes that are looking below the mere accidents of time and place to the everlasting mystery of man's life in God.

And at no time in history perhaps was the Bible ever

studied so wisely and so well as it is to-day. It forms the basis for more real scientific thought than ever before in its history. That it has lost in popularity is not due so much to the changed thought about the Bible as to the lack of interest in religion itself. To place this indifference as the result of the critical studies of the last one hundred and fifty years is to reverse the real order of things. Those who care least for religion know least also about the Bible of modern theological studies. When the spiritual interests of the world assert themselves as against the dull materialism and the selfish struggles of life, it will not be to the Bible of tradition, with its unintelligent understanding and its elementary ignorance of all facts of history, philology, science and theology, but to the book in which science reveals the spiritual history of man in free and untrammeled brightness. The theory of knowledge, of life and the universe which has grown out of the efforts and labors of the last four centuries rests upon foundations which neither ignorance nor orthodoxy so-called, or both, can in any way overcome.

The curious thing is, that in all essentials the Bible has not changed. The real life, the force which made it the guide and comfort of ages past has not in the slightest degree been altered. The great commentaries of the past, in their strange and rather crude forms of expression, show the souls of men resting upon the living faith in God and not upon mere verbal statements. Instinctively one sweeps these local elements away, or regards them as curious illustrations of the intellectual limitations of men who lived in a different world from ours. It is not only in Luther that the real voice of piety and faith is heard, but in Anselm, in Bernard, in Augustine especially, and in Origen. It is the same voice we hear in St. John and St. Paul, the voice of the child rejoicing in the revelation of a divine love, the gratitude of the human heart for the tenderness of a Father it has so wistfully and patiently sought, and found at last in Him who opens the soul to a new vision of the Eternal. The religion of the modern Bible is not hidden by the mechanical and archaic ideas of the past, but stands out in the story, tragic and magnificent, of the upward movement of the soul to God, and of God's manifestation of His essential character through the life and the deeds of Him whom all men bless.

There are few great teachers of the past whom one cannot feel would rejoice in the new Bible and be thankful that so many things which were difficult and obscure to them, are now so much better understood. It has been clear gain in every way. If the great movement of modern thought had produced nothing else for Christian thought and life it would have given to the world in the new Bible a treasure like unto no other. For the rights of reason, the instinct for righteousness, the desire for truth are all met and satisfied, and a larger vision of the future brings new hopes for the Bible in the days that are to come.

The history of theology in the Protestant bodies followed the same course, as has been said, that it did in the Middle Ages. It started with practically the same assumptions or foundations and followed the same method. It took, as the old church had taken them, the Bible, the Creeds and many of the underlying traditions, so far at least as they had been developed or accepted up to the time when the East and the West were separated. It also used the same logic and moved in the same habits of thought, and consequently reached the same conclusions. With this difference, however, that Protestant theology in its later developments became more narrow, lifeless, and meticulous than even medieval scholasticism. This result was bound up in the very nature of the processes used, for the deductive logic, as applied to theology, inevitably involves a scholastic system as its consequence.

For this assumes that theology is a fixed or static science and not a progressive, historical or dynamic one. Hence come verbal refinements, distinctions which are only intellectual and logical, and which lead constantly toward further distinctions and refinements, until the most impossible and unreasonable conclusions are drawn from premises which have been in no way either tested or proved. The fundamental basis of course was the Scriptures, but as these were regarded as simply the product of a mechanical theory of inspiration, the result was only a mass of texts, without any historical significance and no real value, except as proofs for theories or assumptions which were to be defended or justified. Therefore no other results could issue out of such a lifeless and uninspiring interpretation of the biblical literature than what we find.

The same process has repeated itself in all the other religions which had as their foundation a book or a literature, when these were taken in the same way as sacred and impeccable documents. The Jewish theology which grew up in the hands of the rabbis was supposed to be based upon the Hebrew writings. The Mohammedan has treated the Koran in the same way. In each case there developed a theology which in its internal character was scholastic, subtle and without much spiritual value. In each instance also there grew up an orthodoxy which was insistent, dogmatic and intolerant.

The great difficulty had always been that no calm and deliberate examination had ever been made concerning the real nature of theology. It was long before men ever recognized that it was essentially an historical science. That is, it is relative to the knowledge, the experience and the intellectual powers of any individual or age. Man uses what he has to state what he has been able to know of the life and experience of his own soul. Theology is the imperfect and inadequate attempt to put into language the breadth and the depth of all those spiritual facts as man is able to see them, and as they are related to his own experience. Whatever statements are made, however full the experience may be, and however universal the truth appears, the possibilities of larger and wider expressions are necessarily involved in the mere fact of life and thought. Theology is not a fixed and final product even in the case of those truths which are felt to be the most vital and fundamental, for God is a living God and theology is a progressive and not a static science.

In the emphasis upon theology or orthodoxy the question is asked, What is the relation between theology and religion? Can it in any sense be said that they are identical? Then in that case knowledge is essential to salvation, and not knowledge merely, but correct knowledge. If so, then who can be saved? The Roman Church, by implication at least, accepts this conclusion, but the moral and spiritual instincts of men as a whole decline to accept any such inference. Moral values are not to be submerged in ecclesiastical orthodoxy, and the spiritual interests of the soul are not to be determined by purely intellectual considerations. Protestant scholasticism had ultimately brought forth an opposition which was the real counterpart of the reaction from medieval scholasticism. In the Middle Ages this reaction expressed itself in the life and writings of the great mystics. The same process took place in the reply which the spiritual revolt uttered in what is known as German Peitism. And this reaction occupied very much the same geographical territory, as did its earlier expression. Here was found a type of piety not only sincere but profound, and yet apparently in no way interested in or based upon theological speculations or scholastic definitions. Its influence was the only really living force working in the interests of the spiritual life of man. It was consequently the most powerful element in the religious life of the day. The contrast between this

and the dull and lifeless orthodoxy together with the
prevalence of a low and indifferent moral tone, struck
most painfully the earnest spirits who were struggling
with their own problems and were, at the same time, profoundly moved by the contrast between these two elements in the national life. Out of this contrast, the same
contrast which the Wesleyan movement revealed in England a generation later, the question of the relation between theology and religion rose into prominence and
demanded an answer. In view of the actual and visible
facts it could not longer be maintained that they were
identical: and if not, the further question pressed for an
answer, What was the relation between them? The only
one who could be qualified to solve this problem would be
one who was familiar with the facts on both sides, and
also one who was endowed with a spirit of earnestness and
had a real anxiety to establish the limits, if any, between
these two fields of life.

The man at last came. Schleiermacher was the greatest theological mind of his age and one of the greatest
spirits that has ever devoted itself to the highest spiritual
interests of mankind. He was the greatest religious
genius since the Reformation. With his splendid gifts,
his wide interests, his original and creative power he
opened a new path in the study of religion and has
rightly been called, "The Origen of the Nineteenth Century." Realizing the religious needs of the times as few
others did, he felt it necessary to go to the root, if possible, and determine, in the first place, what religion
actually is. This being done, its relation to all the other
phenomena of life could be more easily determined. He
found the intellectual world of his own day filled with
contempt for the empty controversies, the ecclesiastical
futilities, and the bitter animosities of the theological
world. It accepted the position occupied by the theological world which assumed that theology and religion were

identical, or inseparable, and therefore would none of either. Europe was shaken by the outburst of the French Revolution, and the wars of Napoleon were destroying many, if not most, of the old institutions, as well as the traditions of the past. The Church in France had been broken and crushed, and evidence was not wanting that the whole existing body of religious institutions and ideas was on the way to a like fate.

It was under these circumstances that the young Schleiermacher, now only thirty-one years of age, published in 1799 a small volume called, "Ueber Religion," "On Religion: Addresses to the Cultivated among its Despisers." The volume is interesting to us chiefly because it is the first attempt to deal with this problem which, so long as it was unsolved, left men in a real intellectual uncertainty. In his investigations he stands on the same plane with Descartes in his effort to reach the ultimate ground of certainty. His method is psychological, as was that of his great French predecessor. His effort is to discover what are the inner grounds of religion, and what is the character of its psychological factor. As religion is a personal experience, or it is nothing, there must be some basis in the psychological state which will determine what it is and furnish evidence for its reality. If it is a spiritual experience, it must also be primarily a personal one; that is, each individual is religious from the very nature of his being. The further question, what is the essence of this religious element, or the element out of which religion flows to expression. Schleiermacher also attempted to answer. His answer as to the fact of a distinctive religious nature belonging to man as such has been almost universally accepted by all who have studied the problem. But as to his specific definition or description there have been many modifications and additions. The important thing, however, was that he made clear once for all that whatever the value or the need of the-

ology, it was not identical with religion. The relation
between them has been stated by one, if not the greatest,
of his successors, in the field of religious thought. In his
Theologische Ethik, Rothe has defined theology as, "The
effort to know and define the contents of the religious
consciousness."

Consequently the outward form and expression of religion is not theology but piety, for the standard of knowledge is not and cannot be the measure of piety. Thus he
felt that in seeking the psychological basis in which and
out of which religion as a subjective experience grew, he
had solved the question as to whether religion and
theology were identical or not. He believed that in thus
penetrating to the very center of the soul he had discovered what religion is. This process, he was convinced,
was the only way to reach the truth and by adopting it,
he attained conclusions which settled the relation which
religion, in its essence, stood to all other spiritual phenomena. As a result he declared that religion, thus discovered, renounced, and must renounce, all pretensions
to determine any matters in the sphere of science or of
ethics, and, so far as possible, to confine itself to its own
essential reality. Piety, which is the expression of religion and springs from it, is, in itself, neither a knowing
or a doing, but simply an inclination and determination
of the feelings. This feeling is, however, rather a spiritual
sensitiveness than an emotional or pathological state.

Starting from these general statements, based as they
are upon analysis and investigation of religious as distinguished from theological data, the whole of modern
thought on the fundamental subject of religion has
sprung. The dogmatic authority of theology has therefore declined and it has taken a secondary and relative
place in the whole study of man's religious history. The
key which was found, or was thought to be found, in
psychology, has led many serious students to feel that

along this path lies the way to future progress in the spiritual life, and not in the affirmation or reiteration of intellectual formulas.

All the coördinated studies which have sprung up in the general field of religious investigation have further contributed to this end. The fact that religion is a personal experience, that it consists essentially in a vivid religious consciousness, has profoundly influenced the sense of personality and contributed enormously to its growth. At its roots religion is primarily individual, that is, it is a personal relation, essentially a matter between God and the soul of man. Its social aspects are like the social aspects of law, government, and ethics, mainly derivative and not primary. The whole course of modern thought has emphasized the significance and centrality of the human soul, and the whole social order with its intense and often violent assertions of the worth of personality has been only an echo or manifestation of this new religious interpretation of life.

The new readings of the past and of life have been destructive of the whole scheme of life which rested upon the idea of the hopeless depravity of man. The profound mystery of man's nature does not seem to be revealed in any of the theories which were once held to be so conclusive, and in spite of the complex and confusing elements in his nature man is felt to be something more than ever before. All the forces of human thought, all the revelations of science, the whole universe and its history, the mystery and the passion of Christ all point to a being far beyond any earlier conception of his nature. Strange emotions and impulses, hidden hopes and wonderings flow in a steady stream into the rising vision of the future and help form a figure as yet unknown in its greatness, but having affinities with a fate no man can surely read. Amid the vast number of facts which absorb so completely the modern thought of life man stands out as the one thing of supreme interest and a figure of singular and unique impressiveness.

It is in this new atmosphere that the Gospel takes upon it a new value in the sense that the primary facts of life stand out unshaded by the overarching influences of tradition. It is now nearly a century since Strauss wrote his "Leben Jesu," and the smoke of that conflict has been dissipated by the passing years. But out of that battle sprang much that we live by. The New Testament Strauss attacked has largely disappeared and another has taken its place. In this new one the great thing is not the words but the Person. Rich with all the reverence and spiritual affection of the past, isolated by a spiritual and moral supremacy no other has, He stands in His lonely greatness the one supreme figure whose meaning for men is the best in their lives. As we look back over two thousand years, as we see the pain and travail of many races we also see the slow advance, through much confusion and tumult, of a clearer vision of His Face. This progress has been greater than we know. If the past throws any light upon the future it will be greater still in the generations that are to come. For what has been achieved has been largely, by the providence of God, through the action of the laws of thought and the passion of the human soul for God. The scientific method, or the historical, call it what you please, has only begun to point the way to still greater light and higher truth.

Four hundred years have passed since Luther raised his voice in that quiet little German university town, the four greatest centuries the world has ever known. They have been centuries of conflict, contrast, contradiction and paradox. The universe itself has added to man's wonder and amazement. The little world with its center in the Mediterranean lands widened into a great world of new continents, shoreless seas, strange races and miraculous wealth. Then this new world suddenly shrank into a

tiny ball, wandering in unknown space whose depths man
still strives in vain to measure. Discoveries, and new
knowledge far past the imagination of man to conceive,
have come to deepen and enrich life. New nations have
come into being to make their contribution to civilization.
New and powerful states have been established and organized into civilized communities. Literatures more
splendid and more rich than any the world has known
since Greece first lighted "the victorious fires" of human
thought have filled the world with undying light.

Yet before the political vision of mankind the earth
seems to be a huge range of volcanoes which explode one
after the other, and in the lurid glow one sees the old
world pass away forever, buried in the ashes out of which
new nations and new life shall rise and flourish. Revolutions, French and others, have shaken into ruins institutions and ideas hoary with age. Dynasties have risen,
fallen and disappeared. Emperors and kings have moved
across the stage as in the vision of Macbeth. And as they
cast a backward glance before they faded into the night
of time they saw a huge gigantic figure, half naked, half
clad, haggard-eyed and sorrowful, tragic and brutal like
some Caliban called forth by the magic wand of some
unseen Prospero, the People, something never seen before
until these later centuries and the cause of new fears and
terrible hopes in the hearts of many. Yet no centuries in
all the world's long story have given so many great names
in art and literature, war and science, philosophy and
religion as these mighty years. And now this whole vast
complex civilization may go down in a smoking ruin,
plunging the world into a catastrophe more resounding
and possibly more prolonged, than the Fall of the Roman
Empire.

Two factors at least, of creative power, emerge and
stand out above the confusion and the tumult. The one
new and original, the other permanent and more potent

than ever. The first is the new and vivid self-consciousness of the individual everywhere, realizing for the first time in anything like fullness, the meaning of Personality. Impatient, proud, violent, and lawless, waiting for a new spirit to organize and develop into fullness and power the spiritual and hidden wealth of human character. The other force stood already facing human history in those dark days when the fierce tribes of the north swept down upon the old civilization and tore it to pieces. It was He who furnished the inspiration and the courage, which in those days of despair faced the new age, and out of the ruins of the old world and the wild energies of barbarian tribes slowly it was He who fashioned the world we know, Jesus Christ.

It is the same Christ to-day and yet another. It is not the Christ of Nicea, clad in the filmy garments which were woven out of the subtle threads of Greek metaphysics; not the Roman Christ armed with the sword of justice and of vengeance, nor the Medieval Lord with His Gothic sternness and His awful sorrow. But like His ancestor of old He has cast aside the armor with which he was clad and faces the world clear, serene, compassionate, pure and holy as He met John and Peter long ago by the Galilean sea. He stands on the threshold of the new world as He stood on that of the old, and binds men to Him by the same power of love, unselfishness, sacrifice and truth. The best of the past has sprung from this life, and the future is full of hope for a world that does not fear to trust Him.

Above the travail and the pain of life, above the silent drudgery of the weary years He holds the vision still that once won a great soul to cry out of its new birth agony, "I am crucified with Christ: nevertheless I live: yet not I, but Christ liveth in me: and the life which I now live in the flesh I live by the faith of the Son of God who loved me and gave himself for me."

INDEX